Crockett at Two Hundred

Crockett at Two Hundred

NEW PERSPECTIVES

ON THE MAN AND THE MYTH

*Edited by Michael A. Lofaro
and Joe Cummings*

The University of Tennessee Press
KNOXVILLE

Library of Congress Cataloging-in-Publication Data

Crockett at two hundred : new perspectives on the man and the myth /
    edited by Michael A. Lofaro and Joe Cummings.
        p. cm.
    Bibliography: p.
    Includes index.
    ISBN 0-87049-592-5 (cloth : alk. paper)
    1. Crockett, Davy, 1786-1836. 2. Crockett, Davy, 1786-1836
—Legends. 3. Legends—United States—History and criticism.
4. Pioneers—Tennessee—Biography. 5. Tennessee—Biography.
I. Lofaro, Michael A., 1948- . II. Cummings, Joe. III. Title:
F436.C95C76 1989
976.8'04'0924—dc19
[B]   88-29369 CIP

For the Durish family
M. A. L.

For the Cummings family
J. C.

Contents

Illustrations

Preface

During the colonel's first winter in Washington [1828], a caravan of wild animals was brought to the city and exhibited. Large crowds attended the exhibition; and, prompted by common curiosity, one evening Colonel Crockett attended.

"I had just got in," said he: "the house was very much crowded, and the first thing I noticed was two wild cats in a cage. Some acquaintance asked me, 'if they were like the wild cats in the backwoods?' and I was looking at them, when one turned over and died. The keeper ran up and threw some water on it. Said I, 'Stranger, you are wasting time. My looks kills them things; and you had much better hire me to go out here, or I will kill every varmint you've got in your caravan.' While I and he were talking, the lions began to roar. Said I, 'I won't trouble the American lion, because he is some kin to me, but turn out the English lion — turn him out — turn him out — I can whip him for a ten dollar bill, and the zebra may kick occasionally during the fight.' This created some fun; and then I went to another part of the room, where a monkey was riding a pony. I was looking on, and some member [of Congress] said to me, 'Crockett, don't that monkey favour General Jackson?' 'No,' said I, 'but I'll tell you who it does favour. It looks like one of your boarders, Mr.———, of Ohio.' There was a loud burst of laughter at my saying so; and, upon turning round, I saw Mr. ———, of Ohio, within about three feet of me. I was in a right awkward fix; but I bowed to the company and told 'em, 'I had either slandered the monkey, or Mr. ———, of Ohio, and if they would tell me which, I would beg his pardon.' The thing passed off; and the next morning, as I was walking the pavement before my door, a member came up to me, and said, 'Crockett, Mr. ———, of Ohio, is going to challenge you.' Said I, 'Well, tell him I am a fighting fowl. I s'pose if I am challenged I have a right to choose my weapons?' 'Oh yes,' said he. 'Then tell him,' said I, 'that I will fight him with bows and arrows.'"[1]

One would give a great deal to see the expression on the gentleman from Ohio's face as Crockett's message is related to him and even more to know if this story is true or to what degree it is true. Herein lies the joy and the problem of dealing with the congressman from the canebrakes of West Tennessee. History melts readily into myth in Crockett's own hands as he helps to craft the flesh and blood David into the legendary Davy and even more easily in the hands of eager writers and editors who seek to provide a seemingly omnivorous public with more and more remarkable tales about the heroic frontiersman.

The elusive origins of the story recorded above serve as an excellent example of the problem of Crockett's on-again off-again construction of his myth. The story itself bears the earmarks of some currency in oral tradition. In 1833, the same year that the story quoted in the headnote appeared, a newspaper printed a slightly different version of the tale. The version quoted above is extracted from the *Sketches and Eccentricities of Col. David Crockett, of West Tennessee,* a volume penned anonymously by Mathew St. Clair Clarke with much information supplied by his friend Crockett. Yet in his campaign autobiography issued the next year in 1834, Crockett denied his part in the production and, in the main, repudiated the book because of the undignified nature of many of the sketches: "I don't know the author of the book—and indeed I don't want to know him. . . . In parts of his work there is some little semblance of truth. But I ask him, if this notice should ever reach his eye, how would he have liked it, if I had treated *him* so?—if I had put together such a bundle of ridiculous stuff, and headed it with *his* name, and sent it out upon the world without ever even condescending to ask *his* permission?"[2] Crockett obviously wished to distance himself from the work he had helped in large part to create; he seemed to feel that the comic and exaggerated nature of his legendary self might undermine his bid for reelection to the House of Representatives as well as his presidential hopes.

The confusion was compounded after Crockett's death at the Alamo. David could no longer hold the reins on Davy and his undisputed elevation into the pantheon of American heroes made him an eminently marketable and malleable public property. He was resurrected and recreated countless times in the media of the nineteenth and twentieth centuries, usually as the darling but sometimes as the butt of their various fictional projections, and appeared in almanacs, sporting gazettes and other newspapers, songsters and minstrel shows, dime novels, dramas, films, and on radio and television.[3] Much of the present volume is devoted to the examination of these commercial manipulations of Crockett's legendary image and the evaluation of their impact upon American life. The extent to which writers and the media generate controversy to provide sensational copy is an equally fascinating topic touched on throughout the book. Hero worship, it seems, is not nearly as stimulating to an audience as hero bashing, but it is often just as revealing.[4]

The challenge of attempting to analyze the composite and ever-changing nature of Davy Crockett delights the authors whose work appears in this volume. But Crockett fans one and all, they too come to Crockett for the same reason as the interested reader, to participate in the joy and the exuberance that sparkles through the man and the myth. It captivates them whether, like Walter Blair, their fascination with Crockett began a half-century ago at the start of an eminent scholarly career or whether, like many of the other authors, it began as children riveted to a television or movie screen staring spellbound at Fess Parker's Crockett from 1954 to 1956.

As the subtitle to this volume indicates, the authors offer up new perspectives on the man, the myth, and their interrelationships in many areas. They deal with crucial issues that have proved provocative, such as the details surrounding Crockett's death at the Alamo, the reactions to his death over the last 150 years, and the myth-making processes of authors and the media that improve history to suit the popular imagination. They also focus their examinations on entirely new matters: how David is the champion of a campaign style that is still a mainstay of Tennessee politicians; how celebrations in his home state prefigure his rise as a national hero by more than fifty years; the impact of his life and legend upon the nineteenth-century popular music scene; the discovery of a "lost" silent film, *Davy Crockett at the Fall of the Alamo*; the double-edged satire of the "riproarious shemales" who complement the male ring-tailed roarers of the backwoods and have their own tall-tale adventures in the Crockett almanacs; how Crockett points back in time as an American equivalent of the ancient European tradition of the Wild Man in his portrayals on the stage and forward to Owen Wister's character of the Virginian; and how the ultimate source of Crockett's legend is the style of the man, which fit the collective imagination so well that it serves as an authentic representation of America's idea of itself. No less important is the publication of the most complete bibliography of works by and about the frontiersman ever assembled. All these studies seek to enlighten and enliven the understanding of Crockett as a man and as a vital cultural force.

Although Davy's perennial best-seller status means that economic motives are behind the creation of many of the different Crocketts, that fact need not tarnish our enjoyment of them; Davy, in whatever guise he appears and for whatever reason, almost always gives his audiences more than their money's worth. Neither should the Gordian tangle of man and myth obscure the essential unity of Crockett. Glance again at the headnote and note how many Crocketts exist in this one episode. He is congressman, superman, blazing patriot, boisterous braggart, and backwoods trickster,

John Gadsby Chapman's portrait of the historical David Crockett painted in 1834. The Alamo, San Antonio, Texas.

"Crockett Delivering his Celebrated War Speech," a depiction of the mythical Davy Crockett as a savage and jingoistic patriot. From *Davy Crockett's Almanac. 1847. Daring Adventures in the Back Woods; Wonderful Scenes in River Life; Manners of Warfare in the West; Feats on the Prairies, in Texas and Oregon* (Boston: James Fisher), [19]. St. Louis Mercantile Library Special Collections Department.

but all these roles are smoothly dissolved by a broad, puckish, good humor and recast into a single fun-loving, dominant presence. The characterization presented is not fragmented or contradictory but whole. Like Whitman in "Song of Myself," Crockett is large; he contains multitudes. Invested in him, man and myth, are the hopes and beliefs, the virtues and values, and the shortcomings and triumphs of each generation that takes him up as their hero. Approach him, therefore, with the same enthusiasm and anticipation that moved a nineteenth-century reader to inscribe on the cover of his 1841 Crockett almanac: "Go in boys, hurrah for Davy."[5]

Michael A. Lofaro
UNIVERSITY OF TENNESSEE

NOTES

1. [Matthew St. Clair Clarke], *Sketches and Eccentricities of Col. David Crockett, of West Tennessee* (New York: J. & J. Harper, 1833), 177–79. This work, noted on the title page as a "New Edition," was a reprint of *The Life and Adventures of Colonel David Crockett of West Tennessee* (Cincinnati: For the Proprietor, 1833). The story was also printed in the Boston *Daily Evening Transcript* on June 21, 1833. Other than the fact that the newspaper version does not mention the American versus British lion comparison, the accounts differ only in minor detail and punctuation. For a more readily available transcription of the newspaper tale, see C. Grant Loomis, "Davy Crockett Visits Boston," *New England Quarterly* 20 (September 1947):397.

2. David Crockett, *A Narrative of the Life of David Crockett of the State of Tennessee* (Philadelphia: E. L. Carey & A. Hart, 1834), 4–5.

3. For the Crockett Almanac illustrations from the St. Louis Mercantile Library Association, I am indebted to Dr. Charles F. Bryan, Jr., Director, and Mr. John Neal Hoover, Rare Book and Special Collections Librarian.

4. My personal favorite for the "pursue the sensational—it sells" award occurred in early August 1986 at the hands of an interviewer for Capitol Radio, London, who had added a new twist to what he perceived as the demythicizing of Crockett and who refused to be dissuaded from his theme. After I agreed to the telephone interview based on *Davy Crockett: The Man, The Myth, The Legacy, 1786–1986*, a collection of essays that I edited, he began taping and opened with: "Dr. Lofaro, I understand that you have proved in your book that Davy Crockett was fat, bald, and gay . . . [ten-second pause]. . . . I assume that your protracted laughter means that you have *indeed* proved that Crockett was fat, bald, and gay." At that point, I composed myself long enough to explain that I had done no such thing, nor was there any evidence that I had ever uncovered to support such a notion. He was

markedly disappointed and soon cut short his interview after I assured him that I had neither printed or proved a bizarre enough reversal of the historical Crockett's character to warrant his attention.

5. The inscription is at the top of *The Crockett Almanac. 1841. Containing Adventures, Exploits, Sprees & Scrapes in the West, & Life and Manners in the Backwoods* (Nashville, Tenn.: Published by Ben Harding). The almanac is in the collection of the Newberry Library.

Acknowledgments

On August 15, 1986, a symposium was held on the campus of East Tennessee State University in Johnson City, Tennessee, as part of the celebration of the two-hundredth birthday of David Crockett. At this meeting, many of the authors were able to meet as a group for the first time to discuss and analyze Crockett's role in American culture. The editors wish to thank the sponsors of the symposium—the Tennessee Department of Conservation, the Center for Appalachian Studies and Services at East Tennessee State University, and the Department of History at East Tennessee State University—for this opportunity. They also wish to thank Ms. Kathryn B. Croxton for her assistance in helping to bring this volume to fruition.

A NOTE ON EDITORIAL METHOD

This edition follows the standard convention of referring to the historical Crockett as David and the fictional Crockett as Davy. It also retains the often inconsistent original spelling and punctuation of the primary texts.

A Crockett Chronology

Michael A. Lofaro

1786 On August 17, David is born to John and Rebecca Hawkins Crockett in Greene County, Tennessee.

1796 Tennessee joins the Union. The Crocketts open a tavern on the road from Knoxville to Abingdon, Virginia.

1798 John Crockett hires his son out to Jacob Siler to help to drive a herd of cattle to Rockbridge County, Virginia. Siler tries to detain David by force after the contract is completed, but the boy escapes and eventually arrives home in late 1798 or early 1799.

1799 David starts school, prefers playing hooky, and runs away from home to escape his father's punishment. He works as a wagoner and a day laborer and at odd jobs for two and one-half years.

1802 David returns home and is welcomed by all his family.

1803 David willingly works and discharges his father's debts of seventy-six dollars.

1805 He takes out a license to marry Margaret Elder of Dandridge, Tennessee, on October 21, but she decides to marry another.

1806 Crockett courts and marries Mary (Polly) Finley on August 14 in Jefferson County, Tennessee.

1811 David, Polly, and their two sons, John Wesley and William, leave East Tennessee after September 11 and settle on the Mulberry fork of Elk River in Lincoln County, Tennessee.

1813 Crockett leaves Lincoln County to settle on the Rattlesnake Spring Branch of Bean's Creek in Franklin County, Tennessee, near the present Alabama border. He names his homestead "Kentuck." In September, Crockett enlists in the militia in Winchester, Tennessee, to avenge the Indian attack on Fort Mims, Alabama, and serves as a scout under Major Gibson. Under Andrew Jackson, he participates in the retributive massacre of the Indian town of Tallussahatchee on November 3. David's ninety-day enlistment expires on the day before Christmas and he returns home.

1814 Jackson defeats the Creeks at the Battle of Horseshoe Bend on

March 28. Crockett reenlists on September 28 as third sergeant in Captain John Cowan's company and serves until March 27, 1815. He arrives the day after Jackson's taking of Pensacola on November 7, 1814. Crockett attempts to ferret out the British-trained and supplied Indians from the Florida swamps.

1815 Discharged as a fourth sergeant, David returns home to find himself again a father. His wife, Polly, dies the summer after Margaret's birth, although David found her in good health on his return.

1816 Crockett is elected a lieutenant in the Thirty-second Militia Regiment of Franklin County on May 22 and marries Elizabeth Patton, a widow with two children (George and Margaret Ann), before summer's end. In the fall, he explores Alabama with an eye toward settlement, catches malaria, and nearly dies. He is reported dead and astonishes his family with his "resurrection."

1817 By about September, the Crocketts have settled in the territory soon to become Lawrence County, Tennessee, at the head of Shoal Creek. David becomes a justice of the peace on November 17.

1818 He becomes town commissioner of Lawrenceburg before April 1. Crockett is also elected colonel of the Fifty-seventh Militia Regiment in the county.

1819 Crockett resigns his position as justice of the peace.

1821 On January 1, he resigns as commissioner, having decided to run for a seat in the state legislature as the representative of Lawrence and Hickman counties. After two months of campaigning, Crockett wins the August election. From the very first of his political career, he takes an active interest in public land policy regarding the West. The House adjourns on November 17, and David, and his son John Wesley, and Abram Henry, explore the Obion River country.

1822 The Crocketts move west and settle near the Obion River after the second legislative session ends.

1823 Crockett defeats Dr. William E. Butler and is reelected to the state legislature.

1824 Crockett ends his state political career on October 22, when the House adjourns.

1825 In August, Crockett is defeated in his first bid for a seat in Congress.

1826 Nearly dying as his boats carrying barrel staves wreck in the Mississippi River, Crockett is brought to Memphis and is encouraged to run for Congress again by M. B. Winchester.

1827   Crockett defeats General William Arnold and Colonel Adam Alexander for a seat in the United States House of Representatives.

1828   Andrew Jackson is elected president.

1829   Crockett is reelected. He splits with Jackson and with the Tennessee delegation on several issues during this term in office.

1830   Crockett attacks the Indian removal bill.

1831   James Kirke Paulding's play *The Lion of the West,* with James Hackett playing the leading character of Nimrod Wildfire, opens in New York City at the Park Theater on April 25. In his campaign for a third congressional term, Crockett speaks openly against Jackson's policies. He is defeated by William Fitzgerald in a close election.

1833   Mathew St. Clair Clarke's *The Life and Adventures of Colonel David Crockett of West Tennessee* is deposited for copyright on January 5. It is soon reprinted under the title *Sketches and Eccentricities of Colonel David Crockett of West Tennessee.* Crockett defeats the incumbent Fitzgerald and again wins a seat in Congress.

1834   Crockett publishes his autobiography, *A Narrative of the Life of David Crockett of the State of Tennessee,* written with the help of Thomas Chilton. On April 25, he begins his three-week tour through the eastern states in an anti-Jacksonian alliance with the Whigs.

1835   Two Whig books are published under Crockett's name: *Col. Crockett's Tour to the North and Down East* in late March and *Life of Martin Van Buren* less than three months later. The earliest known copy of "The Crockett Victory March" (*"Go Ahead" a march dedicated to Colonel Crockett*) and the first Crockett almanac are published. (The almanac was very likely published in 1834 for 1835.) Adam Huntsman defeats Crockett in the election for Congress, and Crockett, together with William Patton, Abner Burgin, and Lindsey K. Tinkle, set out for Texas on November 1.

1836   In January, Crockett and Patton sign the oath of allegiance to the "Provisional Government of Texas or any future republican Government that may be hereafter declared. . . ." In early February, Crockett arrived in San Antonio De Bexar. On March 6, he is captured and executed after Santa Anna's army captures the Alamo. Early in the summer *Col. Crockett's Exploits and Adventures in Texas* is compiled and fabricated by Richard Penn Smith. That fall, Jackson's handpicked successor, Martin Van Buren, is elected president. A "new edition" of *Crockett's Free-and-Easy Song Book* is published.

1839   "Colonel Crockett: A Virginia Reel" is published. *Colonel Crockett's Free and Easy Recitation Book* is announced as "in press."

1846   The first known publication of "Pompey Smash: The Everlastin and Unkonkerable Skreamer" occurs in *The Negro Singer's Own Book; Containing Every Negro Song That Has Ever Been Sung or Printed.*

1856   The last Crockett almanac is issued for this year.

1860   Reuben M. Potter's study, "Fall of the Alamo," is published.

1871   To honor the frontiersman, Crockett County, Tennessee, is created, and its county seat is named Alamo.

1872   The play *Davy Crockett; Or, Be Sure You're Right, Then Go Ahead,* by Frank Murdock and Frank Mayo, begins a twenty-four year run in this country and in England that terminates only with the death of Frank Mayo, who played Davy, in 1896.

1873   W. P. Zuber first publishes his "improved" account of the last dramatic days at the Alamo.

1889   The first major Crockett celebration is organized by Benjamin Rush Strong at Crockett's birthplace.

1909   The New York Motion Picture Company brings out a silent film entitled *Davy Crockett—in Hearts United.* Charles K. French plays the lead.

1910   The film *Davy Crockett* is released by Selig Polyscope Company.

1911   Davy is a minor character in the film *The Immortal Alamo* (Melies).

1915   Davy, played by A. D. Sears, again has a small part in *The Martyrs of the Alamo,* released by Fine Arts–Triangle, but his is the title role in *Davy Crockett Up-to-Date,* a slapstick farce released by United Film Service.

1916   The Oliver Morosco Photoplay Co. produces *Davy Crockett* starring Dustin Farnum. It is released by Pallas (Paramount).

1926   The last Crockett silent film, *Davy Crockett at the Fall of the Alamo,* is released by Sunset with Cullen Landis playing Crockett.

1934   Constance Rourke publishes *Davy Crockett.*

1937   Lane Chandler stars in the first "Crockett talkie," *Heroes of the Alamo,* which is produced by Sunset and released by Columbia.

1939   Richard Dorson extracts 108 tales from the Crockett almanacs to produce *Davy Crockett: American Comic Legend.* Robert Barrat portrays Crockett in *Man of Conquest,* a film released by Republic.

1940   Walter Blair delineates "Six Davy Crocketts," in *Southwest Review* 25 (1940):443–62.

1950   The film *Davy Crockett, Indian Scout* is released by Reliance. George Montgomery plays Davy Crockett, "cousin" of the hero.

1953   Trevor Bardette plays Crockett in the film *Man from the Alamo* (Universal).

1954   Walt Disney broadcasts "Davy Crockett, Indian Fighter" in his *Frontierland* series on December 15. Fess Parker stars. "The Ballad of Davy Crockett," written by George Bruns and Tom Blackburn, also makes its debut.

1955   The year of the Crockett craze. Two more episodes, "Davy Crockett Goes to Congress" (January 26) and "Davy Crockett at the Alamo" (February 23), were shown and then combined with the first episode to form the Disney movie *Davy Crockett, King of the Wild Frontier*. Two more episodes, "Davy Crockett's Keelboat Race" (November 16) and "Davy Crockett and the River Pirates" (December 14), were also shown. Franklin J. Meine's *The Crockett Almanacks: Nashville Series, 1835–1838* is published. Arthur Hunnicutt portrays Crockett in the film *The Last Command* (Republic).

1956   The last two Disney television shows are combined into a movie, *Davy Crockett and the River Pirates,* that is released in July. James A. Shackford publishes *David Crockett: The Man and the Legend,* the definitive biography of the historical Crockett. The film *The First Texan* is released by Allied Artists with James Griffith playing Crockett.

1959   Fess Parker portrays Crockett in a walk-on part in the film *Alias Jesse James* (United Artists).

1960   John Wayne produces, directs, and stars as Crockett in *The Alamo* (United Artists).

1961   Walter Lord publishes his study of the Alamo, *A Time to Stand.*

1975   José Enrique de la Peña's *With Santa Anna in Texas: A Personal Narrative of the Revolution* is translated and edited by Carmen Perry.

1978   *How Did Davy Die?* is published by Dan Kilgore.

1982   Richard Boyd Hauck publishes *Crockett: A Bio-Bibliography.*

1984   James Wakefield Burke's "imaginative"/fictional biography of Crockett is published.

1985   Michael A. Lofaro's *Davy Crockett: The Man, The Legend, The Legacy, 1786–1986* is published. *Alamo Images: Changing Perceptions of a Texas Experience* is published by Susan Prendergast Schoelwer with Tom W. Glaser.

1986   The bicentennial of the birth of David Crockett and the sesquicentennial of his death, the battle of the Alamo, and the founding of the Republic of Texas are celebrated. On June 14, the exhibit "Davy Crockett: Gentleman from the Cane" opens in the Smithsonian Institution's National Portrait Gallery and is later displayed in the Tennessee State Museum. Walter Blair's 1955 work on the life and tall tales of the frontiersman is reprinted as *Davy Crockett: Legendary Frontier Hero*. Gary Foreman's pictorial compilation *Crockett: Gentleman from the Cane* is published.

1987   *The Tall Tales of Davy Crockett: The Second Nashville Series of Crockett Almanacs, 1839–1841* is published by Michael A. Lofaro. Crockett's autobiography is reissued with a new introduction by Paul Andrew Hutton. The television film *The Alamo: 13 Days to Glory* is aired.

1988   The Disney studios bring Davy back on *The Magical World of Disney* in a new series. The first episode, "Davy Crockett: Rainbow in the Thunder" (November 20) starred Johnny Cash as the elder Crockett reminiscing about his exploits in the Creek Wars. Tim Dunigan played the young Crockett.

1989   *Crockett at Two Hundred: New Perspectives on the Man and the Myth* is published.

Crockett at Two Hundred

Introduction

Walter Blair

Although many Americans abominate historic dates and believe that only pedantic schoolteachers cherish them, when such dates come along in century and half-century sizes, a large number of Americans not only tolerate them but actually join in celebrations of them. So in 1986 the 200th anniversary of David Crockett's birth and the 150th anniversary of his death were enthusiastically commemorated. As a result, our country's most durable legendary hero enjoyed still another of many resurrections.

The 150th anniversary of Crockett's demise concatenated with the sesquicentennial of a memorable event, the siege and the fall of the Alamo between February 23 and March 6, 1836, a battle that itself is unforgettable in part because it was the sort of a clash that has fascinated and moved mankind for more than three thousand years. In each such a battle, a brave but hopelessly outnumbered force was completely annihilated by a much larger one, and the defeated leaders became heroes — Saul at Mount Gilboa; Leonidas at Thermopylae; Custer at Little Bighorn; and in San Antonio, Texas, Travis, Bowie, and Crockett. The 1836 massacre gave Texans a battle cry that helped them drive the Mexican army across the Rio Grande: "Remember the Alamo!"

In 1986 Texans urged Americans to recall that slogan and the Alamo's most famous defender, Crockett. And since Texans were simultaneously celebrating their state's sesquicentennial, they did things on a huge scale, staging ten thousand special events, ranging from visits by two or three presidents to an oatmeal cookoff and a bike race in Oatmeal, Texas, presided over by Miss Bag of Oats.

On June 14, 1986, an exhibit commemorating Crockett's birth and death opened in the Smithsonian Institution's National Portrait Gallery in Washington, D.C. — "Davy Crockett: Gentleman from the Cane." The gallery displayed memorabilia such as its subject's rifle, his watch, and his snuff box; a complete collection of portraits of him and of famous American contemporaries: Jackson, Webster, Clay, and others; and books, almanacs, and other publications featuring the Tennesseean.

This exhibit would later be displayed in the Tennessee State Museum in Nashville as part of a third celebration which Tennessee, as the state of Crockett's birth, initiated in the Davy Crockett Birthplace State Historic Area, in Limestone, August 15. It would be continued there through the two-hundredth birthday on August 17.

The Limestone festivities featured a parade, displays of folk crafts, black-powder musket shooting, mountain music concerts, country dances, horse races, and—for more modern touches—fireworks and a film festival. The academic contribution to this commemoration was the presentation at East Tennessee State University in nearby Johnson City of a symposium in which a number of the papers collected in the present volume were presented and discussed. This gathering, as well as the Limestone festivities, was arranged by Joe Cummings of the Tennessee Department of Conservation. The symposium was sponsored by the Center for Appalachian Studies and Services and the Department of History at East Tennessee State University, and the activities at Limestone were sponsored by the Limestone Ruritan Club, the Tennessee Folklore Society, the National Endowment for the Arts, and the Tennessee Department of Conservation.

Other areas in Tennessee also joined in the birthday party. Fittingly, the first occurred on the July 4 weekend at Alamo, Tennessee, and another at Lawrenceburg, held at the David Crockett State Park, coincided with the events at Limestone. A pair of Tennessee towns held celebrations later—Morristown, home of the Davy Crockett Tavern and Museum, August 23–25, and Rutherford, October 6–12.

Since the Nashville showing of the Smithsonian exhibition, accompanied by various events, opened October 9 and continued until the end of 1986, Texas, the District of Columbia, and Tennessee, between them, drew attention to Crockett's biography and his repute for almost a whole year.

The celebrations attracted nationwide attention and inspired a number of newspapers, magazine articles, and books about Crockett. Inevitably therefore Davy, as has been said, enjoyed the latest of a remarkably large number of rebirths.

His first, it might be asserted, took place during the man's lifetime—in 1816, when he had just started his rise by winning fame as a Tennessee hunter, fighting Indians, and getting elected a militia lieutenant. He'd left his family to explore a new frontier in Alabama. Laid low by malaria, he couldn't write home, his horse came back riderless, and his wife received reports that he'd died and had been buried. When at long last he turned up, Mrs. Crockett understandably was "utterly astonished."

Crockett's second reincarnation would occur twenty years later. Meanwhile, he'd risen from local officeholder to three-term U.S. Congressman and national celebrity. A reason: he was exactly the kind of fellow Americans were going for—a garish eccentric from the section then building power under Andrew Jackson. Speeches and tall tales attributed to him, whether justifiably or not, were cited as his typical frontier talk.

An instance: his name as a hunter even spread among the animals. So the minute a treed raccoon recognized him, it yelled, "Don't shoot! I'm a-comin' down!" And though political opponents spread anecdotes about his horrible gaucheries, he and his backers played up a favorite democratic paradox—that if a man has experience and horse sense, a lack of book learning actually helps him be smart and amusing. So he coined a personal motto perfect for flush times: "Be sure you're right, then go ahead." And his warning to his constituents was tense and clear: "Vote for me or not; but if you don't yawl can go to hell and I'll go to Texas."

They didn't, he did, and his death fed posthumous fame that promptly took the form of a second comeback. During two decades a play about him, *The Lion of the West*, showed him still boasting, storytelling, and cracking wise. Gossip, books about him (some purportedly his), and minstrel show songs sung countrywide repeatedly told about his exploits.

Most notably, Crockett almanacs, published for every year from 1835 to 1856 in Boston, New York, and other cities, told not only old anecdotes about him but many new ones about travels and adventures of his that took place years after the Alamo fell. Over fifty almanacs were published, and these illustrated pamphlets—the calendars, weather forecasts, feature sections, and comic books, so to speak, of that day—had huge readerships: few homes were without one.

And for them, journalists concocted some of the best and most often repeated tall tales about Davy; e.g., one about his deflecting Halley's comet from a collision course and one about his unfreezing the earth's axis one cold morning by pouring bear oil onto it, thus saving the planet and all its flora and fauna a couple of times.

Between 1871 and 1896, writings of two then very popular sorts brought another Crockett recycling. Six Beadle & Adams dime novels, chiefly about the hero's hunting exploits, fetched legions of childish buyers of all ages.

And a melodrama, *Davy Crockett; Or, Be Sure You're Right,* was a vehicle for an admired actor, Frank Mayo, that had more than two thousand performances before Mayo's death ended its run.

Paying minimal attention to biographical facts, this dramatization turned Davy into one of nature's noblemen—one who strikingly resembled Natty Bumppo and who even, like Natty, forsook his dialect at crucial times. In one big scene, for instance, a pack of ravenous wolves tried to break down a cabin door and dine on him and the heroine. Davy vowed he'd hold it closed all night by using "the strong arm of a backwoodsman" for a bar, did so, and only after hours remarked, "This is kind of monotonous."

And when, on a stallion, he rescued the girl from an unloved groom, he hollered, "Whoop, I'm Lochinvar! Who dares to follow?" The script was so much admired that in 1916 it was recycled into a movie starring matinee idol Dustin Farnum.

Between 1954 and 1956, the most awesome of all the Crockett resurrections so far triggered a national craze. A popular new toy—television—brought into American homes a Disney Studio series about Crockett, with its haunting theme song. The program attracted an obsessed viewing audience of parents and their many baby-boom offspring, ripe for exploitation by modern merchandisers.

Everybody had to watch telecasts in which big, handsome Fess Parker, as Davy, played a role sort of based upon the historic frontiersman's biography and the legends about him, gussied up for mid-1950s viewers. As portrayed, Crockett now and then was a humorist, but more often he was so wise, noble, brave, athletic, and ept as a hunter and warrior that he seemed rather too good to be true. More memorable as a comic character was his sidekick, Georgie Russel, played by Buddy Ebsen, later a star clown in "Beverly Hillbillies."

The spinoffs were prodigious. Every Spock-marked kid had to have a coonskin cap, and raccoon-tail prices shot up 1,900 percent. Three thousand other Crockett items amassed huge sales—seven million records of that theme song, for instance; millions of new books and reprints of old ones; an industry with a total gross of $400 million in two-and-a-half years.

In 1960, a little late to partake in Davy's Disneyfied resurrection, John Wayne produced, directed, and starred in *The Alamo,* which recreated Crockett in the Duke's own blowsier (and historically more accurate) image. The movie, the show, and scores of woodcuts, drawings, and paintings had convinced many viewers that they knew for a fact one thing about the battle of the Alamo: that Davy had died heroically during the siege.

But in the 1970s, several reputable scholars reexamined some previously discounted old evidence and uncovered some new evidence with startling results. They decided that—though no less heroically—Davy actually had been killed after the fortress had been taken that fateful morning. When Dan Kilgore, a former president of the Texas State Historical Association, offered strong support for this thesis in *How Did Davy Die?*, outraged Crockettophiles fiercely attacked him and suggested that he and others who agreed with him were probably atheists, Communists, or intellectuals, or maybe all three.

The roundhouse swings some Texans took at Kilgore's book suggest how Crockett's latest reincarnation differs from the earlier ones. Each earlier postmortem reincarnation had been appropriate for its period. In the 1830s, '40s, and '50s, a comic demigod was popularized by tall tales that the man himself, his acquaintances, political backers, political opponents, newspaper reporters, and almanac makers told about him. In the 1870s, '80s, and '90s, the updated Davy was a sentimental and sensationalized creation of melodrama and dime novels. In the 1950s and '60s, affectionate heroic portrayals in television series, motion pictures, comic books, cartoon strips, and popular biographies gave the world the idol of the masses, the "King of the Wild Frontier."

As early as 1927, Vernon L. Parrington, in the second volume of his in many ways admirable *Main Currents in American Thought*, had noticed that two representations of Crockett contrasted sharply. One was of "the real man"—a "wastrel," "an assertive, opinionated, likeable fellow, ready to fight, drink, shoot or brag, the biggest frog in a very small puddle, first among the Smart Alecks of the canebrakes." The other was the mythical Davy—"a deliberate fabrication," Parrington believed, resulting from "the exploitation of Davy's canebrakes waggery, the exploitation of his anti-Jackson spleen, and the exploitation of his dramatic death at the Alamo."

In the years that followed, other writers studied contradictory portrayals of Crockett and decided that reasons for disparities were more complex, even, than Parrington had claimed. "The real man," for instance, had been more of a mixture of admirable and not so admirable traits. And the "mythic" Davy was the product not only of "exploitations" but also of imaginative tales spread by different kinds of narrators—fireside yarnspinners, East Coast almanac makers, newspaper feature writers, and the authors of cinema and television scripts.

Two kinds of reactions to the contrasting representations resulted. Members of one group championed one kind of picturing and attacked other picturings. James A. Shackford, the author of *Davy Crockett: the Man and the Legend* (1956), the best account so far of the life of the historic Crockett, did his best to say some kind things about the mythical Davy but, in the end, dismissed him in favor of his own documented representation of "the man himself." And during subsequent decades, admirers of "the mythical Davy" — in fact both admirers and some detractors of contrasting versions of "the mythical Davy" — have voiced resentment toward those who differed with them.

A second kind of response has been the one embodied in recent symposiums and books, including the present volume. Typically, its practitioners are eager to sort out historical facts and fanciful legends and, as appreciatively as possible, to explore the significance of both. The first two chapters of Richard Boyd Hauck's *Crockett: A Bio-Bibliography* (1982) are entitled "The Facts" and "The Fictions." *Davy Crockett,* edited by Michael A. Lofaro and published in 1985, reveals its concerns by its subtitle, *The Man, the Legend, the Legacy, 1786–1986.* And a book of the same year much concerned with Crockett, the fat, handsomely illustrated *Alamo Images,* edited by Susan Prendergast Schoelwer with Tom W. Glaser, has as its appropriate subtitle *Changing Perceptions of a Texas Experience.*

New Perspectives on the Man and the Myth, this volume's subtitle, emphasizes its dual concern. Co-editor Joe Cummings had made this palpable in his organization of the Limestone birthday party, with part of its program recalling folk and popular roots of the legend and part — the symposium — defining, contrasting, and relating the legendary Davy and the historic David. Readers certainly will find such contrasts and interrelationships fascinating. And they also just may somehow find useful in our democracy a study of the procedures that contributors have used to discriminate true history from tall tales.

Why Davy Didn't Die

Dan Kilgore

David Crockett was born in Tennessee on August 17, 1786, and for over forty-nine years lived as a proud resident of the state. During those years he acquired a national reputation as a frontiersman, a bear hunter, and as West Tennessee's representative in Congress. After his defeat in 1835 for re-election to Congress, he departed for Texas, where he would live for only two months. He died there on March 6, 1836, one of a small band of defenders overwhelmed and massacred by Mexican troops at the Alamo.

Within days after the Alamo's fall, two very different reports of Crockett's final moments were in circulation. One version of Crockett's death was that the Tennessean fought herocially to his last breath against the massive onslaught of Santa Anna's army. Published a few months after his death, the 1837 Crockett almanac is an early example of this account. The almanac reported to its readers that:

> Colonel Crockett's body was found in an angle of two buildings with his big dagger in his hand, and around him were lying seventeen dead Mexicans, eleven of whom had come to their deaths by his dagger, and the others by his rifle and four pistols, which laid beside him. In the dark he had a decided advantage over them, as they could not get behind him, and he stabbed them as they passed by in the charge. He had received two musket balls in his body, both of which were mortal. A smile of scorn played on his features. . . . Thus perished Crockett in a noble cause.[1]

This account and others that are similar, including the modern film and television portrayals of Crockett by Fess Parker in 1955 and John Wayne in 1960, have become a familiar part of our nation's mythology. It must be remembered, however, that none of the Alamo's defenders survived the battle to relate Crockett's final moments and that Mexican observers reported that the frontiersman met his demise in an equally gallant, but very different manner. José Enrique de la Peña, an aide to Santa Anna who fought in the final battle, recorded in his diary that:

> Shortly [after the fall of the Alamo and] before Santa Anna's speech, an unpleasant episode had taken place, which . . . was looked upon as base murder. . . .

> Some seven men had survived the general carnage and, under the protection of General Castrillòn, they were brought before Santa Anna. Among them . . . was the naturalist David Crockett, well known in North America for his unusual adventures. . . . Santa Anna answered Castrillòn's intervention in Crockett's behalf with a gesture of indignation and, addressing himself to . . . the troops closest to him, ordered his execution. The commanders and officers were outraged at this action and did not support the order . . . ; but several officers who were around the president and who, perhaps, had not been present during the moment of danger . . . thrust themselves forward, . . . and with swords in hand, fell upon these unfortunate defenseless men just as a tiger leaps upon his prey. Though tortured before they were killed, these unfortunates died without complaining and without humiliating themselves before their torturers.[2]

Several eyewitness accounts to his death, such as that of de la Peña, confirm that Crockett's emergence as a modern folk hero is rooted in a foundation that he himself helped lay and that is both fact and fiction. His heroism is as undisputable as his style of talking and of telling stories is entertainingly distinctive, and both helped to create his legendary image. Crockett employed his wit, imagination, and charm to establish his position as a great American frontier character in the mind of the public.

Fortunately, Crockett was an author as well as a storyteller. In 1834, he recounted his own life story, *A Narrative of the Life of David Crockett of the State of Tennessee,* in response to a bogus [auto]biography, *Sketches and Eccentricities of Colonel David Crockett of West Tennessee,* written the year before by Mathew St. Claire Clarke. Both volumes significantly increased his national popularity and were the sources for many of the legends about him.[3]

The printed works most responsible for spreading his legend over the longest period of time, however, were the Crockett almanacs. The first of these, the 1835 issue, went to press the same year as *A Narrative,* his true autobiography. These almanacs contained a calendar along with the usual weather statistics and predictions. But more important for the developing legend, they included many tall tales in a contrived frontier dialect that promoted a good-old-boy image of Crockett. A second issue for 1836 reached the printers in late 1835, probably about the time Crockett departed for Texas.[4] After his death at the Alamo, the Crockett Almanacs were widely read and continued to pour forth for twenty years. Until the final issue in 1856, thirty-three distinct issues in at least fifty imprints by several different publishers kept the frontiersman's name and legend alive.

Two hundred years after his birth, Crockett is the most widely known folk hero of the United States and has attained mythical status because of his heroic death at the Alamo. While he gained wide renown during his lifetime, it is not likely that he would be remembered today any more than numerous other colorful characters who appeared on the American scene and then were forgotten. He is remembered and revered today because of his final sacrifice rather than for his lifetime accomplishments.

The 1837 Crockett almanac, printed only a few months after the battle of the Alamo, was one of the first publications to capitalize on his death with one of the most exaggerated accounts of his last stand as well as his prowess during the siege and helped to create and build his legend with an incredible account of the Tennessean's unerring aim during the siege.

> Fear was a word he [Crockett] knew not the definition of. It was calculated that during the siege he killed no less than 85 men, and wounded 120 besides, as he was one of the best rifle shooters of the west, and he had four rifles, with two men to load constantly, and he fired as fast as they could load, nearly always hitting his man; but the distance was so great that he could not put the ball through a mortal place every time.[5]

The true story of the fall of the Alamo is that of one of the great symbolic battles of all time, a classic last stand of dedicated men fighting against insurmountable odds for their deeply held beliefs. The historical David Crockett, not the legendary Davy of the almanacs, and the other defenders willingly chose to remain in the fortress with full knowledge that they would receive no quarter in their inevitable defeat. Their heroic defense, often likened to an American Thermopylæ, is especially revered by Texans who attribute their state's independence from Mexico to the delay of Santa Anna's army created by the defenders of the Alamo.

All great battles have their heroes, and three men, William Barrett Travis, James Bowie, and David Crockett, emerge as the "trinity of heroes" of the Alamo. But Crockett always looms large over the other two because more attention has been focused on the details of his legendary final stand. It is now generally accepted that Travis was shot on the north wall of the fort early in the onslaught. The ailing Bowie, noted as a hand-to-hand fighter, lay propped up on his cot, and, according to legend, died firing his two pistols.[6] Although the final moments of these two men are usually not questioned, Crockett's death is shrouded in mystery and was mythicized from the earliest reports of the battle.

Although eastern newspapers carried accounts of Crockett's execution, in Texas the frontiersman was soon remembered as dying a more valiant death. Only twenty days after the massacre, a resolution adopted at Nacogdoches on March 28, 1836, laid the foundation for the 1837 almanac account by declaring that "David Crockett (now rendered immortal in Glory) had fortified himself with sixteen guns well charged, and a monument of slain foes encompasses his lifeless body." A letter from San Augustine, dated March 29, declared: "The Honorable David Crockett . . . was found dead with about 20 of the enemy with him and his rifle was broken to pieces it is supposed that he killed at least 20 or 30 himself."[7]

The development of the legend of Crockett's death is so closely entwined with the legend of the Alamo that the two cannot be distinguished. As a recent study points out, "There have always been two Alamos – the Alamo of historical fact and the Alamo of our collective imagination."[8] The Alamo of our collective imagination, however, so dominates that of historical fact that no professional historian has even undertaken a definitive study of the battle. Amelia Williams's doctoral dissertation, published in the *Southwestern Historical Quarterly,* is considered to be the best academic study of the battle, but has been described as "of stunningly poor quality." Most of the large body of literature on the battle merely repeats the legends and false stories that have been told before.[9]

The drama and mystery of the battle captured public interest and are responsible for the legends. Not one defender survived to tell the story, and accounts from noncombatant survivors and other sources vary so widely that most of them obscure rather than clarify any questions. Did Travis really draw the line with his sword? Did he even deliver his impassioned speech? Was Crockett the last to die, and how did he meet his death? These and other questions have been debated ever since the smoke of the battle cleared.

Most of the details of the Alamo of our collective imagination derive from the writings of two Texas historians, Reuben M. Potter and W. P. Zuber. Today only serious students of the battle know their names. While neither gave particular attention to the death of Crockett in their studies, both Potter and Zuber vigorously denounced anyone who questioned that he did not die fighting to his last breath. Both men were committed absolutely to the idea of the Alamo as a great heroic epic and took vehement exception to any suggestion that Crockett died under other circumstances. Both men lived until after 1900, and both stoutly defended their accounts by reiterating and revising their positions and by attacking anyone who questioned their views.

Potter's "Fall of the Alamo" was the first major study published after the event and remained the principal source for writers for many years.[10] In 1914, the distinguished Texas historian, Eugene C. Barker, described it as the most thorough study of the battle then available.[11] Potter's study first appeared in pamphlet form in 1860, twenty-four years after the battle. It received much wider circulation after the *Texas Almanac* reprinted it in 1868. A revised and enlarged version, published in the *Magazine of American History* in 1878, gave Potter's account national attention. Later works on the battle, supported by documents not available to Potter, proved the error of some of his conclusions but could not overcome his powerful influence on earlier historians.

As public interest in the Alamo saga increased in the late nineteenth century, the manner of Crockett's death first emerged as an issue. The eyewitness account of Francisco Becerra, a Mexican sergeant, who said that Crockett was captured after the battle and shot by Santa Anna's order, received wide circulation following its publication in 1875.[12] The noted historian Hubert Howe Bancroft denounced the report that Crockett was put to death as a captive as "utterly unworthy of credence."[13]

Over the years Potter criticized the Becerra story and in 1880 stated that "David Crockett never surrendered to bear or tiger, Indian or Mexican." An 1883 article in the *Magazine of American History* that dared to suggest otherwise drew his wrath. He remained convinced that Crockett and every other man in the garrison fell fighting at their posts—with the exception of "a few skulkers." Even these skulkers did not surrender but were dragged from their hiding places and slain.

In 1886, Potter again blasted the tale of the Mexican sergeant; "This infamous fiction confounds [Travis and Crockett] with a group of skulkers already referred to and ought never to have been cited, even as a rumor, in any matter which claims to be historical." Potter did not justify his views by hard evidence but by his preconceived notion that "in a fight . . . [when the hopelessly outnumbered] know they have all got to die, the bravest fall first; the last reached is certain to be a sneak. Thus it was at the Alamo. Travis and Crockett fell early on the outworks." His preconceptions required the events to follow a given sequence. Travis and Crockett had to be among the first to die. Any purported evidence to the contrary would be inconsistent with his theory.[14]

Besides his writings, Potter contributed greatly to the Alamo image through his friendship with Henry Arthur McArdle, the noted Texas historical painter. McArdle's famous *Dawn at the Alamo* is probably the most widely reproduced depiction of the battle scene and reflects the fact that Potter was McArdle's principal advisor on historical matters. He corresponded with the artist for more than ten years—from about 1874 until well after the completion of the painting in 1883. In his early letters to McArdle, Potter advocated wide artistic license by suggesting that the buckskin-clad Crockett hold the widowed Mrs. Dickenson with one hand while firing his last shot with the other. In his final advice to the artist, he changed his mind and suggested the scene that appears in the finished painting: "In that area Crockett, too, actually died; and there we behold him, with clubbed rifle-barrel dealing death to all within his reach and dismay to others who shrink into a safer distance."[15]

The other early historian of the battle, W. P. Zuber, who recorded and probably created more Alamo folklore than any other person, first published his ideas of Alamo history in 1873. Zuber is the single source for the most dramatic episodes during the siege. Only through him do we know of Travis's impassioned speech—which Zuber composed himself "during a phenomenal refreshment of memory."[16] Only on Zuber's word do we know that Travis etched the legendary line in the dirt of the Alamo courtyard with his sword. Only Zuber reported that the ailing Bowie asked his comrades to lift his cot over the line, and that Moses Rose was the only defender who did not step over.

Rose was the last man to leave the Alamo and lived to recount these heroic moments for posterity, and it is through Moses Rose that Zuber gained knowledge of these dramatic incidents. During his flight, Rose recuperated at the home of Zuber's parents. He stayed with the family a week or two, relating many times the speech of Travis and the story of the sword-etched line. Although young Zuber was away with the Texas army at the time, he later learned the speech from his mother, who repeated Travis's stirring words to him over and over. He completed his first version of the speech in 1871, after rewriting and rearranging it many times. Throughout his life, he continued to revise, enlarge, and elaborate on his version of the incidents of the battle, even changing the words of Travis's speech from time to time.

His account of these dramatic scenes appeared in his article, "An Escape from the Alamo," in the 1873 *Texas Almanac*. Travis's speech and the crossing of the line quickly became fixed in the public mind. An expanded version of the incident appeared in a revised edition of Anna J. Hardwicke Pennybacker's *A History of Texas for Schools*, a textbook that was the most widely available history of the state from 1888 until the 1920s. It contained

many tales, both false and true, and became a prime factor in the developing of the Alamo legend.

Zuber, like Potter, maintained that the stories of Texans found hiding
after the battle were certainly fabrications. He said flatly that not one Texan
"escaped or surrendered, or tried to do so; but every man of them died
fighting."[17] The capture by the enemy or the surrender of even one man
would violate his vision of the Alamo as a great heroic epic.

In 1904, Zuber wrote in a letter what Dr. George M. Patrick told him
about the capture of Crockett. Dr. Patrick said that he visited General Martin Perfecto de Cos, Santa Anna's brother-in-law, while Cos was being held
prisoner after his capture at San Jacinto. Patrick asked the general if he had
seen Crockett and if he knew how he had died. Cos answered that he had
found Crockett, who was well dressed and locked alone in a room in the
barracks. Zuber then composed a fanciful entreaty by Crockett, presumably
based on what Patrick had told him years earlier. Zuber quoted Crockett
as explaining that he came to Texas to explore and to become a loyal Mexican citizen, and that he had done no fighting. Following this, Zuber
presented a similar flowery plea by Cos, who had taken Crockett before Santa
Anna with the supplication that his brother-in-law spare the distinguished
former congressman. Zuber had Santa Anna answering impatiently, "You
know your orders," and turning away. Crockett struck at Santa Anna with
a dagger, but "was met by a bayonet-thrust by the hand of a soldier through
the heart."

In the same letter, Zuber declared that the tale was a gross falsehood
based on fabricated stories by Texans who had no knowledge of the actual
events of the Alamo. He maintained that somehow General Cos had learned of the wild stories and adapted them to portray himself as the attempted
savior of Crockett in order to save his own life. Zuber actually denounced
the story because of inaccurate details that he himself had provided. Yet
when he later wrote his memoirs, he again gave differing versions of the
same details. It appears that Zuber, as he once accused a historian who questioned him, "sometimes relied too much on his memory in stating historical
facts."[18]

The work of Potter and Zuber, with some assistance from others, created
the story of the Alamo as it is known today. Controversy over the details
of the battle which arose during their era foreshadowed the recent discus-
sions over the circumstances of Crockett's death. An early commentary on
the battle by a leading Texas humorist a hundred years ago could just as

(Above) Henry A. McArdle's seven-by-twelve-foot oil painting entitled *Dawn at the Alamo* begun in 1876 and completed in 1883. A youthful Crockett can be recognized in the lower right of this work as the figure brandishing his broken rifle over his head. McArdle, one of Texas's most noted historical painters, portrayed Crockett according to the advice given him by Reuben M. Potter. Archives Division, Texas State Library. (Below) Robert Jenkins Onderdonk, *The Fall of the Alamo*, 1903. The original title, *Crockett's Last Stand*, more accurately describes the theme of this famous oil painting which reflects the popular perception of Crockett's final moments. Friends of the Governor's Mansion, Austin.

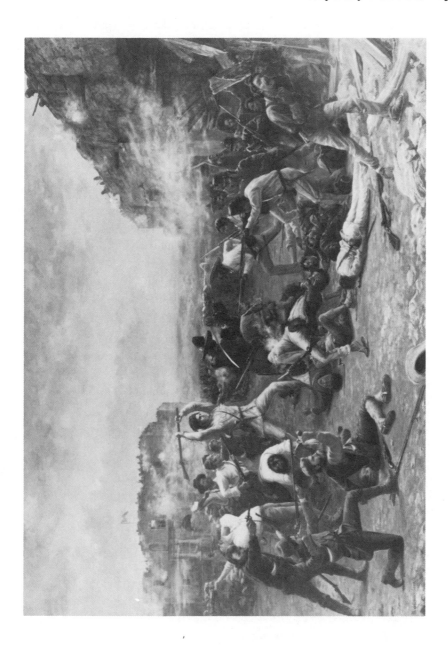

well have been written today. This exaggerated account from a volume of Texas humor describes a tourist's visit to the Alamo in the early 1880s. After hearing an "aged gentleman" give a graphic, but confusing, account of the battle, the tourist comments:

> There are a great many different and conflicting accounts of the battle; so many, in fact, that I, who have heard all of them, or nearly all, am harassed with doubts about any battle ever having been fought there at all. If what all the old residents and historians say to be true, then there is not a spot within a quarter of a mile of the Alamo where Travis did not yield up his life rather than submit to the hireling foe, who would have shot him, anyhow. There is not a hole or corner in the whole building where Crockett did not offer up, with the butt of his rifle, from eleven to seventy-five Mexicans, most of them of high rank. Adding up all the Mexicans the historians have killed, it aggregates a number that is fearful even to think of. I have read everything that has been written on the subject, including some very poor poetry I made myself; I have had strangers from the North tell me all about it; and I have come to the conclusion, that, after all, I know very little about the battle of the Alamo.[19]

During the visit, the "aged gentleman" recited his opinion of Crockett's death: "'Here he took his position close to the door and piled up dead Mexicans on top of each other, until the doorway was full, and he was killed by a bullet that entered that little window up there.'"[20]

Much the same image dominates the public mind today—a dead Crockett surrounded by bodies of fallen Mexican soldiers he had slain. Crockett's death, like the Alamo, is a symbol arising from our collective imagination. Modern technology through the mass media continues to spread his legend worldwide for all to hear, see, and accept as fact. Crockett today is Fess Parker of the television series and movies of the mid-1950s or John Wayne of the 1960 film, *The Alamo*. The historic David has become "Davy, Davy Crockett,/King of the Wild Frontier." In fact, many people today vigorously object to the documented accounts that he and several others were captured and executed at the end of the battle. Thus it is that the historical David died at the Alamo, but the mythical Davy will live forever.[21]

Ironically, in their efforts to pay homage to Crockett and his death, the early perpetuators of the legends, as well as many other writers who followed, have denied the historical Crockett the true dignity of his final hours. James A. Shackford, who attempted to extract the historical Crockett from his legendary persona in a biography of the frontiersman, agreed when he wrote:

Too much has been made over the details of *how* David died at Alamo. Such details are not important. What is important is he died as he lived. His life was one of indomitable bravery; his death was a death of intrepid courage. His life was one of wholehearted dedication to his concepts of liberty. He died staking his life against what he regarded as intolerable tyranny. A poor man who had long known the devastating consequences of poverty and who all his life had fought a dedicated fight for the right of the dispossessed to a new opportunity, he died defending a poor and insecure people and proclaiming their rights to participate in the arts of self-government.[22]

And, as Shackford reminds us, "Tales of melodrama as have been told are not necessary to establish David Crockett's courage, for that is indelibly imprinted upon his whole conduct throughout his life; they but cheapen, by gilding, a very real and quiet luster which requires no such tawdry aids."[23] There is no conclusive evidence that Crockett surrendered, and no stigma has ever been attached to the capture of an exhausted soldier by an overwhelming foe. The men of Bataan, for example, were forced to surrender by the thousands to an enemy superior in numbers but not in spirit. Like the men of the Alamo, they became heroes, not because they died, but because they delayed the enemy.

As one of the last survivors in a desperate last stand, Crockett faced impossible odds, and the facts are not detrimental to his image. As de la Peña wrote, even though the frontiersman and his comrades were tortured, they died without humiliating themselves before their enemies. Crockett faced death with courage and dignity and thus fulfilled the legend he helped create.

NOTES

1. *Davy Crockett's Almanack 1837* (Nashville: published by the heirs of Col. Crockett; reprint in facsimile, San Marino, Calif.: Huntington Library, 1971), 46.

2. José Enrique de la Peña, *With Santa Anna in Texas: A Personal Narrative of the Revolution*, trans. and ed. Carmen Perry (College Station: Texas A & M University Press, 1975), 52–53; J. Sánchez Garza, ed., *La Rebelion de Texas: Manuscrito inedito de 1836, por un oficial de Santa Anna* (Mexico City: 1955), 70.

3. Richard Boyd Hauck, *Crockett: A Bio-Bibliography* (Westport, Conn.: Greenwood Press, 1982), 45–46, 153.

4. Michael A. Lofaro, "The Hidden 'Hero' of the Nashville Crockett Almanacs," in *David Crockett: The Man, The Legend, The Legacy, 1786–1986*, ed. Michael A. Lofaro, (Knoxville: University of Tennessee Press, 1985), 48, 76.

5. *Davy Crockett's 1837 Almanack,* 46.

6. Walter Lord, *A Time to Stand* (New York: Harper & Brothers, 1961), 155, 165.

7. John J. Jenkins, ed., *The Papers of the Texas Revolution, 1835–1836* (Austin: Presidial Press, 1973), 5: 224; 9: 160.

8. Paul Andrew Hutton, Introduction to *Alamo Images: Changing Perceptions of a Texas Experience,* by Susan Prendergast Schoelwer with Tom W. Glaser (Dallas: DeGolyer Library/Southern Methodist University Press, 1985), 3.

9. Ibid., 3–5.

10. John Henry Brown, *History of Texas, from 1685 to 1892* (St. Louis: L. E. Daniel, 1892), 1: 569, and Dudley G. Wooten, ed., *A Comprehensive History of Texas, 1685–1897,* 2 vols. (Dallas: William G. Scarff, 1898), 1: 410.

11. Frank W. Johnson, *A History of Texas and Texans,* ed. Eugene C. Barker and E. W. Winkler (Chicago: American Historical Society, 1914), 1: 410.

12. "A Mexican Sergeant's Recollections of the Alamo and San Jacinto," *Texas Mute Ranger* (April 1882: 169–172), in John S. Ford Papers, University of Texas Archives, Austin; and *Albert Hanford's Texas State Register for 1878* (Galveston: A. Hanford, 1878), 30.

13. Hubert H. Bancroft, *History of the North Mexican States and Texas,* 2 vols. (San Francisco: A. L. Bancroft and Company, 1889), 2: 211.

14. Clipping from the *Independent Hour* (?), January 26, 1880, in Reuben M. Potter scrapbook, 278–279, University of Texas Archives, Austin; R. M. Potter, "Colonel David Crockett," *Magazine of American History* 11 (February 1884): 177–78; Marcus J. Wright, "Colonel David Crockett of Tennessee," *Magazine of American History* 10 (December 1883): 489; G. Norton Galloway, "Sketch of San Antonio: The Fall of the Alamo," *Magazine of American History* 15 (June 1886): 532–33; and R. M. Potter, "The Legendary Alamo," *Magazine of American History* 16 (September 1886): 211–12.

15. Henry Arthur McArdle, McArdle Companion Battle Paintings Historical Documents 18, 22 (8), 39, Texas State Archives, Austin.

16. W. P. Zuber, "The Escape of Rose from the Alamo," *The Quarterly of the Texas Historical Association* 5 (July 1901): 5; 6 (July 1902): 68.

17. Anna J. Hardwicke Pennybacker, *A New History of Texas for Schools: Revised Edition* (Palestine, Tex.: Percy V. Pennybacker, 1895), 139–40, 183–88; and, W. P. Zuber to Charlie Jeffries, "Inventing Stories about the Alamo," in *In the Shadow of History* (Austin: Texas Folklore Society, 1939), 47.

18. Ibid., 45–47; W. P. Zuber, "Eighty Years in Texas; Reminiscences of a Texas Veteran from 1830 to 1910" (manuscript), 208–214, Texas State Archives, Austin; and, R. B. Blake, "A Vindication of Rose and his Story," in *In the Shadow of History,* 29–34.

19. Alex E. Sweet and J. Amoy Knox, *On a Mexican Mustang through Texas, From the Gulf to the Rio Grande* (Hartford, Conn.: S. S. Scranton & Company, 1883), 291–92.

20. Ibid., 290.

21. For a discussion of these sources, see Dan Kilgore, *How Did Davy Die?* (College Station: Texas A & M University Press, 1978).

22. James A. Shackford, *David Crockett: The Man and the Legend* (Chapel Hill: University of North Carolina Press, 1956), 238–39. Despite his efforts, Shackford also may well have been affected by the legendary Crockett and, as a result, decided to select, from among the many different accounts of Crockett's demise, the least glamorous. According to Shackford the frontiersman was struck down early in the siege by a stray bullet. See pp. 227–35.

23. Ibid., 235.

Davy Crockett

AN EXPOSITION ON HERO WORSHIP

Paul Andrew Hutton

When they held a birthday party for Davy Crockett near Limestone, Tennessee, in August 1986, it got lost amidst the hoopla and hysteria over the Texas Sesquicentennial, was generally forgotten after the national hangover from the Statue of Liberty centennial bash, and did not even receive a tenth of the media coverage lavished on Harvard's 350th anniversary. Nevertheless, the home folks in Tennessee celebrated the fact that Crockett was born two hundred years ago on August 17, 1786.

California real-estate entrepreneur Fess Parker, who enjoyed international fame in the mid-1950s as the title character in Walt Disney's "Davy Crockett, King of the Wild Frontier" television programs and movie, was to be the guest of honor. Parker, whose own birthday is August 16, had to cancel out at the last minute, but the party went ahead without him. There were black-powder shooting competitions, horseraces, a Miss Davy Crockett contest, a Crockett family reunion, and a film festival screening both the Disney version as well as John Wayne's 1960 epic of Crockett's Texas exploits.[1]

It was only fitting that Fess Parker should be invited as the guest of honor to Davy Crockett's two-hundredth birthday party, and that his movie *Davy Crockett, King of the Wild Frontier* be used as the grand finale of the whole affair. Parker and his film remain the key elements of the modern perception of the Crockett legend. The baby boomers who once sported coonskin caps or "Polly Crockett" costumes and endlessly wailed – "Born on a mountain top in Tennessee,/Greenest state in the Land of the Free,/Raised in the woods so's he knew ev'ry tree,/Kilt him a b'ar when he was only three" – have now grown up to be busy yuppies making stock deals, delivering babies, writing legal briefs, selling used cars, and teaching history to kids who never heard of Davy. Times are busier now than in the idyllic summer of 1955, when childish personal visions of Davy's life were acted out in America's backyards. The battle of the Alamo was often replayed, with the tensest moments coming during the arguments over who could be Davy and who had to be the Mexicans (to achieve the proper ratio Mexicans could be killed several times and then get up to renew the attack, but Davy only died once, and he always died hard). Often, of course, Davy won the battle at the Alamo, for historical fact is pleasantly irrelevant to six- and seven-year-olds. Affluent kids donned a full set of accoutrements—coonskin caps, fringed shirts, Old Betsy replicas—but many others made do with a stout stick and a vivid imagination.

Fess Parker was their idol, and they thought of him only as Davy Crockett. While their teenaged sisters swooned over Elvis, they were captivated by Fess. He was tall and handsome, strong and brave, but, more important, he always stood firm for truth and justice. When he fought the Creek Indians, he worked not to spill blood but to end the war, speaking not of slaughter but of the brotherhood of man and the golden rule that you should never kill. (Of course, Davy still had to fight a tomahawk duel with Chief Red Stick to convince him of the power of peace.) When he went to Congress he fought for the rights of the underprivileged and downtrodden—finally sacrificing his chance to be president to defend the rights of the Indians. Then he went to Texas to offer a helping hand to folks fighting for their freedom. Even though their parents told them that he died there, defending the Alamo, many never believed it for a minute. They saw him in that final episode of the Disney television show swinging Old Betsy and clubbing enemy soldiers right and left, but they never saw him die. There was only a fade to the Lone Star flag, and they knew for sure that Davy had whipped all those Mexicans and won the battle—and that's the way it was played out in countless backyards.

Even when they grew up, they never forgot Davy Crockett. Little wonder that when handsome John Kennedy came along and spoke of the brotherhood of man, and fought for the poor and downtrodden, and issued a clarion call to fight for freedom in a distant land, they eagerly followed him. They knew well what he was talking about, for they had been brought up on those same liberal values by Disney's Davy Crockett.

Fess Parker, visiting Vietnam in 1968, was struck by the fact that the American warriors he met were in some ways his own creation. "I suddenly realized that all these kids fighting this war were the Davy Crockett generation," he told *Texas Monthly* contributing editor Stephen Harrigan in a 1986 interview. "That was very painful. Some of those guys I was talking to flew off in their planes the next day and didn't come back."[2]

It would be foolish, of course, to make too strong a connection between

A young Crockett fan from Massachusetts helps to celebrate Davy's two-hundredth birthday at Limestone, Tennessee. Photo by Kelley Scott. *Greeneville [Tennessee] Sun.*

early support for the Vietnam War and the values represented in a 1955 television series. Many serious commentators, however, have rightly pointed out the strong connection between Lyndon Johnson's lifelong fascination with the Alamo and his commitment to make a stand against Communism in Southeast Asia. Many of the young Americans who fought that war had grown up with the Davy Crockett craze. They were undoubtedly influenced by the values Parker so vividly projected on the screen. Just as Parker, as Crockett, had answered the call of destiny and volunteered to fight for freedom in a distant land, so now the Davy Crockett generation was called on by their president to make the same sacrifice. In the beginning, at least, many responded with enthusiasm.

Raised amid the false quiet of the 1950s, buffeted by war, political upheaval, and social revolution in the 1960s and 1970s, the Davy Crockett generation appears to be seeking security and comfort in the 1980s. Now in their mid-thirties and early forties, they are a nostalgic group easily captivated by sugar-coated visions of the decade of their childhood. Davy Crockett, along with Elvis, Ike, and Marilyn, remains a powerful nostalgic symbol. He is at once a historical icon as well as a reminder of idyllic childhood.

Despite the lack of national attention given to Davy Crockett's birthday, there nevertheless remains considerable national, and even international, interest in Crockett among the now-adult members of the Davy Crockett generation. They have provided a ready audience for a cottage publishing industry that has sprung up around the Crockett persona. Although this latest round of publishing cannot compare in quantity of spilled ink to the burst of Crockett books during the mid-1950s craze, it nevertheless has produced a large number of notable Crockettiana titles.

Both the University of Tennessee Press and the University of Nebraska Press have published new editions of Crockett's classic autobiography. The autobiography, full of the rough humor and backcountry dialect eventually enshrined in our highest literary traditions by Mark Twain, is a book of enduring popularity. Peculiarly American in form and tone, it is an important social history of day-to-day pioneer life, a strongly partisan political document, and perhaps most important—the success story of that most beloved of American types, the self-made man. The Tennessee edition, perhaps the most valuable edition from the scholar's perspective, reprints James A. Shackford and Stanley J. Folmsbee's heavily annotated 1973 version of the autobiography. Crockett's narrative is reprinted in facsimile from the first edition with insightful annotations by the editors in wide margins.

The Nebraska edition also reprints the 1834 first edition in facsimile and includes a choice selection of illustrations and a long introduction by this writer. It will prove of more interest to the general reader and casual student.[3]

The University of Nebraska Press also reprinted two other Crockett titles in its highly successful Bison Book paperback series. Virgil E. Baugh's *Rendezvous at the Alamo: Highlights in the Lives of Bowie, Crockett, and Travis* curiously recounts Crockett's Texas adventures based on Richard Penn Smith's 1836 potboiler, which claimed to reprint Crockett's journal found at the Alamo. Smith's book was, of course, long ago discredited as a hoax. Far more useful and interesting is the Bison Book edition of Richard Boyd Hauck's *Davy Crockett: A Handbook,* first published by Greenwood Press in 1982. Hauck, a master of the vast Crockett literature, carefully untangles legend from fact and traces the bumpy evolution of the American romance with the Tennessee pioneer-politician-martyr.[4]

Another notable reprint is Walter Blair's *Davy Crockett: Legendary Frontier Hero.* Blair, along with Richard Dorson and Constance Rourke, was instrumental in rediscovering Crockett in the 1940s and establishing him as an authentic American folk hero. His wonderfully folksy book was first published in 1955 at the height of the Disney craze and was aimed at a mainly juvenile audience, but its warm humor will entrance all readers. Blair's *Tall Tale America,* first published in 1944, has also been reprinted and contains much on Crockett in the same folkloric vein.[5]

The University of North Carolina Press has reissued James Atkins Shackford's standard biography of Crockett, with a new introduction by Michael A. Lofaro. Shackford's 1956 book is oppressively scholarly in tone and can be rather rough going for the general reader, but it remains the best biography and for the most part is a model of careful research. The only Crockett biography to appear since Shackford is James Wakefield Burke's *David Crockett: The Man Behind the Myth* (1984). Burke believes, according to this book's introduction, that a "biographer must be allowed a certain range to his imagination," and then proceeds to prove just how far afield his imagination can run. Fictional characters, invented dialogue, and some fascinating detail on Crockett's sex life mark the book. ("Polly was standing ankle-deep, and naked, in the crystal spring, droplets of water dripping from her, gleaming in the late sunlight like jewels . . . ," begins one of the biography's more interesting paragraphs.) Burke's 1975 Alamo novel *The Blazing Dawn* was the source for this inspirational material.[6]

Considering the televised origins of modern interest in Crockett, it is surprising that a pictorial biography was not attempted until 1986. Gary L. Foreman, who received national attention in 1982 with his proposal to renovate the Alamo site, is another baby boomer who never quite recovered from the Disney Crockett-craze infection. His *Crockett: The Gentleman from the Cane* is a nice paperback compilation of a wide range of Crockett iconography. Not surprisingly, Fess Parker's image shows up four times in the little book. A considerable portion of Susan Prendergast Schoelwer's *Alamo Images,* a lavish catalog based on a Texas sesquicentennial exhibit developed at Southern Methodist University's DeGolyer Library in 1985, is devoted to Crockett as well. It is a treasure trove of Alamo and Crockett imagery.[7]

The best of the Crockett birthday books is Michael A. Lofaro's 1985 anthology published by the University of Tennessee Press, *Davy Crockett: The Man, the Legend, the Legacy, 1786–1986.* These eight essays, although scholarly in tone, are well worth "going ahead," as Crockett would say, since the reader's efforts are rewarded with marvelous insights into both the real David and the invented Davy. Lofaro, along with Richard Boyd Hauck, John Seelye, Catherine Albanese, Margaret King, and Charles Wolfe, has created an eminently successful anthology. All of the essays are interesting, some are downright witty, and most of them quite readable. The Crockett legend at age two hundred, Lofaro reminds us, "reflects the range and diversity of the country whose hero he became and documents as well the ever-changing mental image we have of ourselves as a nation and as individuals." That Crockett's bicentennial should come hard on the heels of the republic's own birthday bash is indeed fitting.[8]

Some folks, however, were decidedly unimpressed with Lofaro's efforts. "Professor shoots holes in Crockett myth," ran the headline in the *Knoxville Journal* for April 17, 1986. "Davy Crockett never wore a coonskin cap, didn't go to Texas to fight for independence, and wasn't killed clubbing Mexicans to death at the Alamo. In fact, he never went by the name 'Davy' . . . ," lamented the newspaper article, emphasizing sensational trivia rather than the book's solid scholarship. A column by that newspaper's metro editor followed two days later, castigating the book as "Davy Dearest" (in allusion to the Joan Crawford biography of 1978) and accusing Lofaro of stripping Davy naked and "turning our own East Tennessee hero into a frontier streaker." Columnist Doug Morris, who probably never read the book, went on to plead: "Our heroes are precious few. Don't make us learn history all over again."[9]

No less of an authority than Fess Parker bemoaned the publication of the book. "I think it's really too bad [that the scholars] call attention to themselves by going back and trying to be provocative," Parker sadly lamented in the July 10, 1986, *Wall Street Journal.* "I understand it, but I deplore it."[10]

Lofaro also received some interesting hate mail, including a letter from one irate lady labeling him a "wimp" fit for nothing better than the lowly profession of college teaching. Pretty rough stuff, but mild compared to the perennial reaction of hard-core Texans when Davy's reputation is besmirched below the Red River. The usual epithet instantly cast at wayward Texan scribblers is *Communist* or, even worse, *intellectual!* "Davy Crockett died fighting at the Alamo. He did not surrender. He did not ask for quarter . . . ," emphatically declared San Angelo *Standard Times* city editor Bob Boyd. The current story that he was captured was an effort by "his detractors to sully his reputation. Such effort is waged now by revisionist and sloppy historians eager to make a name by claiming spurious proof that Crockett tried to surrender after the Mexicans broke into the Alamo." It is never enough for many of the Crockett defenders to simply disagree and present counter arguments, they must always attack the motives and abilities of those with whom they disagree. "I think we have a few invaders whose sole intention is to destroy any of the heroism of the Alamo," huffed a spokeswoman for the Daughters of the Republic of Texas from behind the sanctified walls of the shrine of Texas liberty.[11]

Lofaro, neither wimp, Communist, nor publicity seeker—although he is indeed an intellectual—seeks in his book to explain a personal lifelong fascination. He was seven when the Disney Crockett craze swept the nation, and that event led to his initial fascination with history. Indeed, the work of such "revisionists" may be entirely oedipal—an effort by baby-boomer scholars to slay the story that first captured their imaginations and led them eventually into their professions. By exposing the truth about this most cherished tale, they may hope to prove their maturity and credibility as scholars. It is, alas, wasted effort, for their scholarly peers continue to sneer at work on subjects such as Davy Crockett no matter how many footnotes are attached. A dissertation on the origins of Gregorian chants or another demographic study of a seventeenth-century New England town will win scholarly plaudits—but never a book on Davy Crockett that seeks, by exploring a popular hero's legend, to explain so inconsequential a subject as the American national character. Lofaro undoubtedly finds himself sneered at by his academic peers for wasting his time on trivia while being attacked by the press and hero-worshippers who are in fact the only ones who recognize the importance, and ultimately subversive nature, of his work.

Of course, it all matters little anyway, for few will read the book. "We don't care what the scholars say," declared Ann Tillman, the librarian at the Crockett County Public Library in Alamo, Tennessee, where debunking books do not litter the shelves. "True or false, he's still our folk hero."[12]

I watched the furor over Lofaro's book with considerable interest, and not without amusement, as I had been working for some time on a book on the Alamo as an American icon. Having studied the development of the Crockett legend, I found the controversy quite predictable. I had felt the mild stings of the defenders of the true historical faith over my article on the Alamo published in the March 1986 *American History Illustrated*.[13] My narrative included the story of Crockett's surrender and had raised the hackles of quite a few readers of that magazine.

I had no intention, however, of ever tackling the Crockett story, despite the fact that the Disney film and a wonderful Dell comic book, "Davy Crockett at the Alamo," had first sparked my interest in history. My fascination with Crockett's story, or at least the Disney version of it, somehow got lost among New England Puritans, revolutionaries, slaves, abolitionists, robber barons, New Dealers, and all the others one studiously encounters along the road toward a doctorate in American history.

My work on the Alamo, however, induced the editors of *Texas Monthly* to ask me to write an article on Crockett to mark the anniversaries of both his birth and death. Delighted at the opportunity to write for an audience beyond my academic peers, I set to work.

I worried, however, about producing a narrative that would satisfy the requirements of an iconoclastic magazine such as *Texas Monthly*. Crockett was, of course, a nineteenth-century celebrity of sorts—perhaps the first American briefly to make a living off his own celebrity status—but that did not make him a charlatan. How could I write an article that would prove appealing in a cynical age of media hype that produced wretched, violent heroes like Rambo? The essential decency of the real Crockett, as well as the Davy of my youth, would never play in 1986. Davy was too unburdened by psychosis and overburdened with decency, too hateful of violence and loving of peace, and far too caring for the underprivileged to sell as a hero in the era of Reagan. He was a truly admirable human being, well worth our admiration. So what that he wasn't born on a mountaintop, didn't kill a bear when he was three, didn't care much for fighting Indians, didn't look like Fess Parker (in fact his authentic portraits show a stocky, middle-aged politician), didn't go down swinging Old Betsy at the Alamo (he left his favorite rifle in Tennessee and he surrendered at the Alamo), and perhaps didn't even wear a coonskin cap? He nevertheless was a talented, self-made man who fought for human rights and democracy and was defeated in politics because of his independence and honesty. At the Alamo he fell in defense of his vision of freedom, no matter the details of his death. In all my research and writing I was animated at all times by Davy Crockett's lifelong motto, as apt for our times as it was for his: "Be always sure you're right – then go ahead!"

So hopelessly hero-worshipful was my final draft of the article that I worried that the editors at *Texas Monthly* would not like it. My worries were unfounded, for the editors, also members of the Davy Crockett generation, were captivated by Davy. To spice things up the cover of the issue ran a photograph of Fess Parker under the bold headline: "Davy Crockett – Hero or Hype?"[14]

The answer, clearly stated inside the magazine, was that he was a genuine hero. The response was incredible. Repeatedly in newspaper articles and on the radio and television, I was portrayed as a revisionist destroying cherished beliefs (usually accompanied by a photograph of Fess Parker or John Wayne). The media was mild and detached, however, compared to the avalanche of mail I received. While some of it was quite favorable, and some of it offered intelligent counter-interpretations of detail, much of it was incredibly reactionary.

I may have knelt before the Crockett shrine, but I clearly had the catechism all wrong. "I am a Texas history Teacher in McAllen, and what Mr. Hutton wrote amounts to blasphemy," huffed Jean Mangano in a letter to *Texas Monthly.* "In this Sesquicentennial year Texas heroes should be revered, not destroyed. . . . I will never teach my students what he wrote. A real Texan would not." Jim Dumas, president of an outfit called the "Descendants of David Crockett," chided *Texas Monthly* for publishing such a scurrilous "witch-hunt on David Crockett."[15]

The letters to the editor were gentle compared to many of the ones I received at my New Mexico office. The most emphatic came from a lady in Algood, Tennessee. "Why don't you find something or somebody to write about (you call it research?) besides Americans who were *real men,* not like you gutless wonders of today, who call yourselves men," exclaimed

Virginia Byrd. "What would you have kids of today have for their heroes? The longhaired, dirty stinking, foul mouthed noise makers who call themselves singers, but really are a bunch of garbage? 'Historians' such as you could never measure up to these great men, so stop trying."[16] It was encouraging to learn from these letters that folks still cared about history.

Of course, what really got folks upset with my article was my statement that Crockett had surrendered at the Alamo and had been executed on order of Santa Anna. Kent Biffle, in his *Dallas Morning News* Texana column, got right to the point when discussing the controversial parts of the essay: "Well, nobody gives a rat's tail about Davy's altitude at birth. And his fans could probably adjust to the notion of Davy in a tractor hat or a Bosox cap. But the *surrender* part warms them to incandescence."[17]

There really is very little room for doubt that Crockett was captured and executed at the Alamo. It is in fact rather surprising just how much detail we have on this incident. It is even more surprising that so many still refuse to believe the story since there is not a single, reliable eyewitness account of Crockett's death in battle. This resistance to the reality of Crockett's death, however, has grown to such proportions *only* since the vast popularity of the Disney Crockett programs and the 1960 John Wayne film. It is an entirely modern media-inspired response.[18]

The story of Crockett's surrender was quite well known at the time of the battle and throughout the nineteenth and most of the twentieth century, and seemed to upset no one. Early newspaper accounts of the battle often stated that Crockett had been captured and executed by the Mexicans, and this was used as further evidence of Santa Anna's barbarity.

In Mary Austin Holley's *Texas*, published in Lexington, Kentucky, in July 1836, Crockett and six others "cried for quarter, but were told there was no mercy for them." They then continued fighting until butchered. Nobody called Holley a revisionist, and her book has become a classic of Texas history.[19]

Even more influential, however, would be the version of Crockett's surrender and execution in Richard Penn Smith's *Col. Crockett's Exploits and Adventures in Texas*, also published in 1836. Carey and Hart of Philadelphia, the publishers of Crockett's 1834 autobiography and the 1835 ghostwritten *An Account of Colonel Crockett's Tour to the North and Down East*, engaged Smith to hurriedly write the book in order to capitalize on public interest in Crockett and Texas. Basing the book on a few Crockett letters, newspaper accounts of the Texas war, and his own vivid imagination, Smith churned out the manuscript with incredible speed. Pages were delivered to the printer each day as he wrote them. The finished product was marketed by Carey and Hart as Crockett's Texas journal, retrieved by General Castrillón after the frontiersman's death, and then liberated by a Texas soldier at San Jacinto. It sold well and helped the publisher unload a large remainder of *Crockett's Tour* as well. The hoax of authorship was not uncovered for years, and many believed it was truly Crockett's diary.[20]

The final words of the bogus Crockett diary are "Pop, pop, pop! Bom, bom, bom! throughout the day. No time for memorandums now . . . Go ahead! Liberty and independence forever!" The editor then adds a final chapter describing Crockett's capture by Castrillón. The kind Mexican officer takes Crockett and five other prisoners before Santa Anna, but is ordered by his commander to execute them. Writes author Smith: "Colonel Crockett, seeing the act of treachery, instantly sprang like a tiger at the ruffian chief, but before he could reach him a dozen swords were sheathed in his indomitable heart; and he fell and died without a groan, a frown on his brow, and a smile of scorn and defiance on his lips."[21]

Smith's book is fantasy of course. Although unrecognized as such at the time, it is our first Alamo novel. Nineteenth-century readers, however, accepted it as fact and did not protest the Crockett death scene. It was repeatedly reprinted for over one hundred years as part of Crockett's autobiography, and thus had an enormous influence far beyond the first edition.[22]

Edward S. Ellis, whose popular *The Life of Colonel David Crockett* was published in 1884 and went through numerous editions, also recounted the surrender story in such a way as to cast Crockett in a heroic light:

> At last only six of the garrison were left alive. They were surrounded by General Castrillon and his soldiers. The officer shouted to them to surrender, promising that their lives should be spared. In the little group of Spartans were Davy Crockett and Travis, so exhausted they were scarcely able to stand. . . .
>
> There were a few brave and humane officers, and among them were General Castrillon and Burdillon. They spoke sympathizingly to Crockett and Travis, and with several other officers walked to where the scowling Santa Anna stood and asked that the surrender of the few survivors might be received.
>
> The reply was an order that all should be shot. Seeing his treachery, the enraged Crockett roused himself, and swinging his Bowie aloft, made a furious rush for the Mexican Nan Sahib. The intrepid Tennessean was riddled with bullets before he could pass half the intervening distance. Almost at the same moment, the other five were shot down.[23]

This version of Crockett's death is certainly fanciful. We know with some certainty, for instance, that Travis was killed on the north wall early in the final assault. The point to be made here is not that the Ellis or Smith versions are correct in every detail, but rather that they were accepted by most readers without argument. As late as the early 1950s, encyclopedias, juvenile histories, and comic books were repeating this version of Crockett's death.

In the years following the Civil War, Americans were not much interested in Crockett or how he died. Industrial America took little interest in him, and although he remained a popular figure for boys' fiction, usually in tales about the Alamo, he was eclipsed by new frontier heroes such as Buffalo Bill Cody, Wild Bill Hickok, and General George Custer. By 1930, when Vernon Louis Parrington characterized Crockett as "a true frontier wastrel" in his classic *Main Currents of American Thought,* nobody cared enough to challenge him. Parrington's vision of Crockett as "the biggest frog in a very small puddle, first among the Smart Alecks of the canebrakes," was somewhat adjusted by the 1940s work of Walter Blair and Richard Dorson. They partially rehabilitated Davy's reputation and created a new scholarly interest in the folkloric version of the Crockett story. They were concerned, however, with the tall-tale character of the post-Alamo almanacs and had little concern for the real David Crockett or how he died.[24]

Then, in December 1954, the Disney television show on ABC aired the first episode of a three-part series on Davy Crockett. By the time Fess Parker as Crockett went down swinging his rifle, Old Betsy, at the advancing Mexicans in the final episode, a craze of unprecedented proportions was sweeping the nation.

After seven incredible months of a merchandising bonanza in which every conceivable kind of item carried the Davy Crockett label—coonskin caps, toy soldier sets, toy guns, bicycles, towels, pajamas, soap, wallets, pillows, bedspreads, purses, and even ladies' underwear—the Crockett craze began a sharp decline. But the Disney version of Crockett was fixed on the minds of a whole generation of Americans. Seven million copies of "The Ballad of Davy Crockett" record were sold and every one of those buyers now knew for certain just how Davy had died—fighting to the bitter end with his rifle as a club.

This was all a bit much for John Fischer, the editor-in-chief of *Harper's Magazine.* Fischer was a good ol' boy who had grown up on the high plains at Texhoma and had even cowboyed on his uncle's ranch in the Texas Panhandle. He had first gone wrong by attending the University of Oklahoma instead of the University of Texas, and then had compounded his error by going off to Oxford University as a Rhodes Scholar. This foreign influence was obviously fatal to his Texan mindset, for it gave him a high regard for truth and an intense disdain for historical mythology that about obliterated all the good influences of his Panhandle upbringing. In July 1955 he unleashed a thundering attack on the current Crockett insanity in his monthly *Harper's* column. The blast rolled across the Red River and re-echoed throughout the Lone Star State.

The gullible youth of America, Fischer declared, had been "brainwashed" into "worshipping a Crockett who never was—a myth as phony as the Russian legend about kind Papa Stalin." Crockett, Fischer noted, was nothing but a "juvenile delinquent," who became a "poor farmer, indolent and shiftless," and an even worse soldier who hired a substitute to finish out his enlistment term. Davy, Fischer huffed, was never "King of anything, except maybe the Tennessee Tall Tales and Bourbon Sampler's Association."

It was no wonder that America's youth were so captivated by "a simonized, Disneyfied version of history," the editor charged, for their parents had set a terrible example. Clearly warming to his subject, Fischer characterized the Alamo as "the worst military blooper in American history, short of Pearl Harbor." He was amazed that despite the fact that the battle impressed him more for Texas incompetence than heroism, "every Texan—little or big—venerates [it] as his national shrine." He contended that the Texans had deluded themselves for so long about Crockett and the Alamo that they could never accept the truth: "Indeed, such inaccuracy has now become a matter of self-defense; for on this subject—and a few others—the Texans have brain-washed themselves so thoroughly that any speaker who told the whole truth would invite a lynching."

What bothered Fischer was that this regional self-delusion had now, thanks to Walt Disney and Fess Parker, become a national obsession. "Maybe real history always has two strikes against it," he mused. "Ever since the fall of Troy, the mythical heroes and comforting legends have always seemed to find a more eager audience than the workaday fact. They still do."[25]

The response was immediate and emphatic. "Magazine Triggers Hero Slurs," and "This Story Treason! Writer Says Crockett Myth Phony" ran bold headlines in the *San Antonio Light*. "Anti-Davy Crockett fever flared across the nation Friday, kicked off by a snide appraisal of the Texas hero in Harper's magazine," reported the paper.[26]

"Even though what you have written is no doubt true, I feel it would have been much better to have allowed the children to continue to believe that Davy Crockett was a hero," wrote an irate *Harper's* reader from Lookout Mountain, Tennessee. "It takes a great man to praise but a little man to criticize.[27]

Maury Maverick, Jr., a Texas state legislator and heir to a grand Texas political tradition, fired off a salvo from his San Antonio home. "Jack Fischer is an Oklahoma hillbilly who ran away to New York at a tender age," declared Maverick, who personally knew the unfortunate *Harper's* editor, "and has since gone to hell by associating with characters like Bernard DeVoto and drinking dry martinis instead of corn whiskey and branch water." Maverick, his tongue firmly planted in his cheek, was happy to criticize Fischer, but refused to go so far as to defend Davy. He confessed that he had studied history at the University of Texas under J. Frank Dobie, and thus was so jaundiced by the truth that he couldn't rush to the defense of the hero of the Alamo.[28]

Far to the north the editors of the *Indianapolis Times,* emboldened by Fischer's audacity, formed the "Anti Davy Crockett Society of Indiana." The *Times* invited readers to join the society by tearing up any available picture of Davy and mailing it to the San Antonio postmaster for "inclusion with other Crockett trivia at the Alamo." Absolutely shameless, the *Times* editors then added insult to injury by publishing the story that Crockett was one "of six skulking prisoners caught and put to death afterward by Santa Anna."[29] Mrs. R. G. Halter, DRT hostess at the Alamo, wasted no time in contemptuously branding the *Indianapolis Times* story a lie. It was a common tale, she admitted, even cited in encyclopedias, but it had been fabricated years ago by a Texas jokester "to impress some greenhorns from the states." She pointed to the narratives left by Susannah Dickinson and San Antonio *alcalde* Francisco Ruiz, who both had seen Crockett's body after the battle. The crusade to correct this wild falsehood was never-ending, she admitted, especially since the Disney programs had increased the number of tourists visiting the Alamo by nearly a third. "It's very tiresome," Mrs. Halter sadly concluded.[30]

For the most part, however, Crockett partisans and detractors alike kept their sense of humor about the whole debate. Within two weeks the editors of the *Indianapolis Times* capitulated to legions of coonskin cap–bedecked moppets picketing their office. In desperation they wired *Harper's* editor John Fischer for help. He proved as useless as Fannin had been to Travis.

"Can't find Fischer. Presume he's gone coon-hunting," came back the reply from the New York editorial office of *Harper's*. In repentance, the *Indianapolis Times* renamed its club the "Davy Crockett Fans of America."[31] The whole controversy was delightfully entertaining, if nothing else, but in the future a sense of both humor and perspective would desert those who resumed this historical argument.

Both the 1955 film *The Last Command* and the 1960 film *The Alamo* depict Crockett's blowing up the powder magazine as the Mexicans rush upon him. This is a version of Crockett's death that is based upon nothing except a Hollywood scriptwriter's imagination. Robert Evans, in charge of the Alamo's powder, reportedly attempted such an act near the end of the battle but was shot before he could torch the magazine.

Walter Lord's *A Time to Stand* (1961), the best book to date on the Alamo, trod a careful middle ground concerning Crockett's death. He included the story of the execution of the captured Texans but did not identify any of them. In an appendix he addressed the question of Crockett's death and noted that several reliable Mexican eyewitnesses agreed that the famous frontiersman was captured and then executed on order of Santa Anna.[32]

Of these Mexican sources on the Alamo battle, none was more reliable than the diary of José Enrique de la Peña, an officer of Santa Anna's staff, written in 1836. In 1975 a new translation of de la Peña's diary was published by Texas A&M University Press entitled *With Santa Anna in Texas*. Translated and edited by Carmen Perry, former director of the Daughters of the Republic of Texas Library at the Alamo, the 202-page book contained a single page relating the execution of Crockett.

Perry's book set off quite a controversy as journalists picked up on the Crockett death scene as a quick way to get a headline. "Students of American history and John Wayne fans take note. The legendary story of the Alamo may need revision," declared the Denver *Post*. "Has the King of the Wild Frontier been relieved of his coonskin crown?" asked the *Jackson* [Tennessee] *Sun*. "Naturally, it will be hard for a generation that grew up singing 'Born on a mountain-top in Tennessee' to accept the mental image of a cowardly Crockett goveling in the Alamo corner," noted the *Jackson Sun* reporter, who had obviously not even bothered to read the one page in the book that she was writing the article about.

"Did Crockett die at the Alamo? Historian Carmen Perry says no," read the headline in the October 13, 1975, issue of *People* magazine. Above a picture of Carmen Perry, the magazine ran a photo of John Wayne as Crockett.

The press, ignorant of any historical works on the Alamo, consistently used movie versions of Crockett's death as a reference point for their readers. That, of course, made perfect sense since the source of information on Crockett and the Alamo for most people is what they have seen on television or in the movies. They react to everything from the perspective of these popular culture sources.

Miss Perry was uncomfortable with all the publicity, and especially with the anonymous hate mail and late night phone calls. Nevertheless, she staunchly defended de la Peña's account. "People don't believe his account because they don't want to believe it," she stoically noted. "We prefer to live by legend."[33]

Partly in response to the controversy over the diary, Dan Kilgore, a certified public accountant in Corpus Christi who served as president of the Texas State Historical Association in 1977, delivered a speech on Crockett's death as his presidential address to that association. He expanded that speech into a carefully researched and intelligent little book published in 1978 entitled *How Did Davy Die?* Kilgore concluded that the mass of evidence supported the de la Peña account of Crockett's death. The reaction to Perry's book was mild compared to the rantings directed at Kilgore. "Them's Fightin' Words. Davy's Legend Smudged," ran the headline in Kilgore's hometown newspaper, the *Corpus Christi Times*. "Any Texan worth his lizard skin cowboy boots and Willie Nelson albums knows better than to smear the legend of Davy Crockett."[34]

Critics seemed to lump intellectuals and Communists together in their defense of Crockett. A letter to Kilgore from Alabama labeled the author "a mealy-mouthed intellectual" who deserved to "have his mouth washed out with soap." Under pictures of Davy Crockett and John Wayne, a scandal-sheet tabloid called *World Weekly News* noted that "some smarty-pants historians now claim Davy didn't die fighting at the Alamo—but instead surrendered when he ran out of ammo and was then executed." The paper noted that John Wayne must be rolling in his grave over such lies, which were labeled "a commie plot to trash our heroes." A letter to Kilgore from Fort Myers, Florida, agreed: "We know the reason for this. This is one of the Communists' plans to degrade our heroes. . . . He's still king of the Wild Frontier."[35]

Peggy Dibrell, chair of the Daughters of the Republic of Texas Alamo Committee, disputed Kilgore's version of Crockett's death and then amazingly suggested that the version in John Wayne's movie was correct. "There were plans made before the battle to blow up the gunpowder stored in the main shrine if it was overrun," Dibrell was quoted as stating in the San Antonio *Express News* for March 6, 1985, "and Davy Crockett was attempting to do that when he was killed." This statement is reflective of the absolute triumph of popular culture over historical fact.

Dan Kilgore watched in amazement as the controversy swirled around him. He remained good-natured about it all, but did note sarcastically: "I wouldn't have minded all this if they'd bought my books. Nobody even read the damn book."[36]

The Alamo has become a civil-religious shrine, and—as John Fischer, Carmen Perry, Dan Kilgore, Michael A. Lofaro, and I have all discovered—any attempt to tamper with the official, sanctified version of its story is to invite sharp reaction from defenders of the true faith. To suggest that Davy Crockett, the premier demigod of the shrine, surrendered, is to dismantle the props under a powerful symbol of heroic defiance that many Americans have come to embrace as part of their self-identification.

It is understandable that the Daughters of the Republic of Texas, who are responsible for preserving the Alamo, should be so strong in their condemnation of those who would chip away at their polished marble image of the Alamo heroes. They protect their shrine with a zealot's fire that surely outshines that of the vestal virgins of the temples of pagan Rome. Their version of history exists only to advance the heroic myth that they so zealously, and even touchingly, guard. Membership in their organization is based on genealogy; their reason for existence is ancestor worship, not history.

It is also understandable, although sad, that so many Americans refuse to accept the obvious truth of history, preferring to wallow instead in a child's fairy tale (and a tale that is, in fact, a recent Hollywood creation). In an uncertain age it is comforting to believe in bold, black-and-white heroes, who face adversity with a calm certitude that we can never seem to muster. Unfortunately, the consequence of such ancestor worship is often a dangerous effort to be as bold and decisive as these fantasy heroes, or a pitiful self-loathing because we can never be as great as those who came before. But we measure ourselves against a fictional standard.

The truth—while perhaps not as glamorous—is in fact much more instructive. It makes perfect sense for Crockett and a handful of companions, with further resistance obviously suicidal, to accept an offer of quarter from their foes. It is one of the delightful absurdities of the American mind that we react with righteous horror and cultural indignation at the Japanese kamikaze pilots over Okinawa in 1945 and then raise to the status of cultural demigods a band of Texans who essentially performed the same act. The real Crockett was too wily an old politician, and too full of the absolute joy of life, to have thrown his life away needlessly. That he attempted to talk his way out of a desperate situation is perfectly in character. That he who so represented the pure spirit of American democracy should then perish at the direct order of a megalomanic, despotic dictator is somehow fitting.

Crockett was no warrior chieftain—neither Hector nor Achilles. As a youth he had tasted war and quickly came to view it as the cruel obscenity that it is. So contemptuous was he of the soldier's craft that in his autobiography he falsely claimed part in a mutiny and readily admitted that he had hired a substitute to finish out his term of enlistment. He came to Texas, like so many others, in search of economic and political opportunity. He died in search of that opportunity, not lusting after the blood of his fellow man.

To expect him to perish in terrible combat, ringed by the men he had slain with clubbed rifle and knife, is to expect an end entirely out of keeping with the man's life. To make such a death the litmus test for his hero status is both to trivialize his historic importance and to misread completely what the man stood for. It is not the manner of his passing we should memorialize, but rather his bold defense of the rights of the underprivileged and dispossessed, his simple faith in our institutions, and his ultimate sacrifice to secure our continental destiny.

On Davy Crockett's two-hundredth birthday we should focus on the positive forces he symbolized, not on the details of how he died. The latter proves nothing, the former means everything. It is through his spirit of unbridled democracy and bold egalitarianism that this magnificent American is best remembered.

NOTES

1. For Crockett's two-hundredth birthday party see the tabloid supplement to the *Greeneville [Tennessee] Sun*, entitled *The Crockett Bicentennial Times*, August 1986, and *Tennessee Conservationist* 52 (July/August 1986).

2. Stephen Harrigan, "The Ballad of Fess Parker," *Texas Monthly* 14 (November 1986): 131.

3. James A. Shackford and Stanley J. Folmsbee, eds., *A Narrative of the Life of David Crockett of the State of Tennessee by David Crockett* (Knoxville: University of Tennessee Press, 1987); [David Crockett] *A Narrative of the Life of David Crockett of the State of Tennessee Written by Himself* (Lincoln: University of Nebraska Press, 1987). Another edition of the autobiography, still in print, is Joseph J. Arpad, ed., *A Narrative of the Life of David Crockett of the State of Tennessee* (New Haven, Conn.: College and University Press, 1972), published as part of the "Masterworks of Literature Series." The book has been repeatedly reprinted since 1834 in various authentic, abridged, bastardized, and plagiarized editions.

4. Virgil E. Baugh, *Rendezvous at the Alamo: Highlights in the Lives of Bowie, Crockett, and Travis* (Lincoln: University of Nebraska Press, 1986); Richard Boyd Hauck, *Davy Crockett: A Handbook* (Lincoln: University of Nebraska Press, 1986).

5. Walter Blair, *Davy Crockett: Legendary Frontier Hero* (1955; Springfield, Ill.: Lincoln-Herndon Press, 1986); Walter Blair, *Tall Tale America: A Legendary History of Our Humorous Heroes* (1944; Chicago: University of Chicago Press, 1987).

6. James Atkins Shackford, *David Crockett: The Man and the Legend* (1956; Chapel Hill: University of North Carolina Press, 1986); James Wakefield Burke, *David Crockett: The Man Behind the Myth* (Austin: Eakin Press, 1984); James Wakefield Burke, *The Blazing Dawn* (New York: Pyramid Books, 1975). Interestingly, in Burke's novel Crockett dies fighting, but in the "biography" he surrenders and is executed by direct order of General Santa Anna.

7. Gary L. Foreman, *Crockett: The Gentleman from the Cane* (Dallas: Taylor Publishing Co., 1986); Susan Prendergast Schoelwer, *Alamo Images: Changing Perceptions of a Texas Experience* (Dallas: DeGolyer Library/Southern Methodist University Press, 1985).

8. Michael A. Lofaro, ed., *Davy Crockett: The Man, The Legend, the Legacy 1786-1986* (Knoxville: University of Tennessee Press, 1985). The anthology was reissued in paperback in 1986.

9. *Knoxville Journal*, April 17, 19, 1986.

10. *Wall Street Journal*, July 10, 1986.

11. Bob Boyd, *The Texas Revolution: A Day-by-Day Account* (San Angelo: San Angelo Standard, Inc., 1986), 54; *Wall Street Journal*, July 10, 1986. Also see Knoxville *News-Sentinel*, Dec. 1, 1985; *Memphis Commercial Appeal*, April 20, 1986; *Western Historical Quarterly* 17 (Jan. 1987): 61-62; *New Mexico Historical Review* 62 (April 1987): 217; *Southwestern Historical Quarterly* 90 (April 1987): 417.

12. *Wall Street Journal*, July 10, 1986.

13. Paul Andrew Hutton, "The Alamo: An American Epic," *American History Illustrated* 20 (March 1986): 12-37.

14. Paul Andrew Hutton, "Davy Crockett, Still King of the Wild Frontier," *Texas Monthly* 14 (November 1986): 122-30, 244-48. For the media reaction, see *USA Today*, November 14, 1986; *Dallas Morning News*, November 9, 1986; *Chicago Tribune*, November 9, 1986; *Albuquerque Journal*, December 21, 1986.

15. "The Roar of the Crowd," *Texas Monthly* 15 (January 1987): 10.

16. Virginia Byrd to the author, Oct. 31, 1986.

17. *Dallas Morning News,* Nov. 9, 1986.

18. José Enrique de la Peña, an officer on Santa Anna's staff, left us a gripping, eyewitness account of Crockett's execution. His vivid account is further bolstered by briefer, but similar, versions by Colonel Fernando Urissa, Santa Anna's aide, General Martín Perfecto de Cos, Santa Anna's brother-in-law, and Colonel Jose Sanchez Navarro, who led one of the assault columns against the Alamo. Ramón Martínez Caro, Santa Anna's personal secretary, also reported the capture and execution of several Americans (but did not mention Crockett), as did Sergeant Francisco Becerra (whose tale is not particularly reliable). These eyewitness accounts are supported by how widespread the surrender story was in Texas just after the battle. Sam Houston wrote James W. Fannin, the ill-fated Goliad commander, on March 11, 1836, that "after the fort was carried, seven men surrendered and called for Santa Anna and quarter. They were murdered by his order." The *News Orleans Post-Union* carried the surrender story in late March and it was picked up by newspapers across the country. Finally, Sergeant George Dolson of the victorious Texan army, writing to his brother in Detroit on July 19, 1836, related an interview he had with a captured Mexican officer that agrees perfectly with the account of Crockett's execution by Lieutenant Colonel de la Peña. The mass of this historical evidence, both direct and circumstantial, is overwhelming.

For more on this topic see Dan Kilgore's essay in this anthology. Also see Carmen Perry, ed. and trans., *With Santa Anna in Texas: A Personal Narrative of the Revolution by José Enrique de la Peña* (College Station: Texas A&M University Press, 1975), 53–54; Dan Kilgore, *How Did Davy Die?* (College Station: Texas A&M University Press, 1978); Francisco Becerra, *A Mexican Sergeant's Recollections of the Alamo and San Jacinto* (Austin: Jenkins Publishing Co., 1980); Thomas Lawrence Connelly, "Did David Crockett Surrender at the Alamo? A Contemporary Letter," *Journal of Southern History* 26 (August 1960): 368–76; Carlos E. Castañeda, *The Mexican Side of the Texas Revolution [1836] by the Chief Mexican Participants* (Dallas: P. L. Turner Co., 1928), 103–4; Walter Lord, "Myths and Realities of the Alamo," in *The Republic of Texas,* ed. Stephen B. Oates (Palo Alto: American West Publishing Co., 1968), 18–25. For a defense of the theory that Crockett died fighting, see Phil Rosenthal and Bill Groneman, *Roll Call at the Alamo* (Fort Collins, Colo.: Old Army Press, 1985), 29–37.

19. Mary Austin Holley, *Texas* (Lexington, Kentucky: J. Clarke & Co., 1836), 354. The book was reprinted in facsimile in 1985 by the Texas State Historical Association.

20. For the story of the Smith book see William Bedford Clark, "*Col. Crockett's Exploits and Adventures in Texas:* Death and Transfiguration," *Studies in American Humor* 1 (June 1982): 66–76; and Shackford, *David Crockett,* 273–81.

21. Smith's book was published by T. K. & P. G. Collins of Philadelphia, a front for the Carey and Hart firm. Copies are quite rare today. This quote is from an 1869 edition of Crockett's autobiography, which has the *Texas Exploits* included as if it

were part of the original book. *Life of David Crockett, the Original Humorist and Irrepressible Backwoodsman* (Philadelphia: John E. Potter and Co., 1869), 396–97.

22. Smith's book established the patterns of action and characters that would be repeatedly used by other writers in describing Crockett's Texas adventures. His Bee Hunter and Thimblerig are two of the most durable characters in the Crockett legend. Both characters appear in John Wayne's film *The Alamo* (played by Chill Wills and Denver Pyle), while Thimblerig (as played by Hans Conreid) is a central character of the Disney Crockett film. For further examples of the influence of Smith's book, and the popularity of his characters, see these "nonfiction" versions: Charles Fletcher Allen, *David Crockett Scout* (Philadelphia: J. B. Lippincott Co., 1911); Virgil E. Baugh, *Rendezvous at the Alamo: Highlights in the Lives of Bowie, Crockett, and Travis* (New York: Pageant Press, 1960); or these juvenile histories: C. Richard Schaare, *The Life of Davy Crockett in Picture and Story* (New York: Cupples & Leon, 1935); Frank L. Beals, *Davy Crockett* (Evanston, Ill.: Row, Peterson and Co., 1941); William Weber Johnson, *The Birth of Texas* (Boston: Houghton Mifflin, 1960); Stewart H. Holbrook, *Davy Crockett* (New York: Random House, 1955); or these fictional works: Edwin Gustus Mayer, *Sunrise In My Pocket or The Last Days of Davy Crockett* (New York: Julian Messner, 1941); Dee Brown, *Wave High the Banner: A Novel Based on the Life of Davy Crockett* (Philadelphia: Macrae-Smith Co., 1942); Christopher Bryant, *The Bee Hunter* (New York: Pageant Press, 1966).

23. Edward S. Ellis, *The Life of Colonel David Crockett* (Philadelphia: Porter & Coates, 1884), 260. A version of Crockett's death in which he goes down fighting like a tiger was also common in this period. See, for example, Cyrus Townsend Brady, *Border Fights and Fighters* (Garden City, N.Y.: Doubleday, Page & Co., 1902), 307–26; Edwin L. Sabin, *Boys' Book of Border Battles* (Philadelphia: George W. Jacobs & Co., 1920), 114–34. For other examples of Crockett's surrender and execution, see D. M. Kelsey, *History of Our Wild West and Stories of Pioneer Life* (Chicago: Thompson & Thomas, 1901), 192–94; E. G. Littlejohn, *Texas History Stories* (Richmond, Va.: B. F. Johnson Publishing Co., 1901), 147, 162.

24. Vernon Louis Parrington, *Main Currents of American Thought: The Romantic Revolution in America* (New York: Harcourt, Brace and Co., 1930), 178–79. Also see Richard M. Dorson, ed., *Davy Crockett: American Comic Legend* (New York: Rockland Editions, 1939); and Walter Blair, "Six Davy Crocketts," *Southwest Review* 25 (July 1940): 443–62.

25. John Fischer, "Personal and otherwise," *Harper's Magazine* 211 (July 1955): 16–17.

26. *San Antonio Light,* June 30, July 1, 1955.

27. "Letters," *Harper's Magazine* 211 (September 1955): 5.

28. *San Antonio Light,* July 1, 1955.

29. Ibid., July 17, 1955.

30. Ibid. Susannah Dickinson's account of viewing Crockett's mutilated body lying between the church and long barracks is consistently used to prove he died fighting in the battle and was not captured and executed. She did not see his body, however, until after the fighting was over. The chronology of just when she emerged

from the church under the protection of a Mexican officer is established in a contemporary letter from William Parker of Natchez, who was in Texas seeking information on his son Christopher, a defender of the Alamo. On April 29, 1836, he reported that he had spoken with a man who had seen Mrs. Dickinson soon after the battle: "My informant above quoted states, that on his way in, he saw and conversed with Mrs. Dickerson [sic], the widow of one of the gunners at the fall of the Alamo, and the only white person in the fortress at the time of the final catastrophe of this post, who was spared by the enemy, and permitted to return into the American settlements. He says that Mrs. D. informed him, that of the five who, for a moment survived their campanions, and threw themselves on the victor's clemency, two were pursued into her room, and subjected in her presence to the most torturing [sic] death." This account confirms the execution of Texan prisoners and makes it clear that Mrs. Dickinson did not leave the church until some time after Crockett and the others were executed. Alcalde Ruiz, of course, also viewed Crockett's body a considerable time after his death. John H. Jenkins, ed., *The Papers of the Texas Revolution 1835–1836* (Austin: Presidial Press, 1973), 6:119–23; Antonio Francisco Ruiz, "Fall of the Alamo," *Texas Almanac for 1860* (Galveston: Galveston News Steam Printing Co., 1859).

31. *San Antonio Light,* July 17, 1955.

32. Walter Lord, *A Time to Stand* (New York: Harper & Brothers, 1961), 174–75, 206–7.

33. Paul Andrew Hutton, "A Tale of Two Alamos," *SMU Mustang* 36 (Spring 1986): 26.

34. Ibid.

35. Ibid.

36. Ibid., 27.

David Crockett and the Rhetoric of Tennessee Politics

Michael Montgomery

It was the early summer of 1948. Third-district Tennessee Congressman Estes Kefauver of Chattanooga was waging a tireless but uphill fight in the Democratic primary campaign for U.S. senator. He found himself with three opponents: incumbent Senator Tom Stewart, Circuit Judge John A. Mitchell, and, not a candidate but Kefauver's fiercest and principal adversary from behind the scenes, political kingmaker E. H. Crump, mayor of Memphis, who had controlled Democratic politics in the Volunteer State for more than two decades. The name of Kefauver was foreign to most Tennesseans, and his record as a congressman was being relentlessly attacked by his opponents as too liberal to represent the state in the upper chamber in Washington. On June 10, two months before the primary, a full-page ad was taken out by Mr. Crump in every daily newspaper of the state. The most blistering attack yet on Kefauver, the advertisement branded the congressman as "a darling of the Communists" and likened him to, of all things, a "pet coon." Crump wrote:

> Kefauver reminds me of the pet coon that puts its foot in an open drawer in your room, but invariably turns its head while its foot is feeling around in the drawer. The coon hopes, through its cunning by turning its head, he will deceive any onlookers as to where his foot is and what it is into. If the coon could talk, he would say "You have me wrong—I have made a mistake, look at my turned head. I am sorry about my foot. I couldn't see what I was doing.[1]

Without funds to afford a newspaper rebuttal, the congressman and his staff were momentarily stymied as they scrambled for a response. Then Charles Neese, Kefauver's campaign manager, was struck with an idea—to turn the tables on Crump, seize the raccoon image, and have Kefauver capitalize on it. The following day the Kefauver campaign put out a press release defending, not Kefauver, but the raccoon, from Crump's attacks: "The coon is a clean animal; it washes its food before eating. The coon is an American animal; it is found nowhere else in the world; the coon is a courageous animal; it can lick its weight in dogs any day."[2]

The counterattack was on, and three days later, on June 14, Kefauver gave a lengthier rejoinder to Crump's use of the pet raccoon symbol in a radio address over station WDOD in Chattanooga:

> And speaking of coons – I was interested in Mr. Crump's analogy. This animal – the most American of all animals – has been defamed. You wouldn't find a coon in Russia. It is one of the cleanest of all animals; it is one of the most courageous (Mr. Crump wandered off on the possum when he indicated that the coon was not courageous). A coon, as all of you hunters know, can lick a dog four times its size; he is somewhat of a "giant-killer" among the animals. Yes, the coon is all American. Davy Crockett, Sam Houston, James Robertson and all of our great men of that era in Tennessee History wore the familiar ring-tailed, coon-skin cap. Mr. Crump defames me – but worse than that he defames the coon – the all American animal. We coons can take care of ourselves. I may be a pet coon, but I ain't Mr. Crump's pet coon.[3]

Some of Kefauver's staff were more than a little chagrined over this campaign tactic, fearing that a candidate associating himself with a raccoon wouldn't be taken seriously. But Kefauver knew better and, to the delight of his supporters, the critter became the overnight symbol of the Kefauver campaign. It remained so throughout the senatorial race of 1948 and in his two later campaigns for the Democratic presidential nomination as well.

Why did Kefauver defend the virtue of the lowly raccoon? To an out-of-state observer, Kefauver's counter to Crump's newspaper salvo might have seemed either defensive, answering Crump's attack in kind, or comic, even juvenile, in lowering the campaign to the level of buffoonery. No doubt for many a political campaign such a move as claiming that the raccoon had been defamed would have signaled the degeneration of the race. But Kefauver knew exactly how to use the raccoon idea. What may have seemed a desperate, defensive move that would surely deteriorate the level of the campaign into an old-fashioned tussle of exchanging insults was in point of fact anything but that, for Kefauver was most assuredly reaching back into Tennessee political history and clothing his campaign in tradition. Estes Kefauver knew his state history as well as he knew his animals. Rather than merely laughing at Crump's attack, he thrust himself and his campaign squarely into the cherished political traditions of the Volunteer State in order to assert himself as a credible candidate.

First, he appealed to state pride, citing the actions of stalwart figures of the early days of Tennessee history—Crockett, Houston, and Robertson—as precedents and associating himself with them.

Second, he displayed a native knowledge of hunting and of the woods, in this case his knowledge of the raccoon, giving himself a downhome image, identifying himself with the common people of the state, and showing them he was carrying his case directly to them. And he showed he had the sense not to mistake a possum for a raccoon.

Third, and closely related to the knowledge mentioned above, he used the word *ain't* to show the citizens of the state that he was perfectly comfortable, when he had a point to emphasize, in shifting his speech to a less formal, folksier, more vernacular style that was more natural and closer to the daily lives of the people than any schoolbook style of language.

Fourth, he identified himself as the anti-establishment, the anti–party boss candidate, and proclaimed his political independence.

I believe that the behavior of Estes Kefauver reveals that there is an informal tradition in Tennessee politics that delineates what is acceptable political behavior, especially while electioneering. It is a tradition that can largely be traced back to David Crockett, the three-time congressman from the West Tennessee canebrake. It involves politicians using backwoods symbols, language, and traits to express themselves, to relate to the people, and to establish their image. That is, the actions of Kefauver were not idiosyncratic; they fed upon a thriving tradition in the state.

None of the five elements of this informal tradition that I will discuss are unique to Tennessee, nor have the majority of Tennessee politicians exemplified them. But I contend that they form a set of personal habits and political characteristics that Crockett embodied and represented for many subsequent politicians in the state, a set of resources to draw on, at least in part. All of these traits are richly exemplified in his autobiography, *A Narrative of the Life of David Crockett of the State of Tennessee.*[4]

The first element in this tradition is storytelling. Even more than keeping his audience liquored up, rendering a good story was Crockett's prime campaign tactic. Crockett amazed the polite society of Washington with his coarse backwoods tales about hunting bears and other wild critters. In his autobiography, Crockett gives two delightful accounts of how he spun yarns during his first political campaign in 1821, to represent Lawrence and Hickman counties in the state legislature. Storytelling came to him naturally; besides, to hear him explain it, he did not know what else to do:

A public document I had never seen, nor did I know there were such things; and how to begin I couldn't tell. I made many apologies, and tried to get off, for I know'd too, that I wa'n't able to shuffle and cut with him. He was there, and knowing my ignorance as well as I did myself, he also urged me to make a speech. The truth is, he thought my being a candidate was a mere matter of sport; and didn't think for a moment, that he was in any danger from an ignorant backwoods bear hunter. But I found I couldn't get off, and so I determined just to go ahead, and leave it to chance what I should say. I got up and told the people, I reckoned they know'd what I come for, but if not, I could tell them. I had come for their votes, and if they didn't watch mighty close, I'd get them too. But the worst of all was, that I couldn't tell them any thing about government. I tried to speak about something, and I cared very little what, until I choaked up as bad as if my mouth had been jam'd an cram'd chock full of dry mush. There the people stood, listening all the while, with their eyes, mouths, and ears all open, to catch every word I would speak.

At last I told them I was like a fellow I had heard of not long before. He was beating on the head of an empty barrel near the roadside, when a traveler, who was passing along, asked him what he was doing that for? The fellow replied, that there was some cider in that barrel a few days before, and he was trying to see if there was any then, but if there was he couldn't get at it. I told them that there had been a little bit of a speech in me a while ago, but I believed I couldn't get it out. They all roared out in a mighty laugh, and I told some other anecdotes, equally amusing to them, and believing I had them in a first-rate way, I quit and got down, thanking the people for their attention. But I took care to remark that I was as dry as a powder horn, and that I thought it was time for us all to wet our whistles a little; and so I put off to the liquor stand, and was followed by the greater part of the crowd.

I felt certain this was necessary, for I knowed my competitor could open government matters to them as easy as he pleased. He had, however, mighty few left to hear him, as I continued with the crowd, now and then taking a horn, and telling good humoured stories, till he was done speaking.[5]

Crockett follows almost immediately with a second account:

Their court commenced on the next Monday, as the barbecue was on a Saturday, and the candidates for governor and for Congress, as well as my competitor and myself, all attended.

The thought of having to make a speech made my knees feel mighty weak, and set my heart to fluttering almost as bad as my first love scrape with the Quaker's niece. But as good luck would have it, these big candidates spoke nearly all day, and when they quit, the people were worn out with fatigue, which afforded me a good apology for not discussing the government. But I listened mighty close to them, and was learning pretty fast about political matters. When they were all done, I got up and told some laughable story, and quit, I found I was safe in those parts, and so I went home, and didn't go back again till after the election was over. But to cut this matter short, I was elected, doubling my competitor, and nine votes over.[6]

The second element of the political tradition focuses upon reference to the backwoods or to downhome values and locations. Here a politician shows that he is more comfortable in sporting the apparel of the field than the dress of the political corridor and that he prefers to associate himself with the outdoors, especially to hunting, and with rural rather than city folks. Crockett, the "gentleman from the cane," had no apologies in his first congressional campaign of 1827 about the value of being from the country. In comparing himself to his opponent, he stated that the latter

> . . . had many advantages over me, and particularly in the way of money; but I told him that I would go on the products of the country; that I had industrious children, and the best of coon dogs, and they would hunt every night till midnight to support my election; and when the coon fur wa'n't good, I would myself go a wolfing, and shoot down a wolf, and skin his head, and his scalp would be good to me for three dollars, in our state treasury. . . .[7]

The third element of the tradition involves the politician using the vernacular language and showing that he prefers to use the language of the common man rather than more formal, schoolbook English. In his autobiography Crockett complains about having to put his thoughts into the constraints of the written language:

> I despise this way of spelling contrary to nature. And as for grammar, it's pretty much a thing of nothing at last, after all the fuss that's made about it. In some places, I wouldn't suffer either the spelling, or grammar, or any thing else to be touch'd; and therefore it will be found in my own way.[8]

The fourth element is independence of thought; that is, having views that are anti-Washington, and often anti-intellectual. David Crockett not only preferred to conduct his business in Washington according to his Tennessee manners, but he also added in a mixture of modesty and bravado to his public behavior. Having claimed in his autobiography that he was mystified that "the public seem to feel some interest in the history of an individual so humble as I am,"[9] he goes on to exaggerate his almost total lack of formal education:

> But it will be a source of astonishment to many, who reflect that I am now a member of the American Congress, — the most enlightened body of men in the world, — that at so advanced an age, the age of fifteen, I did not know the first letter in the book.[10]

The fifth element in this political tradition is an aptitude and fondness for stumping. For Crockett, it is clear in his storytelling antics quoted above that stumping soon became second nature to him. But he did not take to the trail only to defend his congressional seat. In the spring of 1834, Congressman Crockett undertook an intensive, three-week, stumping "towar [tour] through the Eastern States," going as far as Boston to rally the anti-Jackson forces for the Whigs and to test the presidential waters for himself.

The elements of this tradition are not unique to Tennessee.[11] Southern politicians have often been accomplished raconteurs.[12] They have often proclaimed great affection for their hunting dogs (viz. Lyndon Baines Johnson) and great prowess in hunting. Nor did they originate with David Crockett. But Crockett perfected this tradition, and through him the combined elements of this tradition became particularly identified with Tennessee and were perpetuated in the Volunteer State by its use by later politicians.

David Crockett embodied this tradition; he was a figure who maintained, exaggerated, and even flaunted his backwoods ways as his accustomed style in the halls of Congress. Many other Tennessee politicians have demonstrated a duality of styles, an ability to shift their style of behavior and speech, and a clear indication of greater comfort with downhome ways that they would often slip into when visiting a small town.

After Kefauver made the raccoon the symbol of his 1948 senatorial campaign almost overnight, he continued to exploit the raccoon-Crockett motif throughout his political career. Following Kefauver's initial counter to Mr. Crump, his little beast began to appear everywhere in his campaign. The most dramatic event took place in Memphis, Mr. Crump's backyard, two weeks after Crump's "pet coon" attack. Here, in his own words, is what Kefauver did next:

> A few days after the pet coon and I had an engagement to speak at a luncheon at the King Cotton [Peabody] Hotel at Memphis—524 people paid $1.75 to hear me talk; *against the advice of Ed Meeman* [editor of the Memphis Press-Scimitar] *and most of my Memphis friends, when I rose to speak, I put on a coon cap* and smiled. The photos flashed and the crowd howled—pictures were carried all over Tenn[essee]. Cha[rle]s Neese advertised for 2 pet coons—they came in [from a supporter in Tellico Plains]. The "un-Crumpled" coon [named Davy Crockett] went on the road with us til he got *too excited—we left him at Dyersburg.* Daniel Boone stayed in the office in Nashville.[13]

On the campaign trail, Kefauver would introduce Davy to the crowd by saying that "this is a pedigreed West Tennessee coon. Notice his big bushy

A photograph from Estes Kefauver's 1948 senatorial campaign featuring the raccoon Davy Crockett. University of Tennessee Library.

tail. This coon has rings in his tail, but I want you to remember I have no ring in my nose."[14]

Kefauver said later that putting on the cap had two purposes. He wanted the cap "to inject some humor, . . . [because] there existed in Tennessee a political machine which was the subject of fear among a great many people. The coonskin cap got the people laughing, and one is not afraid of a man or a machine while laughing at him."[15] He also stated that it "dramatized a grim, determined campaign on the part of thousands of people who set their jaws to free themselves, once and for all, from one-man rule."[16]

Nothing could be more Tennessean than a coonskin cap. In every campaign appearance thereafter, 194 stumped in less than two months, Kefauver posed in his furry headgear. The more rabid of his supporters began sporting caps as well, to such an extent that Kefauver feared they might endanger the raccoon population, and he issued an appeal that the animal not be hunted to make caps. Two hundred thousand picture cards with the candidate wearing the cap were distributed, and placards appeared of the mascot raccoon Davy Crockett admiring Kefauver's photograph.

The coonskin cap was to become Kefauver's trademark for the rest of his career. Once he became senator, citizens deluged him with requests for the cap, one of which apparently was electrified—that is, it had a battery-powered flashlight mounted on it. Soon after he settled into his office, the leader of a delegation of fifteen businessmen from Gatlinburg undertaking an advertising tour through Florida wrote the senator, "I would like very much to borrow your coon skin cap, the one with the tail light to wear on the trip since we are to dress as real East Tenn. Mountaineers."[17] Kefauver wrote back, "I have sent you the coon skin cap equipped with lights and battery. I am not sure it will operate satisfactorily and you may have to fix it up some. Also, I am sending another cap for one of your friends to wear . . . and wish for you and your group a most enjoyable tour."[18] Children around the country wrote the senator to borrow a cap for a school play or to request one for a souvenir. To keep his supply of caps fresh, supporters donated coonskins. One supporter justified trapping of the animal by noting it had "the disposition and characteristics of a Republican, always growling and snapping at everything. He was using McCarthy tactics, 'searching' when he put his foot in my trap."[19]

During the run for the Democratic nomination for the presidency in 1952, Kefauver adopted the coonskin cap to symbolize his independence from the party establishment and Truman (he had announced his own candidacy before anyone else, including Truman himself, indicated their plans). Kefauver and his staff would frequently dispense a cap to a child at a campaign stop and the recipient as well as the candidate would garner the attention in the local newspapers. Furriers pressed him for his advance itinerary so they could market the caps at his campaign stops. From all indications, trafficking in coonskin caps demanded a considerable portion of his staff's time. At the Democratic convention that year in Chicago, Kefauver's delegates were conspicuous by their readily identifiable coonskin headgear.

In using the raccoon as his principal symbol, Estes Kefauver tied himself to the earlier "gentleman from the cane" of West Tennessee. (Ironically, it was Kefauver's own great-great-grandfather, Joel Estes, who lost to Crockett in the 1829 U.S. congressional race.) David Crockett's image had been tied to the wily critter by the character Nimrod Wildfire in James Kirke Paulding's wildly popular play *The Lion of the West*,[20] and ever since, the animal had been associated with the backwoods and with Tennessee, so much so that the Tennessee state legislature made it the official state animal on May 19, 1971, in the closing days of the Eighty-seventh General Assembly.

But the coonskin and the Crockett style had an early currency both inside and outside the Volunteer State. It would be difficult to underestimate the degree to which the ring-tailed cap was used to symbolize backwoods values and political independence in the 1830s. The national Whig party, once the party of the aristocrat and mercantile interests, had determined by the early 1830s that to oppose Andrew Jackson successfully, they should adopt the language and trappings of frontier egalitarianism. According to one historian, it was the "Coonskin Congressman" Crockett himself, "'fresh from the backwoods, half-horse, half-alligator,' who for a time was touted as a Presidential prospect for the party and who first translated the chaster terminology of Whiggery into the vernacular of the canebrake."[21]

In promoting the presidential candidacy of William Henry Harrison against incumbent and Jackson-protégé Martin Van Buren, the Whigs "were so extravagant with coonskins in 1840 and it is somewhat surprising," according to another writer, "to find [the animals] still around. It has been estimated that they decimated the raccoon population by 150,000."[22] In this so-called "Log-Cabin Campaign," the Whigs hauled the sixty-eight-year-old Harrison out of his retirement in Ohio, proclaimed him a man from the backwoods of humble origins,[23] and in lieu of a platform, fashioned a campaign around the symbols of the log cabin, hard cider, and the coonskin.

The "Log Cabin Campaign." The caption reads "*This Log Cabin* was the first building erected on the North Bend of the beautiful Ohio River, with the barrel of Cider outside and the door always open to the traveller. The wounded Soldier is one of *Gen. Harrison's* comrades, meeting him after his celebrated Victory at Tippecanoe and not only does the brave old Hero give his comrade a hearty welcome, but his dog recognizes him as an old acquaintance, and repeats the welcome by a cordial and significant shake of his tail! If the lookeron will only watch close enough he can see the tail absolutely shake in the picture, particularly in a clear day, and if it is held due East and West, so as to feel the power of the *magnetic attraction* from the Great West." Library of Congress.

Senators began sporting coonskin caps in the Capitol building, and to pursue the campaign the party marshaled a force of plebeian orators for the stump trail, including a state legislator and Whig leader from Illinois, Abraham Lincoln, who "regaled audiences with anecdotes and humorous satire in an accent native to the frontier."[24] The strategy was wildly successful, with Harrison beating Van Buren in electoral votes by a ratio of four to one, a margin of defeat rarely inflicted on an incumbent president. Crockett himself, now dead, became associated with the campaign, in the form of *Crockett's Harrison Almanac, 1841,* in which the fictional Davy narrated the life and virtues of Harrison and explained why he should be elected president.

In Tennessee, James Chamberlain ("Lean Jimmy") Jones also exploited the coonskin to displace James K. Polk, an old adversary of Crockett's, from the governor's mansion in 1841. Jones, a political unknown two years before, assumed the Whig stand on all the issues, but he could hardly debate the issues on Polk's level; "according to press reports Jones had very little to say and consumed the time by telling stories and denying all that Polk had said."[25] It was his disarming politicking, however, that unnerved and eventually overcame Polk, during the two months they shared the stump trail. According to one writer, Jones

> would draw the attention of the audience entirely away from the discussion by relating some humorous story or by a declamation on the beauties of coon fur. On one occasion, after Polk had made a long and serious argument against the Whigs, "Jones arose and running one hand gently over a coon-skin which he held in the other, remarked, 'Did you ever see such fine fur?' The effect of Polk's speech went up like chaff in a wind before the mocking laughter which recognized the reference to the Harrison campaign and the implied taunt.'"[26]

Crockett could hardly have foreseen the tradition that we have outlined here. But the political tradition he inspired in Tennessee has turned out to be much more over the past century and a half than all the popular images – Hollywood renditions, far-fetched almanac stories, and tall tales – would allow us to account for. He represents a serious, real-life tradition that politicians, especially Tennessee politicians, can and do use in their favor, a tradition that is less than the wild and unabashed tall talk of the ring-tailed roarers, but more than horsing around on the campaign trail.

Consequently, the Crockett tradition in Tennessee is not so much issues as it is symbols and style and special knowledge; it is exemplified by the individual who shows that he is more comfortable with the local folks than with the Washington crowd and that he is able and prefers to speak and act like the locals.

Perhaps more closely embodying the tradition than anyone else since Crockett was Robert Love Taylor (1850–1912), born in Happy Valley, Tennessee, in Carter County, just a few miles up the road from Crockett's birthplace in Limestone. Robert Taylor was a Democrat, thrice governor and once senator, who was best known for the gubernatorial campaign he shared with his brother Alf, the Republican nominee, in the 1886 so-called War of the Roses campaign. Taylor entered politics in 1878, running for Congress against an incumbent in staunchly Republican territory, the first district of Upper East Tennessee. Portraying himself as "nothing but a poor mountain boy"[27] with no money and no powerful supporters, he undertook a victorious campaign by doing little but telling jokes (recall Crockett's first election campaign), playing the fiddle (Crockett was also a fiddler, but apparently never played during his stumps), and projecting a downhome image of himself. One writer describes Taylor clearly in Crockettesque terms as a naive mountain politician, as "young, fresh, unsophisticated, simple, poor, provincial, and uncorrupted by advanced schooling or the other accoutrements of civilization."[28] In their celebrated campaign tour for the governorship, the Taylor brothers made forty-one stops in less than eight weeks, usually giving four one-hour-long speeches at each stop, these speeches being, according to one account, "pleasing, entertaining, . . . but in no sense were 'ponderous or profound.'"[29]

In his youth, Ben Hooper, later governor of Tennessee in the 1920s, noted Taylor's political success and observed that he

> . . . was thus drawn by only one qualification, namely, his striking ability as a campaign orator. He was a great public entertainer. His audiences were always amused, but rarely, if ever, instructed. His method of campaigning was the one quite prevalent over the South when he entered politics, the telling and acting of funny stories, and in this line he had no superior. This mode of "stumping" was that of Davy Crockett, and he was a past master in it. On the lecture platform, Taylor successfully filled a unique place, but in no public office did he ever distinguish himself by genuine public service.[30]

More than half a century later, another governor exhibited features of the Crockett tradition. Frank Clement, the "Boy Governor" of Tennessee first elected in 1952, was well known for his Methodist-style oratory — Alabama's Governor Big Jim Folsom once characterized Clement's style of speechmaking as "cuttin', guttin', and struttin'."[31] Clement demonstrated this in his impassioned keynote address at the 1956 Democratic National Convention. His stumping prowess was as good as any other twentieth-century politician in the state, and he used it in barnstorming campaigns to reach out to the common folk. His style differed from that of Kefauver and Gore, the state's two senators, in that it was the style of an impassioned crusader, yet Clement participated in the tradition we are describing here. After four years out of politics, Frank Clement again won the Democratic primary for the governorship in 1962. He was anything but shy and non-

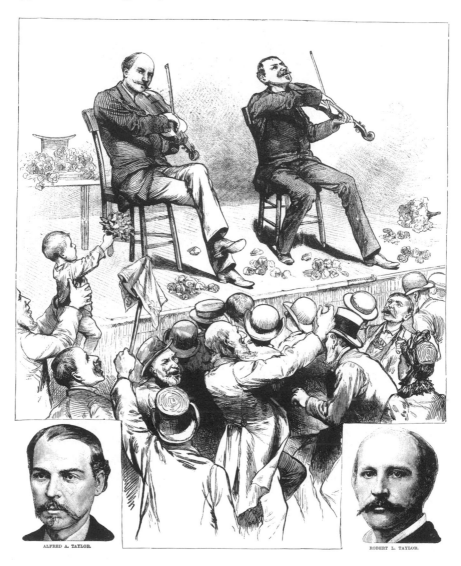

The "War of the Roses" campaign. This cover illustration for the October 2, 1886 edition of Frank Leslie's *Illustrated Newspaper* has a caption that reads "Novel Political Campaign in Tennessee – The Rival Candidates, 'Alf' Taylor and 'Bob' Taylor, Fiddling for Votes." Special Collections and Archives, Rutgers University Libraries.

Frank Clement, the "Boy Governor," in full oratorical swing as he delivers the keynote address at the 1956 Democratic National Convention. University of Tennessee Library.

self-promoting, but the Dickson-born politician knew how to behave with humility and understatement when visiting another small town like Center-ville, forty miles west of Nashville (the same town in which David Crockett made his first campaign appearance 140 years earlier). Portraying himself as "Old Frank" and "just a country boy," he allowed that he would make an even better governor the second time around because he was "ten years older, ten years more mature, and, I hope, ten years wiser."[32] Needless to say, "Old Frank," still in his early forties, was elected handily.

Ten years later, in the summer of 1973, Tennessee Senator Howard H. Baker, Jr., of Huntsville was sitting as the vice-chairman of the Senate Select Committee on Presidential Campaign Activities, better known as the Watergate Committee. As the senior Republican on a committee investigating the reelection of the Republican president, Baker found himself in a most unenviable position. Clearly the Nixon White House expected him to run interference for the administration's positions and to temper the inquisitory ardor of the Democrats. And the Democrats, the majority party in the Senate, were greatly suspicious, especially Committee Chairman Sam Ervin of North Carolina, about how impartial a voice Vice-Chairman Baker would have.

It was a time of grave national soul-searching, and intense attention focused on the hearings. They dominated the front cover of *Time* and were broadcast in full on daytime television for most of the summer. Some of the tensest moments came during the questioning of John Dean, former special counsel to the president, testifying under immunity. Dean's revelations about the personalities and politics of the inner White House had riveted the nation's attention for nearly two weeks. But if we had been in the Senate Hearing Room in early July, towards the end of Dean's two weeks of testimony, we would have witnessed an interesting spectacle. Dean had strongly suggested that President Nixon knew about the Watergate break-in significantly earlier than the president had claimed, and the committee had turned its mind to whether they would try to ask the president himself to testify. At this point in the proceedings, Chairman Ervin and Vice-Chairman Baker were discussing whether there might be any legal precedent for such testimony before Congress. Ervin pointed out that on February 14, 1862, President Abraham Lincoln volunteered to appear and testify before a House committee. Here is what Baker then said:

> Mr. Chairman, I might say in that respect, although my precedent is not nearly as old as your precedent, that I believe in 1919, in junction with the efforts

to ratify the Treaty of Versailles, rather than a President appearing before a committee of the Congress, in fact, President Wilson invited the Foreign Relations Committee to meet with him. *So as we say in Tennessee, there are lots of ways to skin a cat* [emphasis mine] and I wouldn't presume to say how we go about it. But I do hope that there is some way to supply additional information on these crucial important points.[33]

What is remarkable here is Baker's abrupt shift of style (one of many in the deliberations) in citing a proverbial expression and referring to his native state in what could hardly have been a more formal situation. This clearly was not done for comic relief. Baker's quip only seemed to contrast totally with the tone of the proceedings, since it was preceded by a carefully crafted legal statement encumbered with qualifications.

There is nothing distinctively Tennessean in this proverb, of course, but there is something unusual about interjecting a comment of this kind into such a formal hearing. What it signaled was that Baker wanted to draw on an oral tradition, a tradition of folk wisdom, in dealing with a complex political situation in Washington.

Baker was not alone; anyone who remembers the hearings recalls Sam Ervin's folksy efforts to spice up the proceedings with his downhome quips and to upbraid the witnesses with his quotations from and expositions on Holy Writ. On many occasions, such as the one during Dean's testimony mentioned above, the hearing room seemed to revolve around Baker and Ervin, these two seasoned politicians from the southern hills, one from the Cumberland Plateau of East Tennessee, and the other from the Piedmont of North Carolina. They were so much at home with each other swapping anecdotes, trading small talk, and even grandstanding to the television audience that it is hard to remember that there were five other members of the special Watergate committee—Daniel Inouye of Hawaii, Joseph Montoya of New Mexico, Edward Gurney of Florida, Lowell Weicker of Connecticut, and Herman Talmadge of Georgia.

Reading the more than three thousand pages of committee transcripts reveals that Baker and Ervin were the only two senators who called on their experiences from their home state to enlighten the proceedings. At appropriate moments, they would cite the opinion of some stalwart citizen from their home district, call on a legal action back home as a precedent for the goings-on in Washington, cite a lesson learned from a crucial experience growing up, or otherwise draw on their resources back home in Tennessee and North Carolina.

Ervin would often employ an obscure but suggestive mountain term to catch the attention of the audience and the witness. During the testimony of H. R. Haldeman, for example, he quipped, "I am not saying anything is wrong. It just shows there has been a little, what we call in North Carolina, 'connegling together.'"[34] (Ervin later pointed out to Haldeman that this was a compliment to Haldeman's legal dexterity.) At times during the proceedings Baker and Ervin seemed to be more interested in trading rhetorical quips (and, for Mr. Ervin, expounding on Scripture) than in pondering the testimony of the witnesses.

It probably would have been alien to the other members of the committee (excepting perhaps Mr. Talmadge) to have introduced experience from back home and to have shown by their language their roots and the close touch they had maintained with the home folks there. To these other senators, the behavior of Ervin and Baker did not make political sense at a Senate hearing in Washington, although they might have deemed it more appropriate on the front steps of a county courthouse back home. To politicians who had not been nurtured in an oral tradition, the anecdotes of Baker and Ervin must have seemed comic.

Followers of Baker's career over the years can testify to his rhetorical resourcefulness in shifting and orienting his style to his audience and to the occasion, especially when back in East Tennessee. In Washington, he normally displayed a polished, parliamentary style, especially in his role as Senate majority leader, but he often demonstrated that he could make a point more directly in the style of the folks back home in Scott County.

In 1981, for instance, after Baker had become majority leader, a freshman senator noticed that Baker was absent from the majority leader's front desk as the Senate was trying to resolve a territorial dispute between two committee chairmen. A short time later, though, he found Baker relaxing in a third-row seat and asked him why he was not participating. Baker grinned and replied, "There's an old Tennessee saying, 'Ain't got no dog in that fight.'"[35] Notice the style of this expression, especially the double negative and the missing subject pronoun; the "Standard English" equivalent, "I don't have any dog in that fight," hardly sounds like an answer at all! Nor would it lend the lack of dignity to the situation that Baker wanted to express.

Other modern-day Tennessee politicians have shared the values and projected the image of a downhome individual to a degree. Albert Gore, Sr., was well known for entertaining his constituents with his fiddle early in his career. It was his trademark in his upset Democratic primary victory over Senator McKellar in 1952. Lamar Alexander, the recent governor, originally from Maryville, Tennessee, has also demonstrated his desire to keep in touch with the people in several ways. In his gubernatorial campaign of 1978, he made a "walk across the state" in a flamboyant red-and-black flannel shirt, khaki pants, and hiking boots and stayed in the homes of non-politicians overnight along the way. Although both of these two politicians have partaken of the Crockett tradition, neither has been distinguished by their ability to shift their style or their speech. Alexander's accent has not changed since he entered politics nearly twenty years ago, nor does he have much affinity for telling spicy or comic stories, no matter who the audience is. Gore, in the latter part of his eighteen-year tenure in the Senate, impressed the voters as aloof and sounded more like a northerner than a Tennessean. A frequent criticism of him in 1970, when he was defeated by Bill Brock, was that he had lost touch with the people.

Crockett was two hundred years old in 1986, and by any measure the times have changed. In the late twentieth century, far more voters see politicians on television than in person, and political analysts declare that electability depends on being smooth and prepared before the cameras. Is there any place left for the old-fashioned campaigner from the backwoods?

In the late 1980s at least two Tennessee politicians have shown that the Crockett tradition is alive and well. In the summer of 1986, Ned Ray McWherter, speaker of the Tennessee House of Representatives and a country-talking former shoe salesman and college dropout from West Tennessee and dealer of the folksy phrase and humorous quip, won the Democratic nomination for the Tennessee governorship over two urban competitors. In the fall he won by a hundred thousand votes over his urban Republican opponent. About the source of his appeal, here is what one newspaper writer said:

> Being called folksy, he says, is the "highest compliment you can pay me." His speech patterns are a trademark. He professes nervousness when he must make a speech, say at a college commencement or Boys State, "where I have to use perfect grammar and study what I say to set a good example." But he likes it when, as on the stump in informal campaigning, "I can just get up and say what I feel."[36]

A final example comes from when, on a Friday in late February 1987, former Senator Howard Baker answered the Ronald Reagan's rescue call, in the depths of the greatest crisis in the Reagan presidency, to become White House chief of staff and help put the White House in order. Baker immediately showed his folksiness at an afternoon news conference, joking and indulging in anecdotes with the press and exhibiting the un-Washington, downhome style that enabled everyone to forget the humorless demeanor of the just-departed Donald Regan. The media called Baker's style "a breath of fresh air," and *Newsweek* cited his "taste for ritual and tradition back home in Tennessee"[37] as one of his positive qualities as a choice for chief of staff.

Is Crockett's legacy dead? Decide for yourself.

APPENDIX: THE TALL TALK TRADITION

There is another legacy having to do with rhetoric and language that is associated with Crockett, albeit the fictional *Davy* rather than the historical *David*. More accurately, this belongs to those who wrote about him, the unnamed writers who produced over thirty different Crockett almanacs (with more variants and imprints) between 1835 and 1856. This is the legacy of tall talk, of the use of exaggerated and extravagant turns of phrase, of copious language and fantastic elocution in the so-called Humor of the Old Southwest. This literary movement began in earnest in the 1830s, marked especially by the appearance in 1831 of Paulding's play *The Lion of the West* with its hero from "Kaintuck," Nimrod Wildfire, a thinly veiled imitation of Crockett, in whose mouth Paulding put the "I can jump higher – squat lower – dive deeper – stay longer under and come out drier!" oration that Davy Crockett later adopted for his own.[38] Although the movement was best known for its wild stories about the Old Southwest, eastern literary organs, most notably William T. Porter's weekly *Spirit of the Times* newspaper (1831–1856), were its main propagators and in part its originators.

Among the many striking features of the Crockett almanac stories (a number of which, as John Seelye has established,[39] were produced by hack writers in Boston), and much of the other early almanac tall-talk literature, we could discuss the figures of speech, the imagery and startling word-pictures, and the use of eye dialect (i.e., spelling words without silent letters, such as *no* for *know*, so that they appear to the eye to be "dialect"; little genuine regional dialect appears in either the Crockett almanacs or Crockett's own autobiography). Richard Boyd Hauck has discussed several of these matters in Chapter 3 of his *Davy Crockett: A Handbook*.[40]

But perhaps more identified with the Crockett almanac persona than any other aspect of language are the far-fetched, high-flown, mouth-filling, wild-sounding, invented derivations (i.e., such terms as *terrificacious* and *hellifericious*), most often constructed with empty, filler syllables and pseudo-Latinate endings. These tall-talk coinages were a microcosm of the frontier itself, encapsulating the wildness and unabashedness of life beyond the confines of civilization and seeming to be as unbounded and expansive in adding syllables as was the frontier itself. One scholar has captured a small collection of these words from the era in the following statement (not all of which are from the Crockett almanacs):

> The frontiersman, ring-tailed roarer, half horse, and half alligator, described himself as *kankarriferous* and *rambunctious*, his lady love as *angeliferous* and *splendiferous*. With consummate ease he could *teetotaciously exfluncticate* his opponent in a *conbobberation*, that is to say a conflict or disturbance, or *ramsquaddle* him *bodaciously*, after which the luckless fellow would *absquatulate*.[41]

These specimens of tall talk are the antithesis of schoolbook grammar (in whose terms, no doubt, they would be termed 'uncouth' and 'barbaric') and the mockery of Latinate vocabulary. Only a few of them (such as *rambunctious* and *bodacious*) have achieved much currency, and others (such as *humongous*) have come along, but they exemplify the inventiveness that has always been one of the hallmarks of American English. These are "hellacious" for the etymologist, who is little better than the man on the street in pinning down the formative elements of words like *explunctificate* and *humongous* and who can hardly keep track of their proliferation in the tall-talk literature.

That these words are a legacy we can associate with Crockett lies in the fact that their earliest, or very nearly their earliest, appearance in print was in the Crockett almanacs, even though we must again remember that most of these terms are deliberate creations of eastern writers to portray the color and excess of the backwoods. For instance, the following were first used in print in the 1830s (and were very soon afterward employed in the Crockett almanacs: *angeliferous* (1835), "angelic"; *ramsquaddle* (1830), "to overcome"; *savagerous* (1832), "fierce, savage"; *sockdolager* (1830), "a tremendous blow"; *splendiferous* (1837), "magnificent, striking"; *teetotaciously* (1833, in the spurious *Sketches and Eccentricities of Colonel David Crockett of West Tennessee* (1833), "totally."[42]

We could add several dozen of the other terms discussed below to this list, but they have not been included by the lexicographers of American English.[43]

To present and discuss a sample of these derivatives, I have culled from Richard Dorson's *Davy Crockett: American Comic Legend* edition of tales from the almanacs a list of seventy-six such fanciful words for a quick analysis.[44] The primary function of these seventy-six terms is seen in that sixty-three (83 percent) of them are modifiers. Forty-one are adjectives (including *hostilacious, skintearriferous,* and *unscrupulocious*) and twenty-two are adverbs (including *fistifferously* and *suddenaciously*). Eleven of them are nouns (such as *bankruptification* and *terrification*), and only two are verbs (*explunctificate* and *intarmine*). Genuine dialect forms such as *watermillion* are rare in the almanacs, but eye-dialect forms like *steem, vennyzon,* and *wile,* as well as longer forms like *allmynacks, eddycation,* and *pretticularly,* are exceedingly common.

The productivity of the fanciful forms is easily seen in the variety of base words from which these examples of tall talk are derived: "You may fight fistifferously, kick hossiferously, or bite catifferously, but if you attempt to murder another accordin' to fashion . . . you'll find that Col. Crockett's a gentleman accordin' to natur, and won't tolerate any unnatural civilities between nobody."[45] It can also be seen in our sample's derivatives of two common words, *terrific* and *total.* From *terrific* are formed *terrification, terrifications, terrificacious,* and *terrificaciously*; a related form is *tarrifacious.* From *total* are derived *teetotal, tetotalacious, teetotaciously,* and *teetotalaciously.* The derivation of these terms draws on a potential for the endless addition of syllables to produce longer and more far-fetched creations. At first glance, this process may seem unprincipled and unbounded. A closer look, though, shows this is clearly not so. In fact, the creativeness of the word-formation processes involved in these tall-talk terms is clearly limited, and the principal ways syllables and suffixes are added can easily be spotted.

The variety of such words is clearly limited, because we find that forty-six of the modifiers have one of three suffixes: *-ous, -ferous,* or *-acious* ending. We can identify several common processes of inserting or adding the syllables that make the words more "impressive," such as adding *-iferous* or *-ifferous.* These suffixes are based on the Latin verb *ferro,* "to bear or carry" and have the sense of "containing, bearing, or bringing forth a certain quality." They are found in such English words as *somniferous* and *carboniferous.* More than likely they are influenced by the adjective *ferocious* as well. Sixteen words are formed by the addition of this suffix, the result of which is to transform one- and two-syllable words into four- and five-syllable ones.

angel → *angeliferous*
pest → *pestiferous*
skin tear → *skintearifferous*
snore → *snoreifferous*
tooth → *toothiferous*
voracious → *voraciferous*

Six similar sounding but etymologically unrelated forms end in *-erous*, among them:

savage → *savagerous*
swag → *swaggerous*

Twenty forms in the list, fifteen adjectives and five adverbs, have one of several almost identical suffixes, *-acious, -atious, -aceous,* or *-ocious,* including the following:

echo → *echoaciously*
hostile → *hostilacious*
huge → *hugaceously*
monster → *monstracious*
scalp → *scalpaciously*
sudden → *suddenacious.*

One word, *hellifericious,* uses both the *-fer* and *-cious* syllables. What we see, then, is that even though the coinage of these terms seems unconstrained, a very narrow range of processes is used to derive them.

Most of the fanciful nouns in our sample employ a common derivational process as well; seven of the eleven have the noun suffix *-tion.*

steam → *steamification*
test → *testification*

This brief survey of the formation of these outlandish and often fanciful terms shows that they were derived using a small repertoire of processes, but even so, it also confirms that they could surely have a striking effect on the reader and that they were extremely flexible in that they could be attached to an endless number of English word roots.

NOTES

1. E. H. Crump, "Estes Kefauver Assumes the Role of a Pet Coon," Newspaper advertisement, June 10, 1948, n. p. Item from Series 4b, box 3, of the Estes Kefauver Collection at the University of Tennessee Library, Knoxville.

2. Harvey Swados, *Standing up for the People: the Life and Work of Estes Kefauver* (New York: Dutton, 1940), 37.

3. Estes Kefauver [Estes Kefauver Answers Crump Attack], Typescript of radio address over station WDOD, Chattanooga, June 14, 1948, 2–3. Item from Series 10, box 1, of the Estes Kefauver Collection at the University of Tennessee Library, Knoxville.

4. James A. Shackford and Stanley J. Folmsbee, eds., *A Narrative of the Life of David Crockett of the State of Tennessee by David Crockett*, a facsimile edition with annotations and an introduction (Knoxville: University of Tennessee Press, 1973).

5. Ibid., 140–42.

6. Ibid., 142–43.

7. Ibid., 169–70.

8. Ibid., 9.

9. Ibid., 13.

10. Ibid., 43.

11. A general account of the antics of electioneering in antebellum southern politics is provided in William J. Cooper, Jr., *The South and the Politics of Slavery, 1828–1856* (Baton Rouge: Louisiana State University Press, 1978).

12. The best analysis of the role of storytelling in southern politics is perhaps Waldo Braden, *The Oral Tradition in the South* (Baton Rouge: Louisiana State University Press, 1983).

13. Estes Kefauver, untitled typescript, 1948. Item from Series 10, box 1, of the Estes Kefauver Collection at the University of Tennessee Library, Knoxville.

14. Joseph Bruce Gorman, *Kefauver: a Political Biography* (New York: Oxford University Press, 1971), 51.

15. Swados, 40.

16. Estes Kefauver, "How Boss Crump was licked," *Collier's* 122 (October 16, 1948): 24–25.

17. H. F. Frow Letter to Estes Kefauver, January 3, 1950. Item from Series 4b, box 3, of the Estes Kefauver Collection at the University of Tennessee Library, Knoxville.

18. Estes Kefauver Letter to H. F. Frow, January 4, 1950. Item from Series 4b, box 3, of the Estes Kefauver Collection at the University of Tennessee Library, Knoxville.

19. Jim Lewallen Letter to Estes Kefauver, January 5, 1951. Item from Series 4b, box 3, of the Estes Kefauver Collection at the University of Tennessee Library, Knoxville.

20. James Kirke Paulding, *The Lion of the West retitled The Kentuckian, or a Trip to New York: a Farce in Two Acts*, revised by John Augustus Stone and William Bayle Bernard, edited and with an introduction by James N. Tidwell (Stanford, Calif.: Stanford University Press, 1954).

21. Robert Gray Gunderson, *The Log-Cabin Campaign* (Lexington: University of Kentucky Press, 1957), 7.

22. Edward Boykin, "The Coonskin is an Old Political Prop," *Washington Eve-*

ning Star, March 5, 1952, n.p. Item from Series 4b, box 3, of the Estes Kefauver Collection at the University of Tennessee Library, Knoxville.

23. This claim was a disingenuous one, according to Edward Pessen, *The Log Cabin Myth: the Social Backgrounds of the Presidents* (New Haven: Yale University Press, 1984).

24. Gunderson, 212.

25. Ray Gregg Osborne, "Political Career of James Chamberlain Jones, 1840–1857," *Tennessee Historical Quarterly* 8 (1948): 195–228.

26. Ibid., 207–08.

27. Robert Taylor, Jr., "Apprenticeship in the First District: Bob and Alf Taylor's Early Congressional Races," *Tennessee Historical Quarterly* 28 (1969): 34. Other accounts of this fraternal campaign are Rupert P. Vance, "Tennessee's War of the Roses," *Virginia Quarterly Review* 16 (1940): 413–24; and Paul Deresco Augsburg, *Bob and Alf Taylor: Their Lives and Lectures* (Morristown, Tenn.: Morristown Book Company, 1925). Augsburg relates an occasion in Chattanooga on which Bob pilfered his brother's speech and delivered it verbatim before Alf could take the stand. Crockett had pulled the same trick on the campaign many years earlier (James A. Shackford, *Davy Crockett: the Man and the Legend* (Chapel Hill: University of North Carolina Press, 1956), 64.

28. Taylor, 33.

29. Ibid.

30. Everett Robert Boyce, ed., *The Unwanted Boy: the Autobiography of Governor Ben W. Hooper* (Knoxville: University of Tennessee Press, 1963).

31. N. E. Parmentel, "Tennessee Spellbinder," *Nation,* August 11, 1956, 113–17.

32. "Ole Frank," *Time,* August 10, 1962, 13.

33. *United States Senate, Hearings before the Select Committee on Presidential Campaign Activities: Watergate and Related Activities* (Washington: U.S. Government Printing Office, 1973), 1557.

34. *United States Senate,* 3083. The term *connegle* must be either a localism or a nonce creation. It is not listed in any dictionary of American English, including Frederic Cassidy's monumental *Dictionary of American Regional English A–C.*

35. Helen Dewar, "Howard Baker is Senate's 'Political Neutron Bomb,' " *Atlanta Journal and Constitution,* February 21, 1982, 28-A.

36. Tom Humphrey, "McWherter Unafraid of Taking a Chance," *Knoxville News-Sentinel,* June 1, 1986, B-1, B-5.

37. Bill Barol et al., "One for the Gipper: Baker Signs on," *Newsweek,* March 9, 1987, 22.

38. Paulding, 27.

39. John Seelye, "A Well-wrought Crockett: or, how the Fakelorists Passed through the Credibility Gap and Discovered Kentucky," in *Davy Crockett: The Man, The Legend, and The Legacy, 1786–1986,* ed. Michael A. Lofaro (Knoxville: University of Tennessee Press, 1985), 21–45.

40. Richard Boyd Hauck, *Davy Crockett: A Handbook* (Lincoln: University of Nebraska Press, 1986).

41. Albert H. Marckwardt, *American English* (New York: Oxford University Press, 1958), 100.

42. The dates of earliest appearance are from Mitford M. Matthews, *Dictionary of Americanisms* (Chicago: University of Chicago Press, 1951).

43. The historical Crockett's autobiography contains at least half a dozen expressions that had their first appearance there. See Shackford and Folmsbee, 9.

44. Richard M. Dorson, ed., *Davy Crockett: American Comic Legend* (New York: Spiral Press for Rockland Editions, 1939). Dorson's collection of almanac tales is edited and far from complete, but it is the only edition readily available.

45. Passage from a Crockett almanac, quoted from Dorson, *Davy Crockett,* 84–85.

Celebrating Crockett in Tennessee

Joe Cummings

There is an assumed natural progression in American heroes. Generally, the talents and abilities of a hero are first recognized on the local level by his neighbors, then by the citizens of his state, and then by the nation at large. David Crockett, however, because of his unusual career, went from local hero to national celebrity; not until after his death did the already famous frontiersman become a state hero in Tennessee. To understand Crockett's strange journey in becoming a hero in the Volunteer State, it is necessary to understand the nature of Tennessee's regionalism and its effect on the commemoration of Crockett. Similarly, the effects of Crockett's national fame on his former neighbors and their descendants need also to be examined to understand fully Crockett's rise to glory in his home state.

David Crockett is Tennessee's only state hero. This is not because of a lack of heroic examples in the state; but most heroes in Tennessee fall into the other two categories — local and national. The first are men like James White, the Revolutionary War veteran who founded Knoxville, or Casper Mansker, the "long hunter" and friend of Daniel Boone, who founded Goodlettsville, or Nancy Ward, the "Beloved Woman of the Cherokees," who protected the early settlers of Upper East Tennessee. These people are men and women who by their actions within the community perpetuated their community's sense of self. Then there are national heroes like David G. Farragut, Alvin C. York, and Cordell Hull, people who left and became famous away from their community. In addition to adding to their community's sense of self, they are remembered and honored by their former neighbors who look at their lives as examples of the type of greatness that can spring from within.

The third type of hero is the state hero who mediates between the self-identity of the locale and the nation, but who also evokes a sense of state chauvinism. These people are admired and honored by all the citizens of the state. In Tennessee, however, almost all of the local and national heroes are identified with only one of the three sections of the state. Presidents Andrew Jackson and James K. Polk are, for the most part, honored by the people of Nashville and Columbia, where their respective Middle Tennessee homes are found. The same also can be said of Tennessee's third president, Andrew Johnson, who hailed from Greeneville in East Tennessee. And while no president lived in West Tennessee, the "King of Rock and Roll," Elvis Presley, is especially honored in the city of Memphis, the site of his palatial home, Graceland.

The main reason for Tennessee's lack of state heroes is the state's geography. Like a huge parallelogram, the state of Tennessee is superimposed over six major geological regions, which vary from the mountains and valleys of East Tennessee to the Mississippi-delta flatlands that surround Memphis. Since its earliest times, Tennesseans recognized that their state's different geography created different interests and, as a result, they traditionally have separated their state into three grand divisions of East, Middle, and West Tennessee.[1]

The differences perceived by the inhabitants of the three divisions are represented in several ways. The state constitution, for example, requires that the state supreme court meet in all three sections of the state. Many departments of the state government are similarly subdivided into three divisions to serve citizens' needs.

Occasionally, the natural rivalry that exists among the three sections seems humorous to outside observers. For instance, one governor of the state, Buford Ellington, erected signs by roads entering the state that greeted and confused tourists by welcoming them to the "three great 'states' of Tennessee."[2] More recently, when the Tennessee Historical Commission acquired Alex Haley's boyhood home in West Tennessee, and a memorial to Sam Davis, the "boy hero of the Confederacy," in Middle Tennessee, a clamor was raised by some commission members for a similar acquisition in East Tennessee. To placate the commission members' concern, the Bulls Gap home of the East Tennessean Archie Campbell (the recently deceased star of television's "Hee Haw" fame) was made into a state historic site.

Before the Civil War, however, the differences among the three divisions were less jocular. East Tennessee's hilly terrain made a plantation economy unprofitable, and as a result, farmers of that region owned few slaves. Middle and West Tennesseans, on the other hand, considered slaves a necessary part of successful farming. Middle and West Tennesseans, however, also were divided by the latter's suspicions of Jacksonian policies that threatened their land holdings. To the poor homesteading farmers of West Tennessee, Jackson and his Middle Tennessee cronies represented a greedy aristocracy; as a result, Whig candidates like David Crockett were able to campaign successfully against Old Hickory in his own back yard.[3] Similarly, many East Tennesseans were avid Unionists during the Civil War, while the rest of the state joined the Confederacy. In fact, two times during the war, East Tennesseans met and considered seceding from the state just as West Virginia did from Virginia during the same period.[4]

Since the war, regionalism has remained an important part of Tennessee politics, especially between East Tennessee and the other two sections. As late as 1949, V. O. Key reported that mountainous East Tennessee traditionally and overwhelmingly voted for the party of Lincoln, while the rest of the state always supported the Democratic ticket.[5] Several times since the Civil War, East Tennessee legislators introduced bills in the General Assembly to give their people a separate state.[6]

One result of Tennessee's regionalism is that there are very few statewide heroes. In fact, the only Tennessean who is honored in all three "states" of Tennessee is David Crockett. During the last thirty-six years, for example, the Tennessee Historical Commission has had a program that places markers on state highways to commemorate important persons, places, and events in Tennessee history. While the first markers were placed because of nominations by the commission, most have been erected at the public's request. Crockett, with fifteen markers in twelve counties, is the only person to have markers in all three grand divisions of Tennessee.[7]

Crockett is Tennessee's only state hero for several reasons. He passed through the entire state as he followed the frontier and lived in all three of its regions. More important to his becoming a hero, however, was the nature of his character and the popularity that he enjoyed during his lifetime. Throughout his adult life—in the militia, in county courts, and in politics—Crockett was a public man who was concerned about, and who cultivated, his public image. A natural storyteller and effective political campaigner, he was first elected to the state General Assembly in 1821 and the United States Congress in 1827. In Washington, the charismatic qualities of the colorful backwoodsman were recognized by the Whigs, who promoted him as a potential political alternative to fellow Tennessean, President Andrew Jackson. As a result, Crockett leapt from a popular local figure to a man of national prominence.

Soon afterwards, Crockett's fortune changed. When his political enemies back in West Tennessee were able to drive him out of office, his Whig allies abandoned him. At the same time, he was falling deeper into local debt. Disappointed and perhaps bitter about his reverses, Crockett left Tennessee in search of new opportunities in Texas. Gathered with friends at a farewell drinking party in Memphis, Crockett proved that his humor was still intact even though he was at a low ebb in his private life and public career. He concluded a toast by telling those who had gathered that, since the voters of Tennessee had cast their lot with his opponent, "you may all go to hell and I will go to Texas."[8]

Tennesseans recognized a certain gallantry in Crockett that was enhanced by his death. When the news that the Alamo had fallen reached Tennessee, newspapers throughout the state reported Crockett's bravery during the final hours of the siege. The source for many of the stories was a former editor of the *Nashville Banner* named George C. Childress, who claimed to have been present at Washington on the Brazos when the first reports of the battle of the Alamo were made by Travis's slave, Joe. Childress told Tennessee reporters on March 31, 1836, that "the gallant Crockett to the last, . . . continued to 'go ahead'—when he fell the corpses of the enemy were literally, piled around him." Childress's story was confirmed a few weeks later when a letter from Calvin Henderson of Washington, Texas, was printed in the Jackson, Tennessee, *Truth Teller,* a newspaper that served many of the frontiersman's former constituents. Henderson reported that during the battle, Crockett's "example animated every body"; furthermore, he had slain "25 of the enemy during the siege."[9]

In the middle of the state, Nashvillians were so moved that one man remembered "seeing adult men and women shed tears on account of the death of David Crockett." Out of admiration for the old frontiersman, many people began to see him in a new light. Four months after his father's death, John Wesley Crockett wrote to a kinsman that "even his [father's] most bitter enemies here, I believe, have buried all animosity, and joined the general lamentation over his untimely end."[10] The younger Crockett won back his father's seat in Congress during the following election and was able to pass an important piece of land-reform legislation, his father's main unaccomplished project, with the help of some of his father's former political foes.[11]

Crockett's former constituents in West Tennessee were the first to try to commemorate him by naming a county created out the counties that he represented in Congress. On December 20, 1845, an act was passed by the general assembly forming a new county, named Crockett, out of parts of Haywood, Madison, Gibson, and Dyer counties. At the same time the new county seat's name was changed from "Cage" to "Alamo" to honor the frontiersman's final sacrifice. The county did not come into being until years later because of injunctions and other legal efforts by the parent counties to prevent organization. Nevertheless, new legislation was reintroduced, passed, and stymied in the courts four times in 1852, 1866, 1870, and 1871. Crockett County was finally formed in 1871.[12]

In Memphis, an antebellum fire brigade honored Crockett's bravery in a different fashion. Like other fire brigades across the nation, Invincible No. 5 named their hose-reel wagon "Davy Crockett." In 1860, the Invincibles, with "Davy Crockett" in tow, took top honors at a fireman's parade in Nashville. The Memphis firemen marched proudly in colorful uniforms of decorated white flannel Shaker shirts and tightly fitting red pants. The legs of the trousers were tucked into patent leather boots that had "Davy Crockett" emblazoned on white-lined tops.[13]

Crockett's former neighbors in Lawrence County in Middle Tennessee also remembered their former state legislator and were the first in the nation to honor him with a stone memorial. Following the Civil War, when other communities were placing memorial markers to the Civil War dead on the State Capitol grounds, the people of Lawrenceburg placed a marble slab there inscribed "In Memory of David Crockett."[14]

The first major recognition of Crockett as a symbol of the frontier oddly occurred on his 103d birthday in 1889. Benjamin Rush Strong, a wealthy Knoxville real estate broker, took note of the growing interest in the Tennessee frontiersman by purchasing approximately forty-seven acres around Crockett's birthplace near the confluence of the Nolichucky River and Limestone Creek. Capitalizing on one of the many natural springs in the area, Strong built a spa. In an effort to make the spa look rustic, the buildings were sided with pine bark, and the columns on the veranda were undressed tree trunks. Inside the main building, one of the supporting beams was left exposed because, Strong told his guests, it had come from Crockett's birthplace.[15]

Strong, who had an interest in history as well as profit, worked with the Davy Crockett Historical Society of Washington County, Tennessee, to celebrate Crockett's 103d birthday. The real estate developer may have realized that Crockett was an attractive subject for a celebration for several reasons. First was a growing interest in the past by the public that was paralleled by a proliferation of nativist social organizations, like the Daughters of the American Revolution, a group that required for membership a genealogical link with the past. Second, Crockett came from a period in history before the Civil War. In East Tennessee, where both the North and the South had recruited men, Crockett was a person who would have equal appeal to the veterans of both armies.

Whatever Strong's reasons, the public response to his idea was tremendous. Over five thousand people traveled to visit the famous backwoodsman's birthplace for the celebration. Expecting a crowd, the ETV&G Railroad put on extra trains from Knoxville and charged special rates for the day. The trains were swamped. People also came in wagons, hacks, and buggies. N. B. Remine, a journalist from the *Jonesboro Herald and Tribune*, reported that "slopes, rocks, roadway, turf, benches, everything for acres that could afford human foothold and bear human weight held its quota of human beings. A record was kept of the free water from the spa's spring that was given to visitors, and by the end of the day, over 4,300 gallons were served."[16]

Strong and the Davy Crockett Historical Society had a full agenda for their guests. As families picnicked by the Nolichucky River, they listened to a band from Greeneville play patriotic music and watched teams from Limestone, Telford, and Jonesboro play baseball. Rifle companies from Knoxville, Greeneville, and Johnson City also entertained the crowd with military drills and parades. There was even a sham battle during which "the boys killed each other in a great mimic style, and after exhausting their ammunition, the battle was declared a draw . . . much to the relief of the trembling umpires" and to the delight of the spectators.[17]

Inside the Strong Inn, one room was set aside as a museum. On exhibit was a stone ax that Crockett had used during a "battle with the Cherokees in the 1820's," Crockett's grandmother's brass kettle, and a portrait of Crockett when he was in Washington painted by Rembrandt Peale. All of these items were brought to the celebration by Crockett's grandson, R. H. Crockett, who had been invited as a special guest of honor.

Besides the Crockett memorabilia, other artifacts from the pioneer days were exhibited, including a gourd found growing in Andrew Johnson's garden in 1812, a pair of cotton cards used by Andrew Johnson's great-grandmother, a cake plate used at Tennessee's first governor John Sevier's wedding, a flax hackle used by Sevier in 1816, an 1812 skillet that once belonged to President Garfield's grandmother, a local pioneer's tin horn, and a wolf skin taken in 1817.[18] Most of the curios in the small museum belonged to a time that the visitors to the 103d birthday celebration had never known. Like the flax hackle and the wolf, the world of the frontiersman and the pioneer was gone from the Tennessee scene. As the director of the census would report the following year, the American frontier had closed. To the people who gathered at Limestone in 1889, Crockett represented a lost world.

This theme recurred in the speeches made that afternoon at the celebration. According to the first speaker, N. B. Remine, East Tennesseans stood "in the glorious noon day of civilization"; the speaker urged his audience to "not forget their debt of gratitude 'renewable forever.' All honor to the brave pioneers who roamed the misty avenues of unfriendly forests, subdued the dens of savagery, opened up the great Western world, and built the America of to-day."[19]

The Honorable Alf Taylor, a popular local politician, stressed the same themes in his speech. "It is good to make such pilgrimages as this," he told his listeners. David Crockett was a "prince of pioneers" who was "schooled in the hard and trying experience of daily battle" with the forces of nature and who knew "none of the luxuries of our age, nor the elegant indulgences, vices, nor refined conventionalities, manners and customs of our more cultured civilization. He was essentially a child of nature."[20]

After the last speaker left the podium, Crockett's grandson was introduced to the audience. The old man was greatly moved by the welcome he received and struggled to compose himself before he could speak to the crowd.[21] With him was Peale's portrait of his famous grandfather, which was held high like an icon for all to see. The old man shared a few words with the crowd and then passed around the rifle, "Pretty Betsy," that had been presented to David Crockett by the young men of Philadelphia, for the people to inspect and admire. For the people of East Tennessee gathered on the shores of the Nolichucky, Crockett had become the symbol of the frontier. He was, as one speaker said, the "grand in all [people] that goes to make a nature's nobleman."[22]

The following year another celebration was held in Limestone, and amid the music, military exercises, hot air balloons, fireworks, and other entertainment, a cornerstone was laid for a monument honoring the Tennessee frontiersman. In Lawrenceburg, the first of many similar celebrations was also being held.[23] Two years later, five thousand spectators joined two hundred Crockett descendants for a family reunion at Crockett's cabin in Gibson County in West Tennessee.[24]

Throughout the state, the image of Crockett as nature's nobleman was promoted by teachers, orators, and historians. Schoolbooks in Tennessee reinforced the polished this image of Crockett. One schoolbook, written by G. R. McGee in 1899 and used in Tennessee classrooms for over twenty years, stated "that many absurd stories have been told of Colonel Crockett's fondness for hunting, his whiskey drinking, his ignorance and his boorishness." Instead, the author concluded, Crockett was a very moderate and respectable man despite his primitive environment. "Born and reared as he was in the forests of a new country, he was very naturally fond of hunting and adventure, and killed many bears, panthers, and other wild beasts. But hunting was not his business; it was his amusement. He was never in any sense a drunkard. Instead of being ignorant he was really very shrewd and intelligent. His opportunities at school had been very poor, but I [the author] have seen letters, written with his own hand, that show good sense and great information, as well as good writing and fine taste in composition. Instead of being a boor he was a very social and popular man of good manners according to frontier standards."[25]

Interestingly, it was at this time that the famous frontiersman was connected to another important Tennessee symbol—the Volunteer. Originally the Volunteer referred to Tennesseans who answered their nation's call for troops during the Mexican War in 1846. McGee reported that Tennesseans were aware of the murder of Crockett and others by Santa Anna after the fall of the Alamo in 1836 and that their indignation over the Mexican emperor's cruelty inspired Tennesseans to enlist and fight ten years later.[26]

In 1923, another link between Crockett and the Volunteer was forged when the frontiersman's great-great-granddaughter, Beth Crockett, presented the Tennessee State Library with an idealized picture of Crockett as a young man standing in a forest glen with his rifle in one hand and his coonskin cap in the other. Soon after, John Moore Trotwood, historian and state librarian, used the picture in his history *Tennessee: The Volunteer State 1769–1923*.[27] Now, as any diehard University of Tennessee fan knows, the Volunteer often sports a coonskin cap. Similarly, a few years ago when the Tennessee Department of Tourism wanted to promote the adventure and excitement that awaited out-of-state visitors, they dressed songwriter Ed Bruce in Crockett-style buckskins and a coonskin cap and had him urge tourists to "Follow Me to Tennessee."

The turn-of-the-century celebrations inspired a new generation of Crockett commemorations throughout Tennessee. In the early 1920s, state senator C. C. Kelly, who had attended the 1890 celebration, was inspired to

By the start of this century Crockett epitomized the noble aspects of the
frontier. From John Trotwood Moore's *The Volunteer State*. University of
Tennessee Library.

promote Lawrenceburg as one of the early homes of David Crockett by erecting a statue of the frontiersman. To raise money for his project, Kelly published a booklet with a short biography of Crockett and sold advertising space to local merchants. With the money he raised from the booklet and a state appropriation that he pushed through the General Assembly, Kelly was able to construct a twenty-foot bronze and granite statue of the county's founder in 1922.[28]

This figure of Crockett is modeled after the portrait by John Gadsby Chapman. Wearing a hunting shirt and holding a broad-brim felt hat, instead of a coonskin cap, the statue reveals the unique relationship of Lawrence countians to Crockett; they think of their famous founder foremost as a local hero who went on to greater glory, and not the coonskin-capped creature of popular legend. They traditionally have sought to honor the historical Crockett. Similarly, Lawrence countians take great pride in using the historical "David" instead of the more popular legendary "Davy" when discussing their former state legislator.

During the 1920s, 30s, and 40s, large public commemorations of David Crockett dwindled as, first, the Depression made Tennesseans too poor, and then World War II made them too busy. Nevertheless, Crockett continued to be remembered in other ways. During the 1930s, the local chapter of the Daughters of the American Revolution in Franklin County erected a marker honoring the grave of Crockett's first wife, Polly Findley, and the farmer who owned the land that Crockett had named "Kentuck" set aside the area around Polly's grave for visitors.[29] In Gibson County, a banker with a similar desire to save an important Crockett artifact bought the frontiersman's last cabin. Lacking the money necessary to preserve the structure properly, the banker disassembled the cabin and stored it until money could be raised for the restoration.[30]

There were, however, two major celebrations of Crockett that confirmed the backwoodsman's growing importance as a state symbol. In 1936, Crockett's 150th birthday was remembered in Greeneville with a two-day historic festival that attracted thousands. Among the special invited guests were the governors of six states and several United States senators. Many of the guests traveled out to Crockett's birthplace to visit the large stone that Strong had identified as a part of the original cabin; according to one newspaper the rock had become a "shrine" to Crockett's memory.[31] Ten years later, during the state's sesquicentennial, Tennesseans throughout the state

Dedicated in 1922 and located in the town square of Lawrenceburg, Tennessee, this statue was designed from John Gadsby Chapman's 1834 portrait of the frontiersman to mirror the esteem of Lawrence Countians for the historical "David" over the legendary "Davy." Tennessee State Library and Archives.

honored Crockett. He was now often identified as a representative of all three divisions of the state.[32]

Early in the 1950s, Crockett became the focus of many new commemorations. In Limestone and Morristown in East Tennessee, and in Rutherford in West Tennessee, separate citizens' groups were formed to recreate Crockett's birthplace, his father's tavern, and his last cabin, respectively. The recreation of structures reflects the importance of Crockett as a pioneer symbol in Tennessee. Except for the last cabin, all of the buildings Crockett lived in had disappeared many years before. Much of the wood for the last cabin had also been pilfered and used for firewood. To supply the logs necessary to build these structures, the descendants of Crockett's neighbors razed remaining frontier structures in the area to create memorials for their symbol of the frontier.

Not surprisingly, the Walt Disney Crockett craze of the 1950s increased the strong attachment that all Tennesseans had for the frontiersman. Thousands of people began visiting the Crockett sites throughout the state. In Limestone, a rumor was started that a log building belonging to a local farmer, W. L. Carter, was Crockett's birthplace. The farmer had to run off souvenir hunters who wanted slivers of Davy's first home. The problem became so bad that Carter appealed to the Tennessee Historical Commission, who issued a statement that the birthplace was indeed lost.[33]

In Morristown, the tavern was completed in time to be the showcase of the city's centennial celebration, and Crockett, who had died nineteen years before the city was founded, became the chief symbol of the celebration. Other places in Tennessee with even more dubious claims also honored Crockett as a native son. In Fentress County, a local historian published a book claiming that Crockett had played an important part in his county's history because his uncle had resided there.[34] In Overton County, the campsite of a Crockett kinsman was honored with a state historic marker.

It was at this time that the people of Greene and Lawrence Counties began planning to buy land for a park to honor Crockett. The descendants of the frontiersman's former neighbors wanted an area for their annual commemorations. Eventually both of these groups gave the land that they purchased for a park to the state, thus creating the Davy Crockett Birthplace State Historic Area in Limestone, and the David Crockett State Park in Lawrenceburg.

The most recent cycle of commemorations also demonstrates the statewide reverence for David Crockett. Originally the Tennessee Department of

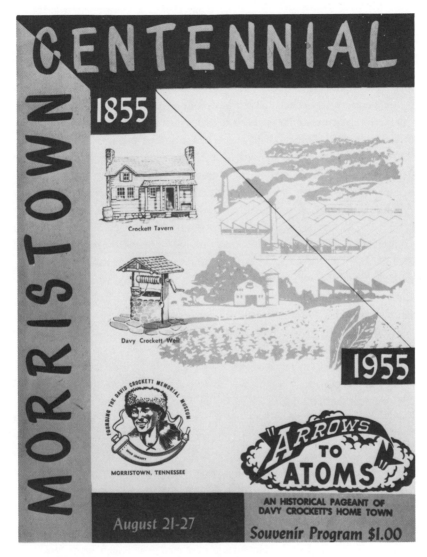

Although Crockett's death preceded the founding of Morristown, Tennessee, by nineteen years, he still played an important part in the town's centennial celebration. Author's collection.

Conservation planned to hold Crockett's bicentennial celebration at the birthplace in Limestone. But officials soon learned that citizen groups throughout the state also wanted to remember the frontiersman's two-hundredth birthday. In Lawrenceburg, the local historical society flatly told the state that they wanted their own special program at David Crockett State Park. Organizers in Rutherford, who planned Davy Crockett Days every fall, expressed a genuine concern that a big program in Limestone would eclipse their program. In Morristown and Alamo, plans were also being made for Crockett celebrations in concert with Homecoming '86, a special program started by then-Governor Lamar Alexander to get communities interested in celebrating their past. As a result, Crockett's two-hundredth birthday became a statewide celebration.

Only Crockett would have been remembered in such a manner. Of all Tennessee's heroes, only he is first a local hero to the communities he passed through, then a national hero, and finally a state hero who was and is both the frontiersman and the Volunteer, the key dual symbols of the state.

NOTES

1. Robert E. Corlew, *Tennessee: A Short History,* 2d ed. (Knoxville: University of Tennessee Press, 1981), 3.

2. In fact, the governor launched a large campaign around that theme in an effort to draw tourist dollars equally into all three parts of the state. For an example, see "Three 'States' of Tennessee" (Nashville: Tennessee Department of Conservation, 1970?).

3. Corlew, *Tennessee* 159–94; and Paul A. Bergeron, *Antebellum Politics in Tennessee* (Lexington: University Press of Kentucky, 1981), 7–8.

4. Corlew, *Tennessee,* 298.

5. V. O. Key, *Southern Politics in State and Nation* (1949; reprinted, Knoxville: University of Tennessee Press, 1984), 75.

6. Eric Russell Lacy, "The Persistent State of Franklin," *Tennessee Historical Quarterly* 23 (1964): 321–32.

7. Crockett is second only to Nathan Bedford Forrest as the subject of historical markers; however, the general's memorials are all located in Middle and West Tennessee. See *Tennessee Historical Markers,* 7th ed. (Nashville: Tennessee Historical Commission, 1980), 1–207, passim; also see Herbert L. Harper, "Tennessee is Crockett Country," *Tennessee Conservationist* 52 (1986): 20–21.

8. James Atkins Shackford, *David Crockett: The Man and the Legend* (1956; reprint, Chapel Hill: University of North Carolina Press, 1986), 212. Communities from Rutherford to Memphis all claim to have had a tavern where Crockett made his "You may go to hell" toast; if true, then Crockett engaged in one of history's greatest "pub crawls."

9. Photostatic copies of Tennessee newspaper accounts about Crockett's death are available in the Special Collections of the University of Tennessee Library; also see Stanley J. Folmsbee and Anna Grace Catron, "David Crockett in Texas," in *Houston and Crockett: Heroes of Tennessee and Texas*, ed. Herbert L. Harper (Nashville: Tennessee Historical Commission, 1986), 214.

10. Folmsbee and Catron, 215.

11. Shackford, 240.

12. Robert M. McBride, "David Crockett and his Memorials in Tennessee," in *Houston and Crockett*, ed. Harper, 233; and Tom Siler, *Tennessee Towns: From Adams to Yorkville* (Knoxville: East Tennessee Historical Society, 1985), 1.

13. James Boyd Jones, Jr., "The Social Aspects of the Memphis Volunteer Fire Department," *West Tennessee Historical Society Papers* 37 (1983): 66.

14. *Lawrenceburg* [Tenn.] *Democrat Union*, undated, author's collection.

15. *Jonesboro Herald and Tribune*, August 19, 1889.

16. Ibid.

17. *Knoxville Journal*, August 22, 1889.

18. *Jonesboro Herald and Tribune*, August 19, 1889.

19. Ibid.

20. Paul Deresco Augsburg, ed., *Bob and Alf Taylor: Their Lives and Lectures* (Morristown, Tenn.: Morristown Book Company, 1925), 276–78.

21. *Knoxville Journal*, August 22, 1889.

22. *Jonesboro Herald and Tribune*, August 19, 1889.

23. "Lawrenceburg, Tennessee, Has the Only Statue of Colonel David Crockett" (Lawrenceburg: Lawrence County Chamber of Commerce, 1955).

24. Marvin Downing, "Davy Crockett in Gibson County, Tennessee: A Century of Memories," *West Tennessee Historical Society Papers* 37 (1983), 57.

25. G. R. McGee, *A History of Tennessee: From 1667 to 1900* (New York: America Book Company, 1900), 169.

26. Ibid., 167–68.

27. This picture of Crockett is still used in state publications like the *Tennessee Blue Book*. See John Trotwood Moore, *Tennessee: The Volunteer State, 1769–1923*, vol. 1 (Chicago: S. J. Clarke Publishing Co., 1923), 401.

28. *Lawrenceburg News*, 22 July 1970.

29. Jesse Arn Henderson, "Unmarked Historic Spots of Franklin County," *Tennessee Historical Magazine* [ser. 2] 3 (1935), 117; and, "Hilltop Grave," *Nashville Tennessean*, August 16, 1936.

30. Downing, 58–60.

31. *Nashville Tennessean*, August 16, 1936.

32. Gov. Jim McCord, "Tennessee Sesquicentennial," *Tennessee Historical Quarterly* 5 (1946): 298. See also related items in this issue on pages 340, 363, 391, 393, and 399.

33. *Nashville Banner*, May 17, 1955.

34. Albert R. Hogue, *Davy Crockett and Others in Fentress County Who Have Given the County a Prominent Place in History* (Jamestown, Tenn.: by the author, 1955), 7–8.

Crockett and Nineteenth-Century Music

Charles K. Wolfe

In a recent essay on Davy Crockett and music, I attempted to explore the effect the Crockett legend has had on two facets of twentieth-century music: the living folk tradition (which had its roots in the 1840s minstrel songs about Crockett), and the pop song tradition generated as a result of the Crockett fad of the 1950s.[1] However, Crockett was as much, if not more, a public figure in his own century, and had an equally impressive impact on the music of that day and time. Not surprisingly, the nineteenth-century popular music scene is less well documented than that of the twentieth century, but enough new research is emerging to allow us to begin to assess some of the ways in which the Crockett image was reflected in this earlier music. This survey will approach the Crockett mystique, then, from two perspectives: that of how Crockett's image was reflected in music of his day, and that of Crockett's actual involvement in the music of his day—primarily through his abilities as a fiddler.

Earlier students of Crockett made vague references to a Crockett songster, one *Free-and-Easy Song Book*.[2] At the time I wrote my earlier essay, I had not been able to inspect a copy of this book, and had tentatively dated its first edition as 1837. Since then, Brown University has made available a copy of the song book on microfilm,[3] and a study of this, as well as further research into songster history, has caused revision in my earlier appraisal of the book. While there is still no proof that Crockett had anything to do with the actual song choices in the book, new evidence suggests that the book came out earlier than was previously thought. An 1836 edition has surfaced, giving no publisher on the title page, but containing 304 pages of songs with the notation that this is a "new edition." This may mean that the songster was published during Crockett's lifetime, and also indicates that it was quite popular: there were at least five known editions from 1836 to 1846, one graced with illustrations by Charles Dickens's famous artist George Cruickshank. In fact, *Free-and-Easy* was so popular that publisher James Kay announced an abridged version of the book (128 pages out of over 320) especially designed "for young men." He also announced as *in press* in 1839 a companion volume called *Colonel Crockett's Free-and-Easy Recitation Book*, "a collection of the best Stage, Dining, and Parlor Recitations, Comic and Sentimental." It was seen "as a companion" to *Free-and-Easy*, "to form a volume of the same size executed in similar style." This publication does not appear in NUC, and I have not inspected it; however, it is worth noting that the recitation has a parallel history to traditional songs; folk audiences often used the two almost interchangeably. Folk recitations are a form of folk poetry, and many can be traced back to such recitation compilations. As we will see, there are a number of such recitation or semi-spoken versions of the most famous Crockett song, "Pompey Smash." In the preface to the 1839 edition, the editors write:

> Since the appearance of the first edition of this very popular Manual for the Vocalist, the remarkable individual whose name introduced it to the notice of the public has paid the debt of nature. . . . It may not be improper to mention that the call for this little work has rather increased than fallen off, since the death of *Colonel Crockett.*

The preface continues to describe the purpose and scope of the new collection, noting that "particular attention" has been paid to adding "Texian songs" and "African" (i.e., minstrel) songs. The collection does contain a wide variety of these songs, as well as Irish songs (or ersatz Irish songs), a number of nationalistic songs (including an early version of "God Bless America"), comic songs, and sentimental songs. Several recitations are also included. Looking at the collection from the standpoint of modern folklore, it is noteworthy that a number of texts here did go into oral tradition; one example is the Irish song "The Exile of Arion," which appeared in the repertoire of Tennessee traditional singer Dee Hicks, and was sung in Nashville in the 1830s at Irish celebrations. But the publishers of the songbook made no claims that any of the songs were in any way folk; they were described as "stage songs," but some had hitherto not appeared in print—a curious admission. Texts had been gathered "from the archives of a most respectable club of vocalists in this city" (Philadelphia). Over three hundred items appear in the 1839 collection, none with music, but a number with the "air" or melody indicated—i.e., newer songs composed to older, familiar melodies. These are technically parodies, but we must remember that in popular and folk music a "parody" is not necessarily comic or lampoonistic— it is simply a new song modeled on an earlier one.

Such is the case with the title song from the 1839 edition of *Free-and-*

Easy, a new piece called "The Alamo; or The Death of Crockett." It was composed by (and credited to) Robert T. Conrad (1810–1858), a well-known poet and politician who was one-time mayor of Philadelphia and the mainstay of the Pennsylvania Historical Society. He published two books of poems, wrote a popular play called *Jack Cade*, and edited *Graham's Magazine* for a time. He was also very active in the cause of Texan independence. Though there is little evidence that "The Death of Crockett" went into oral tradition — it is far too literary and lugubrious to appeal to a folk aesthetic — it has been on occasion reprinted (cf. Walter Blair). It has not, however, been often performed, possibly because author Conrad set it to the melody of "The Star-spangled Banner" — in 1839 a freshly minted parody of the British drinking song "To Anacreon in Heaven," and by no means yet our official national anthem. There *is* evidence (see below) that this was one of the more popular responses to Crockett's death[4] and as such deserves our attention.

The Alamo, or The Death of Crockett

By R. T. Conrad, Esquire.
Air — Star-Spangled Banner.

To the memory of Crockett fill up to the brim!
    The hunter, the hero, the bold yankee yeoman!
Let the flowing oblation be poured forth to him
    Who ne'er turned his back on his friend or his foeman,
        And grateful shall be
        His fame to the free;
        A bolder or better they never shall see.
Fill! fill! to the brave who for liberty bled —
May his name and his fame to the last — GO AHEAD!

When the Mexicans leaguered thy walls, Alamo!
    'Twas Crockett looked down on the war-storm's commotion,
And smiled, as by thousands the foe spread below,
    And rolled o'er the plain, like the waves of the ocean.
        The Texans stood there —
        Their flag fanned the air,
        And their shout bade the foe try what freemen will dare.
What recked they, tho' thousands the prairies o'er-spread?
The word of their leader was still — GO AHEAD!

They came! Like the sea-cliff that laughs at the flood,
    Stood that dread band of heroes the onslaught repelling;
Again! and again! yet undaunted they stood;
    While Crockett's deep voice o'er the wild din was swelling.

"Go ahead!" was his cry,
"Let us conquer or die;
"And shame to the wretch and the dastard who'd fly!"
And still, mid the battle-cloud, lurid and red,
Rang the hero's dread cry—*Go ahead! GO AHEAD!*

He fought—but no valour that horde could withstand;
He fell—but behold where the wan victor found him!
With a smile on his lip, and his rifle in hand,
He lay, with his foemen heaped redly around him;
His heart poured its tide
In the cause of its pride,
A freeman he lived, and a freeman he died;
For liberty struggled, for liberty bled—
May his name and his fame to the last—GO AHEAD!

Then fill up to Crockett—fill up to the brim!
The hunter, the hero, the bold yankee yeoman!
Let the flowing oblation be poured forth to him
Who ne'er turned his back on his friend or his foeman!
And grateful shall be
His fame to the free,
For a bolder or better they never shall see.
Fill! fill! to the brave who for Liberty bled—
May his name and his fame to the last—GO AHEAD![5]

"The Fall of the Alamo, or The Death of Crockett" was one of the more popular songs in the *Free-and-Easy*; not only was it the centerpiece for the book itself, which paralleled the surge of Crockett almanacs between 1837 and 1845, and was reprinted again in 1841, but the song was a legitimate stage hit. During 1841, for instance, audiences in Memphis, not far from Crockett's West Tennessee homestead, wildly applauded singers who performed the song on the stage of John Potter's old stable theater.[6] *Free-and-Easy* also contains at least five songs either completely about Crockett, or making substantial reference to him. A second Alamo song featuring Crockett is "Go Ahead":

Go Ahead

I'll "go ahead!"
The hero said,
Though I should tread
On heaps of dead!
With sack upon his back,

And rifle in his hand,
He made his hasty track
To the patriot's land.
Swiftly the forest ranging through,
He cried, 'mid scenes of danger new
As on he led—
I'll "go ahead!"
And echo said,
I'll "go ahead!"

I'll "go ahead!"
And on he sped,
Through paths that led
To glory's bed;
Nor slacked his rapid pace,
Till on the Texian field
He saw the foeman's face,
And when the war-notes pealed,
His rifle's crack the chorus rung,
And ever then the hero's tongue,
While foemen fled,
'Mid torrents red,
From those that bled,
Cried, "go ahead!"

We'll "go ahead!"
Then each one said;—
"The traitor's head,
Or we are dead!"
The fatal conflict rose,
Hot grew the deadly fight!
By hundreds fell their foes,
And with a tiger's might—
'Mid fiery bolt and burning rocket—
Hard fighting to the last, brave Crockett
Cried, "GO AHEAD!"—
The last he said—
When fell his head
Among the dead![7]

This bloodthirsty little paean makes one wonder if many of the popular press saw the tragedy at the Alamo almost exclusively in terms of Crockett's death. This song, for which we have no possible indication of tune, is an odd contrast to the 1950s Disneyized version of the motto, "Be Sure You're

Right, and Then Go Ahead." It suggests that Crockett's motive for going to Texas was his pioneer spirit; Texas is presented as an odd place of forests and mountain echoes and is "the patriot's land." The short dipodic lines that open and close each verse lend a martial air to the piece, and the strident use of the "dead-red-tread-ahead" rhyme scheme fits in with the rather gory description of the battle.

A similar view of Crockett as a military hero (as opposed to braggart, backwoodsman, trickster, or politician) occurs in "The Yankee Volunteer." I have not been able to find this song in folksong collections, but it resembles, in its word order and diction, a song that has had some oral honing. The song begins by recounting battles at Lexington, Bunker Hill, Trenton, Saratoga, and "Jackson's Deed at New Orleans." Then, almost certainly appended more recently, is a stanza on Crockett:

> The barber his razor did nobly wave,
>   And to lather the foe took off his coat,
> "If I had Santa Anna to shave,
>   By de hokey powers I'd cut his throat.

> The southern hunter drain'd his cup,
>   And slung his rifle over his back,
> "I guess my dander's riz right up,
>   In Texas 'cause I go for a crack."
> Onwards march through prairie wide,
>   With rifle slung and knife in pocket,
> Victory sits on freedom's side,
>   Three cheers for Houston and Davy Crockett![8]

Crockett's heroism here resides not in his death at the Alamo, which is not even described, but in the spirit of volunteerism that makes him go to Texas.

Perhaps the most interesting in *Free-and-Easy*, at least from a perspective of folk tradition, is a minstrel show text called "Zip Coon." Popular music of the 1830s and 1840s, especially that of the minstrel stage, was much more topical than popular music of today, with widespread and sometimes ambiguous references to current events and well-known personalities. It is not unusual, then, to find Crockett a common figure in many of these songs and minstrel or vaudeville stage shows — and to find him often appearing in the kind of songs described by contemporaries as "African" songs in deference to the pseudo-black culture the songs reflected. We have, though, too few examples of just how Crockett was viewed in these songs, or what aspects of his legend the songs dealt with. "Zip Coon" provides us with a rare glimpse of this image. Zip Coon, like the later Pompey Smash, was a minstrel stereotype who appears in countless sketches and songs. He narrates this song, which consists of a series of unrelated stanzas, each portraying Zip Coon as an insouciant, smart-mouthed observer of the current scene. Stanzas 6 and 7 deal with Crockett:

> Dat tarnal critter Crockett, he never say his prayers,
> He kill all de wild Cats, de Coons and de bears,
> And den he go to Washington to make de laws,
> And dere he find de Congress men sucking deir paws.

> If I was de President of dese United States,
> I'd suck lasses candy and swing upon de gates,
> An does I didn't like I'd block em off de docket,
> An de way I'd block em off would be a sin to Crockett.[9]

Other evidence (references to the federal bank) places this song as codifying around 1833, and it does reflect the Crockett legend motifs of might hunter and reformist politician.

By far the most popular song about Crockett, however, is "Pompey Smash," the long minstrel piece that appeared first (as far as we now know) in an 1846 collection entitled *The Negro Singer's Own Book*, a huge compilation of minstrel songs.[10] The song, however, is certainly older than 1846; the book's subtitle *Containing Every Negro Song That Has Ever Been Sung or Printed* attests that this is a "greatest hits" sort of retrospective, and a bibliographic examination of the book's texts and typeface suggests that many of the songs were reprinted directly from earlier songsters or even broadside sheets, song cards, or "ballets." A reference to Halley's comet in the text may date the song to the 1834 era, suggesting that it dated from a time when Crockett was still alive.

What image of Crockett appears in this song? Six of the twenty stanzas deal with Crockett and describe in detail a fight he has with the song's main character, one Pompey Smash, a black minstrel character similar to Zip Coon.[11] The central event of the passage—grinning the bark of a tree during a coon hunt—seems to come from a passage in the *Sketches and Eccentricities* of 1836. However, if the song actually dates from 1834, then it might be that *Sketches* was drawn from the song, or that both were drawn from an incredibly potent oral version of the bark-grinning story. The fight in the river, and the alligator reference found in some texts, have parallel references in the almanacs.[12]

"Pompey Smash" became the most famous Crockett song of all, even more popular than the Disney version. After all, the Disney song was a chart hit for less than a year, and a standard for thirty; "Pompey Smash" has been sung continuously by the American people for over 140 years; it is the real Crockett anthem. The six stanzas dealing with Davy, along with an occasional stray stanza from other parts of "Pompey," probably went into oral tradition about the time of the Civil War; the Crockett almanacs ceased publication in 1856, and the last printing of "Pompey" was about 1850. (Many other minstrel songs made their way into folk tradition during the 1850–60 era.) We know little of the song's progress in the latter half of the nineteenth century, but in the early part of the twentieth century, folk-song collectors found the song prominent among the earliest native-American collections. Collectors gathered versions of the song—now usually called merely "Davy Crockett"—in 1900, 1907, and 1917, and from singers in their sixties and seventies and eighties—singers who would have learned the song as far back as the 1850s or 1860s. Thus the song was kept alive during the late 1800s, and it attained renewed popularity in the early 1920s. Furthermore, though early collections came from Missouri, Texas, and Kentucky, and though the song was often referred to as a "southern" folk song (as in John Cox's book *Folksongs of the South*), later collections by Library of Congress recording teams came from Traverse City, Michigan; Quebec, Vermont; and Chicago, Illinois; as well as Murrells Inlet, South Carolina. The song, in short, appears all over the country; it is a truly national commemoration of Crockett. If more versions appear from the South, the reason might be that more people looked for the songs in the South.

When I wrote my essay "Crockett Songs: From Minstrels to Disney," I felt that almost all traditional versions of the Crockett song derived from "Pompey Smash"—even though a few items in some folk versions did not appear in the "Pompey" text that I had. After examining the *Free-and-Easy Song Book*, and noting that other items from it have been found "on the ground" (i.e., live in folk tradition), I now feel that parts of the "Zip Coon" song might also have found their way into oral tradition. Zip Coon is mentioned in many of the oral versions, and some scholars have suggested that this resulted from a folk confusion between the two minstrel characters, Pompey and Zip Coon. I would suggest now that what happened was that parts of two songs, "Pompey" and "Zip," went into tradition, and later were confused or merged in the folk imagination—especially in the light of Crockett stanzas appearing in *Free-and-Easy*'s version of "Zip Coon." There is no reference to Zip Coon in the printed text of "Pompey," yet a number of folk variants either refer to Zip Coon or even title their song "Zip Coon."

While cheap, popular songsters like *The Negro Singer's Own Book* and the *Free-and-Easy Song Book* accounted for most of the nineteenth-century Crockett songs, other sources offered music supposedly generated by Crockett himself. The most interesting of these is the song-poem "Farewell to the Mountains," which David reputedly wrote himself when he decided to leave Tennessee in 1835. Whether or not he did is uncertain, but the piece has an interesting and long history. It probably first appeared in book form in Buffalo Bill Cody's 1888 book on "The Renowned Pioneer Quartet" of Cody, Boone, Carson, and Crockett, and Cody insists there that it originally appeared in the Nashville *Republican Banner* shortly after Crockett's death.[13] A search of these paper files, however, has yielded nothing resembling it.

A widely quoted version of it appears in Austin P. Foster's account of Crockett's life that appeared in the October 1925 issue of the Tennessee Historical Society's *Tennessee Historical Magazine*:

> Farewell to the mountains whose mazes to me
> Were more beautiful far than Eden could be;
> No fruit was forbidden, but Nature had spread
> Her bountiful board, and her children were fed.
> The hills were our garners—our herds wildly grew,
> And Nature was shepherd and husbandman too.
> I felt like a monarch, yet thought like a man,
> As I thank'd the Great Giver, and worshipped his plan.
>
> The home I forsake where my offspring arose:
> The graves I forsake where my children repose,
> The home I redeem'd from the savage and wild;
> The home I have loved as a father his child;
> The corn that I planted, the fields that I cleared,
> The flocks that I raised and the cabin I rear'd;
> The wife of my bosom—Farewell to ye all!
> In the land of the stranger I rise—or I fall.
>
> Farewell to my country!—I fought for thee well,
> When the savage rushed forth like the demons from hell.
> In peace or in war I have stood by thy side—
> My country for thee I have lived—would have died!
> But I am cast off—My career now is run,

And I wander abroad like the prodigal son—
Where the wild savage roves, and the broad prairies spread,
The fallen despised—will again go ahead!

The more common title for this piece is "His Parting Blessing," and it is widely referred to as "the only poem composed by Davy Crockett." Though he quotes the poem in *Davy Crockett: Legendary Frontier Hero,* Walter Blair, like a number of other modern Crockett scholars, doubts its authenticity, or at least that Crockett wrote it. "It would be pleasant to think that Davy composed it without any practice," he notes.[14] In spite of this, the poem did become associated in the popular imagination with Crockett, and May 1955, it became a national issue.

In that month Walt Disney released the film version of *Davy Crockett, King of the Wild Frontier,* after its successful television debut. Bill Hayes's Cadence recording of "The Ballad of Davy Crockett," which had been released in February 1955, had climbed to Number One on the record charts. Wonderland Music Company, the Disney musical publishing arm, was naturally seeking a follow-up release, and discovered the text of "His Parting Blessing." They asked George Bruns, the composer of the music to "The Ballad of Davy Crockett," to fit music to this as well, and retitled it "Farewell"; promotional advertisements boasted that it was "Davy Crockett's Own Song (He wrote the words)".[15] The text of the new pop song was simplified considerably from the original: Bruns used the first two lines from stanza one, the third and fourth lines from stanza two, and the final couplet for stanza two served as the bridge: a total of six lines drawn from the original text of twenty-four. Bruns's melody is a slow, haunting, folk-like dirge that was probably adapted from background music for the film. The music industry saw it as a natural hit, and at least four recordings were rushed out immediately; one by Bill Hayes (Cadence 1256), one by Tennessee Ernie Ford (probably the best rendition, Capitol 3058), one by Fess Parker (star of *Davy,* Columbia 40450), and even one by legendary crooner Bing Crosby (Decca 29483). Unfortunately, none of these efforts even made the charts: the public seemed as indifferent to "Farewell" as it had been receptive to "The Ballad of Davy Crockett." The song remained an interesting curiosity in the byways of Crockettana—albeit an interesting alternative valediction to the more common quote of Crockett upon leaving Tennessee: "You can go to hell; I'm going to Texas."

While there are few stories about Davy's being a poet who could have written a piece as sophisticated as "Farewell to the Mountains," dozens of tales surround his other claim to musical fame: fiddling. This is not surprising, since many frontiersmen were able to play the fiddle and to appreciate a good fiddle tune; the fiddle was the basic musical instrument of the frontier, light, easily portable, repairable, and capable of a wild variety of sounds and moods. Legends about fiddling have attached themselves to a number of early American heroes, from George Washington to Thomas Jefferson to Andrew Jackson. Thus it is not unusual to find numerous references to fiddling, and to dances by fiddle music in early writings by and about Crockett.[16]

Specific instances of Crockett's involvement with fiddling, however, are less easy to come by. The oft-reported "Colonel Crockett: A Virginia Reel" has earlier been described as an older tune that was renamed in Crockett's honor during the national outpouring over his death.[17] Recent research, though, indicates that "Colonel Crockett" may have had more of a southern folk pedigree than previously thought. The tune appeared in an 1839 collection of fiddle tunes entitled *Virginia Reels,* edited by G. P. Knauff and published in Baltimore by George Willig. It was one of thirty-five tunes in the collection, most of which, modern researchers feel, were transcribed from local fiddlers.[18] The tunes comprise the first published collection of southern traditional fiddle tunes, and the inclusion of "Colonel Crockett" in it strongly suggests that the tune was being widely played by local fiddlers under this title. Indeed, the tune has remained in fiddling tradition to the present day, though the name has often been changed. It was recorded on commercial phonograph records as early as 1925, when a fiddler in Houston, Texas, named Captain M. J. Bonner, recorded it under the name "The Gal on the Log" (Victor 19699), and again in 1928 when a couple of old Mississippi fiddlers, the Carter Brothers, did it as "Jenny on the Railroad" (Vocalion 5297). In the 1960s and 1970s the same tune was collected from West Virginia as "The Route." No one, to my knowledge, has found the tune in twentieth-century folk tradition under its "Colonel Crockett" name. Thus, while it may well have been a tune Crockett was fond of playing, it has not survived as a tribute to him.

Another tangible bit of Crockett fiddle lore is an instrument owned by the Witte Museum in San Antonio, Texas, which is generally referred to as "The Davy Crockett Violin." This instrument, which has been part of the Crockett exhibit since 1934, was actually played on a 1955 recording by Red River Dave McEnery, a singing cowboy star, called "When Davy

Crockett Met the San Antonio Rose." The provenance of the instrument certainly seems to link it to Crockett. It was sold to the San Antonio group by a fiddler and fiddlemaker from Russellville, Alabama, about four counties southwest of the Franklin County, Tennessee, area where Crockett once lived. The violin repairman, in turn, had learned about the fiddle in the early 1930s; it was reportedly in the possession of an old man in Franklin County, Tennessee. The repairman bought it, made certain repairs on it, noted that it contained old rattlesnake rattles (a familiar tradition with old fiddlers), and sold it to San Antonio. In affidavits provided with the instrument, the Franklin County, Tennessee, owner, Frank Hollis, stated that his father, Tom Hollis, who lived near the Crockett homestead in Franklin County, bought the violin from Joseph Crockett ("who was David Crockett's son") in 1859; Tom Hollis died in 1872, and his son Frank inherited the instrument. Apparently during all this time, the violin was kept strung and was presumably played—at least until 1895. After that point, its condition was such that no one felt like stringing it up for play.[19]

The most curious part of the provenance, however, is the inscription written on the inside of the instrument: "This fiddle is my property, Davy Crockett, Franklin County, Tenn. February 14, 1819." By all chronologies, this date seems plausible; Crockett was in the area of south-central Tennessee during that time, albeit serving as an official of the neighboring county of Lawrence. Modern Franklin County is two full counties to the east of Lawrence, and court records show him present in Lawrence as late as May 1819. However, Richard Boyd Hauck's chronology[20] shows that Crockett had settled in Franklin County, on Bean's Creek, southwest of Winchester, in 1813, and stayed there until his move to Lawrence County in 1817. Could the inscription be a misreading, and could the "9" in fact to be a "3" or a "5"?

Another problem is the reference to the fact that the fiddle was sold by Crockett's son Joseph in 1859. Biographies make no mention of a son named Joseph, only of John, William, and Robert, the last-named born in 1816, the two older ones before 1811. None of them would have been old enough to take over the Franklin County homestead when Crockett left it in 1817, though they conceivably could have returned there later. And, again, it is possible that the Hollis family oral tradition of Tom Hollis's getting the fiddle in 1859 is simply garbled, and that Tom Hollis in fact got the instrument from either John or William—neither of whom followed Crockett and his second wife, Elizabeth, and her two children when they moved to West Tennessee or when she later moved the family to Texas after Davy's death.

A third problem with the provenance is the use of the term "Davy" in the fiddle inscription. As Michael A. Lofaro has noted,[21] this term was never actually used in any documents by Crockett himself, who preferred "David." The inscription could have, of course, been done at a later date, by a relative, and may still reflect historical truth. It might still represent David's fiddle, though not his exact inscription. Further research into the Crockett genealogy, as well as the exact status of the "Crockett homestead" in Franklin County, may be needed to resolve this.

The story of the Crockett violin might seem to be a somewhat inconsequential footnote on which to end a survey of Crockett music—until one realizes the iconic value of instruments in traditional and country music. Southern folk musicians tend to venerate instruments almost as much as songs, and most can offer a long and detailed provenance of their particular instrument; instruments are ways of validating an otherwise abstract heritage. In the case of Davy Crockett, the continuing public interest in the Franklin county violin—whether or not the instrument has an unblemished history—testifies to the continuing importance music plays in the public image of the man. More than perhaps any other nineteenth-century legendary hero, Davy Crockett has been validated by music. In the twentieth century, this music was the product of a sophisticated public marketing effort, buttressed by a strong folk impulse. In the nineteenth century, the music was a product of Crockett's own interest in music as an element of the frontier culture, and a product of a less sophisticated but equally influential minstrel and songbook business. Twentieth-century pop music offers numerous barometers by which we can quantitatively judge song popularity—best-seller charts in record magazines, sheet-music sales, royalty figures, distribution patterns, and discographies of recorded versions of songs. Nineteenth-century music offers far fewer clues: scraps of accounts of performances, number of reprints of a song, evidence of song survival in folk tradition. But this evidence, scanty though it be, indicates that the 1950s relationship between Crockett and song was no anomaly, and suggests that it was merely a resurgence of an earlier relationship: one forged in the 1800s and one that helped found the Crockett mystique that continues to this day.[22]

NOTES

1. Charles K. Wolfe, "Davy Crockett Songs: From Minstrels to Disney," in *Davy Crockett: The Man, the Legend, the Legacy 1786–1986*, ed. Michael A. Lofaro (Knoxville: University of Tennessee Press, 1986), 159–90.

2. Constance Rourke, *Davy Crockett* (New York: Harcourt, 1934), 258.

3. This copy is now available at the archives of the Center for Popular Music, at Middle Tennessee State University, to whom I am indebted for assistance.

4. Rourke, 258–59.

5. *The Free-And-Easy Song Book* (Philadelphia: James Kay, Jun. & Brother, 1839), 7–9.

6. Frederick M. Culp and Mrs. Robert E. Ross, *Gibson County Past and Present* (Trenton, Tenn.: Gibson County Historical Society, 1961).

7. *Free-And-Easy Song Book*, 242–43.

8. *Free-And-Easy Song Book*, 51–54.

9. *Free-And-Easy Song Book*, 140–41.

10. The entire text of this version of "Pompey Smash" — of considerable length — is reprinted in Wolfe, "Minstrels to Disney," 163–66.

11. See, for instance, articles by John Seelye and Michael A. Lofaro ("Hidden Hero") in *Davy Crockett: The Man, the Legend, the Legacy 1786–1986*, cited above.

12. Ibid.

13. William F. Cody, *Story of the Wild West and Camp-Fire Chats, by Buffalo Bill (Hon. W.F. Cody): A Full and Complete History of the Renowned Pioneer Quartette, Boone, Crockett, Carson and Buffalo Bill* (Philadelphia: Historical Publishing Company), 1888.

14. Walter Blair, *Davy Crockett — Frontier Hero* (New York: Coward-McCann, 1955), 124.

15. *Billboard*, May 28, 1955.

16. Charles K. Wolfe, "Davy Crockett's Dance and Old Hickory's Fandango," *The Devil's Box* 16 (September 1982): 34–42.

17. See Wolfe, *Devil's Box*, and *Gibson County*.

18. Alan Jabbour, personal correspondence, October and December 1986.

19. Hank Harrison (San Antonio Museum Association), personal correspondence, October 1986.

20. Richard Boyd Hauck, *Davy Crockett: A Handbook* (1982; reprint Lincoln: University of Nebraska Press, 1986), 146–50.

21. See, for example, his Introduction to the paperback edition of James A. Shackford, *David Crockett. The Man and the Legend* (1956; reprint Chapel Hill: University of North Carolina Press, 1986), xi–xii.

22. I am also indebted to Michael A. Lofaro and Joe Cummings for pointing out to me certain sources and references, and to Paul Wells for certain fiddle tune references.

Davy Crockett and the Tradition of the Westerner in American Cinema

William Eric Jamborsky

The American westerner of film and drama is the decendant of some of the earliest characters to appear in American theatre. These characters reflect the differences between the Old World class distinctions and the American revolt against those class distinctions. At the same time, differences between the American easterner, the aristocracy of the early nineteenth century, and the Scotch-Irish settlers of the Trans-Appalachian regions become apparent. The development of Davy Crockett as a western hero in the twentieth century is best understood by examining his origins, his representative American virtues, and how they have been incorporated into film.

David Crockett was of the stock of the borderers of the British Isles, a tough, stubborn people who were conditioned to border wars against the English. In the sixteenth century, they took up the teachings of John Knox, which cemented their deep-seated distrust of both the aristocracy and the poor; in their eyes poverty was a sin. Wealth was measured in land, and land was available in the New World; by 1730 these former borderers arrived in North America by the thousands. As firm believers of the Calvinist work ethic, they believed they had not stations in life, but functions. A man could not be judged by who he was but by what he did. These immigrants shunned the eastern seaboard and its new aristocracy, instead seeking the wilderness inland. Their independence, self-reliance, and dislike of the class system soon became a feature of the American character that was in turn the hallmark of the westerner of drama and film.[1]

Crockett's forebears set the pattern that he would follow as well. His grandfather, David, was among the early settlers who crossed the Appalachians before the American Revolution in defiance of British policy prohibiting settlement west of the Appalachians. After the Revolution began, David and his son William signed the Watauga petition for annexation of the Wautauga region to North Carolina. In 1777 David and his wife

were among a dozen settlers who were killed by a band of Creek and Chero-
kee Indians.[2]

David Crockett was born August 17, 1786, in a land alien to the original
thirteen colonies. By the time he rode into San Antonio, Texas, on February 8, 1836, he was a national figure. He had served as a volunteer in the
Creek war, entered local politics, and risen to state office. By 1827 he was
elected to Congress as a supporter of Andrew Jackson, but soon was driven
to join the opposition due to Jackson's policies regarding Indian removal
and the Tennessee Vacant Land Bill. In doing so, he lost the election of
1835 and effectively ended his political career in Tennessee.[3]

Crockett took his defeat hard and, as he and his ancestors had often done
before in bad times, moved further west. He decided to explore Texas, seeking land and perhaps a new political career. Once in Texas he was drawn
to the fight for independence from Mexico. Crockett traveled on to San Antonio and joined the garrison at the mission fortress called the Alamo. Why
he went there is still unclear. James Shackford claims he was driven by his
opposition to Sam Houston, Andrew Jackson's man in Texas, to support
officers also opposed to Houston. It is also possible he may have been
drawn by the thought of one last adventure or by the presence of another
contemporary legend, Jim Bowie. Whatever attracted Crockett to San Antonio, he stayed to fight with the rest of the garrison.[4]

Crockett's death created a storm of outrage across the United States. The
Natchez *Courier* stated, "Poor Davey Crockett. The quaint, the laughter–
moving, but the fearless upright Crockett, to be butchered by such a wretch
as Santa Anna—it is not to be borne!"[5] Crockett soon became a firm feature
of American history and legend.

Native American theatre began its rise during Crockett's lifetime and
reflected many of the elements of Republicanism. John Augustus Stone
wrote *Metamora* for Edwin Forrest; its theme was that of the noble savage,
which would become popular in silent films in the next century. Many people recognized the importance of American theatre. Andrew Jackson declared, "It is time that the principal events in the history of our country
were dramatized, and exhibited at the theatres on such days as are set apart
as national festivals."[6] One wonders how Jackson's enthusiasm might have
been tempered had he known that one of the popular characters in American theatre would be modeled on one of his bitterest enemies.

Popular figures in American theatre were quite often designed to promote
the virtues of American Republicanism over European aristocracy and

featured characters like Jonathan Ploughboy, Jedediah Homebred, Industrious Doolittle, and Deuteronomy Dutiful. In this spirit actor James H. Hackett commissioned a play that was to feature an American backwoodsman who, though uneducated, would be more than a match for the aristocrats. The 1831 play, *The Lion of the West*, was scripted by James Kirke Paulding, and its hero, Nimrod Wildfire, was based loosely on the image presented by Congressman David Crockett as a westerner.[7]

Crockett was the title character of *Davy Crockett, Or Be Sure You're Right, Then Go Ahead*, a romantic melodrama written by Frank Hitchcock Murdock as a vehicle for the actor Frank Mayo. The play was revised heavily by Mayo and was premiered in Rochester, New York, on September 23, 1872. It marked a firm step forward in the development of Crockett as a western hero, through the introduction of Arthurian material into the growing body of western mythology. *Davy Crockett* owed much to Scott and Tennyson in its heroic and romantic elements.[8]

Murdock's plot is simple. Davy loves Eleanor, but considers her beyond his station. However, when they are trapped in the mountain cabin by wolves, their true feelings are revealed when she reads Scott's "Lochinvar" to Davy, a dramatic device to show that he is no less a man than his high-born rival. In the end of the play, Davy, on horseback like one of Sir Walter Scott's Knights, rescues Eleanor and exposes his rival as a villain. The plot is full of maudlin romantics, with a dash of sometimes subtle humor, and would inspire a number of films.[9]

Following the birth of motion pictures, it was only natural that Crockett would soon become the subject of films. Four motion pictures, *Davy Crockett—in Hearts United* (1909)[10], *Davy Crockett* (1910), *Davy Crockett Up To Date* (1915), a parody, and *Davy Crockett* (1916), were based on the Murdock-Mayo play. *Davy Crockett* (1916), was written by Frank Mayo, grandson of the original star, and directed by William Desmond Taylor. In following the romantic plotline, none of these films dealt with Crockett as an actual person or added to the image of Crockett as a western hero.

David Crockett's first screen appearance as a historic figure was in 1911 in the Gaston Méliès film *The Immortal Alamo*. He was played by Francis Ford, whose younger brother John Ford was soon to become a famous director. *The Immortal Alamo*, although an ambitious film for Méliès, ran only one reel in length.[11] Crockett next appeared in 1915 in the David Wark Griffith production *Martyrs of the Alamo*, directed by W. Christy Cabanne. Played by A. D. Sears, Crockett was a secondary character, the lead being a fictional scout Silent Smith (based loosely on the actual Deaf Smith) played by Sam DeGrasse. This Triangle release ran five reels and was well received on its initial release. A review in *Variety* stated, "Some of its battle scenes excel those in Griffith's immortal 'The Birth of A Nation.'"[12]

Martyrs of the Alamo has Crockett already in San Antonio in late 1835, participating in the ouster of the Mexican garrison commanded by General Cos, Santa Anna's brother-in-law. Crockett is presented in the image familiar to most filmgoers today. He wears a leather hunting jacket and a coonskin cap. His wit is evident; when Bowie teases him with his famous knife, Crockett says, "You might tickle a fellow's ribs a long time with this instrument and never make him laugh." His native intelligence is also demonstrated when he ends the feud between Bowie and Travis.

When the siege begins, Crockett gives evidence of his marksmanship. A title card reads, "Crockett because of his sure aim was placed in command of the wall." When it is certain that no help will come for the garrison, Travis draws the line in the dirt and says, "Those who wish to die like heroes and patriots cross the line to me." Crockett grins and crosses the line. On the morning of March 6, the Mexicans attack and breach the wall; they also discover a secret tunnel leading into the chapel. Attacked from two sides, the garrison quickly falls. Crockett is seen near the door to the chapel, clubbing Mexicans with his gun until he is overwhelmed. A scene after the battle shows him where he fell, surrounded by dead Mexicans.

What becomes evident in this film is the power that Crockett holds over the audience. As written, his part is secondary to Silent Smith and Jim Bowie, yet he is the most memorable character in the film. In a cast of larger-than-life characters, Crockett stands above the rest. It is very likely that it was the magnetism of Crockett's character that influenced William Desmond Taylor in his decision to film a version of the melodrama *Davy Crockett* a year later.

David Crockett's first starring role was in *Davy Crockett at the Fall of the Alamo* (Sunset Productions, 1926).[13] The script by Ben Ali Newman began with Crockett's defeat for reelection to Congress in 1835 and ended with his death at the Alamo. This was a fairly ambitious effort for Sunset, a company that specialized in low-budget historical films. The director was Robert North Bradbury, who would later direct John Wayne in a number of his early films.[14] Wilson Silsby and Paul Cosgrove designed a large set based loosely on the Alamo as presented in the painting by Theodore Gentilz. To star as Crockett the producers chose Cullen Landis.

When first seen, Crockett appears in a beaver high hat and frock coat, the clothes of a gentleman of the period. He has a stocky build and graying hair, very much in the image of the real Crockett.[15] Informed of his defeat for reelection, he goes slowly into his cabin, obviously disappointed. Inside he looks around him and spots his hunting coat and coonskin cap hanging on a peg. Slowly he removes his top hat and frock coat and takes up his hunting clothes. The disappointment is now gone, for he has a new goal; he resolves to go to Texas and fight for independence. The title card reads, "Texas must be freed from Mexican rule." Crockett and a few friends, among them "the Bee-Hunter" and Lige Beardsley, "Champion Spitter of the South," prepare to leave for Texas.

There is little subtlety in the film. Santa Anna was played by Fletcher Norton as an effete, sneering villian; the Texans are all brave and noble.[16] When a messenger (Bob Bradbury, Jr.) brings word that no reinforcements will come and Travis draws the famous line in the dirt asking for volunteers to stay, not a man refuses. On March 6, the Mexicans storm the fort, and the surviving Texans are driven into the ruins of the chapel. "Boys, only 60 of us left," says Crockett. "Show them we're Americans." The fight degenerates into hand-to-hand grappling and fisticuffs in the confines of the chapel. The Bee-Hunter falls and Crockett mouths (without benefit of a title card), "Those Bastards!" Taking up a sword, he attacks a Mexican soldier, and soon both antagonists have dropped their weapons to fight bare-handed. This is no choreographed Hollywood set-to, but a rough and tumble scrap. Soon Crockett has downed his opponent and then proceeds to kick him several times; it is brutal, with no holds barred. Crockett then clubs another Mexican with his gun, hitting him until the gun shatters. Four Mexicans finally drag Davy down as six others stab him with bayonets. It takes ten men to kill Crockett. He dies with a smile of defiance on his lips.

Davy Crockett at the Fall of the Alamo blends the Crocketts of history and legend for the first time in films. The historic Crockett is introduced through a framing sequence when a small boy asks his grandfather to tell him the story of Davy Crockett. The old man holds a copy of William F. Cody's *Story of the Wild West and Camp-Fire Chats* and begins to read to the boy. The film features several rustic characters of the types popular in the early days of Hollywood and introduces the Bee-Hunter from Richard Penn Smith's spurious book about Crockett in Texas.[17] The romantic subplot concerning Bee-Hunter and Kate Kennedy is right out of Cody's book,

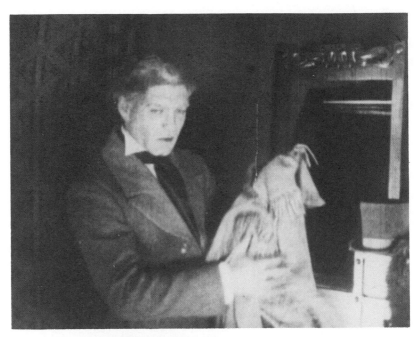

Scenes from *Davy Crockett at the Fall of the Alamo*. (Opposite page, top): Cullen Landis as Crockett decides to go to Texas. "Texas must be free from Mexican rule!" (Opposite page, bottom): From left to right are Frank Rice as Lige Beardsley, Bob Bradbury, Jr. as "Pinky" Smith, and Landis as they prepare to face the next onslaught of the enemy. (Above): It takes ten men to kill Crockett. Author's collection.

which has obviously drawn heavily from Crockett's autobiography and Smith's *Col. Crockett's Exploits and Adventures in Texas*. (An illustration in Cody's book also appears to have influenced the set designers for *Martyrs of the Alamo*.) Also present are many of the conventions of the B western, such as the comic sidekick, but that is to be expected, as the film was directed by one of the inventors of the genre.[18]

Cullen Landis delivers a firm portrayal of Crockett, avoiding many of the overplayed mannerisms common in silent films. There is a naturalness to his playing and to that of Frank Rice as Lige, his tobacco-chewing crony. Landis is a sincere but unfortunately humorless Crockett and thus his characterization omits one of Crockett's key trademarks. This limitation is apparently due, however, to the script and the lack of time to develop subtle humor in a silent film. What comedy there is is of a broad nature and is left to others, primarily Frank Rice.[19]

Davy Crockett at the Fall of the Alamo is a pioneering work in that it establishes Crockett as a film hero in a historical context and not just as the stock lead in a melodrama. It is important in that it does not treat Crockett as a backwoods rube trying to impress a citified girl, as in the Murdock-Mayo play; it also avoids the old plot of the country bumpkin who gets the best of the city slicker. This Crockett is mature and is a genuine hero in the mold established by William S. Hart.[20] It also adds another dimension to the popular image of Crockett, that of Crockett the politician. Despite the film's limitations, it plays an important part of the evolution of the Crockett legend.

The direct descendant of *Davy Crockett at the Fall of the Alamo*, and the next major film featuring Crockett, was the 1937 production *Heroes of the Alamo*. It was Davy's first appearance in a sound film. *Heroes of the Alamo* was a low-budget film produced by Anthony J. Xydias, whose Sunset Productions had made *Davy Crockett at the Fall of the Alamo* eleven years earlier. In fact, as a cost-cutting measure, director Harry Fraser used footage from the 1926 film for most of the battle sequences.

David Crockett is played by Lane Chandler, a popular actor and one-time co-star to Clara Bow and Greta Garbo, and rival of Gary Cooper. In *Heroes of the Alamo* his talent is quite evident, and his Crockett easily becomes the focus of attention, despite a particularly clumsy script. When he arrives at the Alamo, he says he is looking for a fight: "Them numbskull voters in Tennessee wouldn't send me back to Congress for another term. I figured your little war here was the next best thing to Congress." As he enters the fortress, a fiddle case is perched prominently on his pack horse, an image that underscores Davy's fondness for music, which would later be used in Disney's *Davy Crockett* (1955) and the television film *The Alamo: 13 Days to Glory* (1987). Again Crockett becomes a focal point for the action. When the Mexicans arrive, it is Crockett who draws first blood by picking off an enemy soldier at a distance to demonstrate his marksmanship, an act that enrages Santa Anna, who orders an immediate attack. Chandler's Davy is confident but easygoing, and his performance is similar to Fess Parker's almost twenty years later. The battle itself is anticlimactic. The new footage is poorly staged and there is no excitement. After the fighting ends, Santa Anna enters the fort and notices that one defender is still alive. A badly wounded Crockett crawls to a ladder and attempts to stand up. The dictator orders him killed, and a Mexican soldier clubs Crockett. Before he dies, Crockett looks at Santa Anna and says, "And be danged to ya!"[21] *Heroes of the Alamo* was not well received, and one reviewer wrote, "It is one of the most amateurish production efforts of a decade."[22]

The next full treatment of Crockett in a film did not come until 1955 in *Davy Crockett, King of the Wild Frontier,* but is became the protrayal of Davy Crockett that remained foremost in the American mind.[23] In 1954 Walt Disney entered television with a weekly hour-long show called *Disneyland,* designed to promote his new amusement park. The episodes would be based on themes coinciding with the different sections in the park such as Fantasyland, Tomorrowland, Adventureland, and Frontierland. It was decided to base some episodes on the lives of famous Americans, and Davy Crockett was the first of those selected.[24]

The Disney staff decided to film three installments about Crockett, each based on a particular phase of his life. The first, "Davy Crockett, Indian Fighter," concerned his early career as a militia man in the Creek War, 1813–1814. The second, "Davy Crockett Goes To Congress," dealt with his political career, and the final installment, "Davy Crockett at the Alamo," was about his trip to Texas and his death in the Texas Revolution. One installment was aired each month, on December 15, 1954, and January 16, and February 23, 1955. Davy Crockett unexpectedly became an overnight sensation. Walt Disney later said, "We had no idea what was going to happen to 'Crockett.' Why, by the time the first show finally got on the air, we were already shooting the third one and calmly killing Davy off at the Alamo. It became one of the biggest overnight hits in TV history, and there we were with just three films and a dead hero."[25]

The script, by Tom Blackburn, appears to be based primarily on Constance M. Rourke's 1934 book *Davy Crockett,* and also owes a debt to Cody's book.[26] While exaggerating Crockett's exploits as an Indian fighter and Congressman, the script stays a bit closer to the truth than many films of this type. Crockett is an admirable man, but can be violent when he has to be. The Indian battles are fierce and in later years were trimmed by the censors for network broadcast.

For the most part Disney played reasonably straight with history. Elements of the legendary and the real Crockett were blended in the story, along with some of the conventions of the western film. Crockett was given a comic sidekick, but was still allowed humor when the story called for it. The only fictional character retained from Smith's book was the gambler called

Thimblerig. Crockett was presented as an intelligent man capable of wining a hard-fought election and yet politically naive; he allowed himself to be used by President Jackson and his crony Tobias Norton. It was a mature presentation and one not expected by many critics of Disney.

As a result of the Crockett series, Fess Parker quickly became a star, and Buddy Ebsen's career was revived. The popularity of the Crockett programs was so great that Disney had the three episodes edited into a ninety-minute feature and released to theaters as *Davy Crockett, King of the Wild Frontier.*

In the second set of shows, "Davy Crockett And The Keelboat Race" and "Davy Crockett And The River Pirates," released to theaters as *Davy Crockett and the River Pirates* (1956), Disney represents the Crockett of legend. Under the titles are pictured Davy Crockett almanacs, and the song warns the viewer that this is to be a tall tale. Upon encountering Crockett, keelboat captain Mike Fink looks him up and down and says, "You're about a foot shorter than you ought to be." Davy's pal Georgie replies, "He's still growing." We see another side of Crockett in this film. Challenged to a keelboat race by Mike Fink, the self-styled "King of the River," Davy finds himself against a formidable opponent, who will use any means to win. When his boat is sabotaged by Fink, Crockett decides to retaliate. Needing time for the boat to be repaired, Crockett confronts Fink in a tavern and challenges the riverman to a shooting contest. He fakes a shooting trick, pretending to catch a ricocheting bullet in his teeth. Then, needing time to get back to the boat, he cleverly starts a barroom brawl in order to create a diversion. This trickster is the Davy Crockett of legend brought to life. Adding to the feel of the film is the inclusion of the villains Wiley and Micajah Harpe, Sam Mason, and Colonel Plugg, notorious figures of American history and folklore.[27]

Another 1955 film in which Crockett has a role is Republic's *Last Command.* Jim Bowie is the central character and is convincingly played by Sterling Hayden. The film is almost stolen, though, by Arthur Hunnicutt as Davy Crockett. He enters wearing the traditional buckskins and coonskin cap, but he is shorter than usually portrayed, and he is bearded. His fame rests as easily on his shoulders as his rifle, and he is obviously comfortable with his notoriety. When asked to give a speech, he proclaims with mock humility, "I have been persuaded."

He delivers a variation of the "Hell or Texas" speech while getting in a dig at Andrew Jackson: "My friends and constituents. I left Washington and the United States Congress some time ago at the request of a gentleman who had the gall to call himself Andrew Jackson. But his real name, as most self-respectin' Indians know, is the fellow who got the whole thing bollixed up. Anyway, in Washington they told me to either go to Hell or to Texas, so naturally, not wantin' to be took for a coward, I chose Texas. Lookin' over your territory as I come, I want to tell you I think you found somethin'. I don't know what it is, but it sure is full of space. Only thing, a few more people is needed. Men like you could solve that problem in no time at all. But I hear there's another man here who's agin' other people bein' here, a certain general called Santa Anna. Seems like he wants to make it a game preserve for coyotes. And from what I heerd, we might have a run-in, iffin he don't scare me off." This is a Crockett who knows how to use humor, and Hunnicutt's portrayel is superb; it is probably the best rendition of Davy Crockett in films. It is certainly the most believable.[28]

Before Crockett arrives, it is rumored that he is at the head of a thousand men, but in reality he has only twenty-nine. Once the siege begins, Crockett is always where he is needed most. On the last day, he gives the ill Bowie two pistols, places his cot where it faces the door, and reassures him saying, "They'll eat snakes before they get in here, Jim." In the final battle, Crockett takes a torch and plunges it into a keg of powder, taking many of the enemy with him. It is a scene that would reappear in five years; in fact there are several interesting parallels betwen *Last Command* and *The Alamo*. Certain sequences, not in history or legend, are in both films, but it is not clear whether James Edward Grant, writer of *The Alamo*, copied *Last Command* or whether Sy Bartlett, who scripted *Last Command*, had access to the story treatment John Wayne developed while at Republic Pictures.

The next major Crockett film was John Wayne's *The Alamo*, released in 1960. This was a film he had wanted to make for ten years; in fact, he had first proposed it while he was still at Republic, but studio boss Herbert J. Yates backed out, fearing it would be too expensive. In 1955 he turned down the opportunity to play Bowie in *Last Command*, having left Republic in 1952. Unable to sell his project to any of the studios, he decided to make the film himself.

John Wayne as David Crockett is larger than life. He demonstrates surprising depth of character as an intelligent man cloaking himself, in the words of Travis, as a "bumpkin." Unfortunately the film is sabotaged by

From left to right are John Russell as Lieutenant Dickenson, Ernest Borgnine as Mike Radd, Sterling Hayden as James Bowie, Roy Roberts as Doc Summerfield, Richard Carlson as Colonel Travis, and Arthur Hunnicutt as Crockett in *The Last Command* (Republic Pictures, 1956). Author's collection.

James Edward Grant's script, which is long on talk and short on dramatic impact. Neither is Wayne helped by Richard Widmark as a hysterical Bowie nor Laurence Harvey as a boorish Travis.[29]

The Alamo was filmed on a grand scale and, partly for this reason, much of the human element was lost. Only in some of the supporting players, particularly Chill Wills as Beekeeper, does this film come alive. Still, it is a noble failure. Wayne had been strongly attracted to the idea behind the battle at the Alamo and wanted to honor those who had fought to gain Texas's freedom from Mexico. He had wanted to make this film since the 1940s and risked his personal fortune in order to see his dream finally realized. It was to be more a monument to the struggle for freedom than a movie; this reverent attitude is very likely what led to its failure.

The most recent treatment of Crockett was in the 1987 NBC television film *The Alamo: 13 Days to Glory.* Loosely based on Lon Tinkle's book, the film is disappointing due to an uneven script by Clyde Ware and lackluster direction by Burt Kennedy. Fortunately, Davy Crockett is played convincingly by Brian Keith, as a Crockett who can inspire legends and manipulate them. This Crockett is a drinker, a talker, and a fighter.

Even though Keith's Crockett commands self-respect, he does not take himself too seriously: "Every now and then, when I'm right in the middle of speechifyin', I can hear myself sayin' somethin' that makes a whole lot or sense." This Crockett also uses exaggeration easily. "In those days Old Hickory was just a tree instead of a switch," he says in reference to Jackson's trying to whip Congress into line. He can inspire. After watching Crockett in action, Travis says, "You know, I'm beginning to believe you really did wrestle that bear." Crockett grins and says, "Well, I didn't really wrestle him, I just tickled him and he fell off a cliff. Darndest bear I ever did see." Even in trying to debunk a myth, he only makes it grow. All in all, it is a reasonable portrait of the Davy Crockett one now expects, a mixture of history and legend.

The character of Davy Crockett in the movies is an American western hero in the mold of those personified in films by William S. Hart, Buck Jones, Randolph Scott, Joel McCrea, and John Wayne. Beginning with *Davy Crockett at the Fall of the Alamo,* and to a lesser degree with the Murdock-Mayo play, Crockett has been portrayed in the light of the westerner, the hero of the Great American Myth. Crockett displays the courage and determination to fight against any odds for a cause he believes is right. He is flawed but rises up to great heights. It is the myth-making process that transformed George Custer into the hero played by Errol Flynn, or Jesse James into the hero played by Tyrone Power. But in Davy Crockett there is a firmer basis for the popular image. Custer is now recognized as a glory-hungry egotist whose political ambitions led to the deaths of almost three hundred men under his command; and the image of Jesse James as a Robin Hood has long since been proved false. But the mythological Crockett lingers. The viewer can believe that Crockett actually tries to grin a bear into submission or, as in *Last Command* and *The Alamo*, that he will destroy the powder supply and himself in order to take as many of the enemy with him as he can. One can believe it may well take ten of the enemy to bring him down finally, as in *Davy Crockett at the Fall of the Alamo*. Crockett the cinematic hero has eclipsed Crockett the man.

In the confines of film it is not really important to separate the man from the myth, for despite what some would prefer, films are not history; they are drama, and drama requires a hero like Crockett. Through his decision to stay at the Alamo when he could have left, Crockett joined the pantheon of heroes like Roland, whose stand at Roncesvalles saved King Charlemagne. His decision to stand and fight also echoed the borderer ethos of his ancestors that was carried into the New World and became a part of the ethos of the westerner. The idea of fighting against all odds for what one believes is right is also reflected in Crockett's motto, "Be always sure you're right—THEN GO AHEAD."[30] This motto parallels that of the westerner, a man who is usually pictured as fighting alone against great odds, such as Gary Cooper in *High Noon*, or in a small band fighting an overwhelming number of enemies, as in *The Magnificent Seven*.

The end product of almost eighty years of motion pictures, Davy is in many ways the prototype for these modern film heroes. He has grown from a stock figure in melodrama to a hero of almost epic proportions. This transformation is made possible, in part, because the myth that had grown up around Crockett during his lifetime provided the seeds for the images of Crockett that exist today. Davy's death at the Alamo proved both the crowning achievement of his life and his legend and became the cornerstone of much of the ever-expanding myth of the American frontier.[31]

NOTES

1. Fehrenbach, T. R., *Lone Star, A History of Texas and the Texans* (New York: Collier Books, 1980), 85–89.

2. Robert M. McBride, "David Crockett and His Memorials in Tennessee," in *More Landmarks of Tennessee History* (Nashville: Tennessee Historical Society, 1969), 78.

3. Lon Tinkle, *13 Days to Glory* (New York: McGraw-Hill Book Company, Inc., 1958), 255. James Atkins Shackford, *David Crockett: The Man and the Legend* (1956; reprint, Chapel Hill: The University of North Carolina Press, 1986), 8, 20, 84. Fehrenbach, 209–10.

4. Shackford, 219–21; Richard Boyd Hauck, *Davy Crockett: A Handbook* (1982; reprint, Lincoln: University of Nebraska Press, 1986), 49–50. Shackford mistakenly places Colonel Travis in the anti-Houston party, whereas Travis was loyal to both Houston and Governor Smith. See Fehrenbach, 205–15, for one of the better recent accounts.

5. Walter Lord, *A Time To Stand* (New York: Harper & Brothers, 1961), 170.

6. Howard Taubman, *The Making of the American Theatre* (New York: Coward McCann, Inc., 1965), 71–72.

7. Taubman, 72–73; Richard Boyd Hauck, "Davy Crockett In The Theater," in *Davy Crockett, The Man, The Legend, The Legacy, 1786–1986*, ed. Michael A. Lofaro (Knoxville: The University of Tennessee Press, 1985), 104–5.

8. Taubman, 111; Kathryn C. Esselman, "From Camelot to Monument Valley: Dramatic Origins of the Western Film", in *Focus on the Western*, ed. Jack Nachbar (Englewood Cliffs, N.J.: Prentice-Hall, Inc., 1974), 13–14; Hauck, "Davy Crockett In The Theater," 111–12.

9. Esselman, 15; Hauck, "Davy Crockett in the Theater," 113–15.

10. *Davy Crockett—in Hearts United* was produced by Adam Kessel and Charles Bauman for their independent film exchange. The producers borrowed a wolfskin rug from a taxidermist for the scene where Davy and Eleanor are trapped in the cabin by wolves. Kessel in the role of Crockett shot the wolfskin rug with tremendous effect at the climax. The film, which marked the beginning of wild animals in screen drama, was a box-office success. Terry Ramsaye, *A Million And One Nights: A History of the Motion Picture Through 1925* (New York: Simon & Schuster, Inc., 1926), 491.

11. Silent films were usually projected at a speed of sixteen frames per second, and the films were mounted on reels that gave approximately ten minutes of running time, but this could vary, as projectors of this period were operated by hand.

12. Paul Andrew Hutton, "The Celluloid Alamo," *Arizona and the West* 28 (1986), 7–8; Hauck, "Davy Crockett In The Theater," 116; *Variety*, October 19, 1915. For a detailed description of the Murdock-Mayo play and the 1916 Davy Crockett see Hauck, "Davy Crockett In The Theater," 111–15, and Norman Bruce, "A Newly Discovered Silent Film," 125–36, both in Lofaro.

13. Thought by R. B. Hauck to be a lost film ("Davy Crockett In The Theater," 116), a print of *Davy Crockett at the Fall of the Alamo* is in this author's collection. Undoubtedly there are more in existence. The print is not intact, running a little less than forty minutes, where the original film was six reels. A romantic subplot involving the Bee-Hunter and Kate Kennedy appears to be too short and there are

some signs of nitrate decomposition later in the film, but only in the early scenes does the plot suffer from the loss.

14. Robert North Bradbury was noted as one of the directors who shaped the B western in its early years. He was also noted for launching the career of his son, Bob Bradbury, Jr. The younger Bradbury later changed his name to Bob Steele and remained a popular actor through the 1960s. As of this writing, Bob Steele, at age eighty, is the only member of the cast of *Davy Crockett at the Fall of the Alamo* still alive.

15. Cullen Landis (1896–1975) was thirty when this film was made. While gaining some popularity as a second-string leading man since 1917, his career seemed to end when sound films arrived. He is largely forgotten today.

16. Neither *Martyrs of the Alamo* nor *Davy Crockett at the Fall of the Alamo* is sympathetic toward Mexicans, perhaps because of the bitter feelings resulting from raids by Mexican bandits during the years before World War I. Adding to this bitterness was the unveiling of the San Diego Plan, which called for a Hispanic revolt against the Anglo-Texans, and the Zimmerman Telegram, in which the Germans attempted to create a war between the United States and Mexico. Fehrenbach, 690–91. Interestingly enough, starting with *Heroes of the Alamo*, Mexicans received better treatment in most Alamo films, with most of the onus being placed on Santa Anna and his generals.

17. Hauck, *Davy Crockett*, 51.

18. Frank Rice, who played Lige Beardsley, was a familiar face in B westerns for years to come. Also see note 14.

19. The use of a comic sidekick is a common convention of westerns and other adventure films and is noticeable in two later films in which Crockett is the central character. In Disney's *Davy Crockett* and John Wayne's *The Alamo* the broader humor is handled by sidekicks Georgie Russell and Beekeeper. In the B westerns the comic sidekicks became so popular that they sometimes eclipsed the popularity of the nominal star.

20. William Surrey Hart was a Shakespearian actor long popular on stage. He began his film career in 1914 and soon became a star of westerns. His love and respect for the west and westerners led him to demand realism in his pictures. Hart's films were the antithesis of the flashy, juvenile adventures of Tom Mix and were, in the words of film historian William K. Everson, "raw, unglamorous, and gutsy, the costumes and livery trappings accurate." William K. Everson, *A Pictorial History of the Western Film* (New York: The Citadel Press) 1969, 37–40.

21. Crockett's last words are hard to hear due to a poor soundtrack, but after listening closely several times this is what they appear to be. It is typical of the quality of writing on this film.

22. *Variety,* April 6, 1938.

23. Crockett was used as a stock historic character in a number of films during the intervening two decades. *Man of Conquest* (Republic, 1938) featured Robert Barrat as Crockett. In *Man from the Alamo* (Universal, 1953), Trevor Bardette was presented as Travis's second-in-command but without any attempt at an accurate

portrayal. Oddly enough, the chief villains in this film were white renegades led by Victor Jory. Post-Disney appearances include *The First Texan* (Allied Artists, 1956) with James Griffith, normally a western villain, outstanding as Crockett in a short scene where he delivers a speech. In the 1960s science-fiction series "Time Tunnel" (ABC) Crockett is featured in an episode about the Alamo. In the 1971 revival of "You Are There" as a CBS Television Saturday morning program, Fred Gwynne portrayed Crockett in a dramatization of the fall of the Alamo. Crockett has a small part in the "Alamo Jobe" episode of "Amazing Stories" (NBC, 1986). Finally, in "Houston: The Legend of Texas" (CBS, December 1986), Crockett is seen only after the fall of the Alamo, lying dead in the courtyard.

24. Leonard Maltin, *The Disney Films* (New York: Bonanza Books, 1973), 20–21, 122.

25. Hutton, 14–15; Maltin, 122.

26. Constance M. Rourke, *Davy Crockett* (New York: Harcourt, Brace, and Co., 1934).

27. For another look at the Disney Crockett, see Margaret J. King, "The Recycled Hero, Walt Disney's Davy Crockett" in Lofaro, 137–58, and in the same book, Hauck's "Making It All Up," 116–18.

28. Sy Bartlett obviously based Hunnicutt's speech on one of the many versions of Crockett's "Hell or Texas" speech. One version concluded with, "I have a new row to hoe, a long and rough one, but come what will I'll go ahead. I am done with politics and you may all go to hell, and I'll go to Texas." Buffalo Bill (William F. Cody), *Story of the Wild West and Camp-Fire Chats* (Rpt.; Freeport: Books For Libraries Press, 1970), 247–48. Cody is considered an unreliable source by many but has obviously inspired a number of filmmakers. A possible genesis of this speech is in a letter reconstructed by Shackford, " . . . if I don't beat my competitor I will [go to texes]" [sic]. Later, Shackford quotes a speech given by Crockett in Memphis which concludes, "Since you have chosen to elect a man with a timber toe to succeed me, you may all go to hell and I will go to Texas." Shackford, 204, 212.

29. For an opposing viewpoint see Hauck, "Making It All Up," 118–20.

30. David Crockett, *A Narrative of the Life of David Crockett of the State of Tennessee*, ed. James A. Shackford and Staney J. Folmsbee (Knoxville: University of Tennessee Press, 1973), 1.

31. The legend continues. On Sunday, November 20, 1988, as this book was going to press, *The Magical World of Disney* presented "Davy Crockett: Rainbow in the Thunder," the first episode of a new Crockett series. Johnny Cash, an excellent choice, starred as the elder Crockett reminiscing with President Jackson just before starting for Texas. Tim Dunigan was the young Crockett and Gary Grubbs co-starred as Georgie Russel. While handsomely produced, the script strayed much further from the facts than did the first Disney series.

Riproarious Shemales

LEGENDARY WOMEN IN THE TALL TALE WORLD

OF THE DAVY CROCKETT ALMANACS

Michael A. Lofaro

> *Orlando had become a woman—there is no denying it. But in every other respect, Orlando remained precisely as he had been. The change of sex, though it altered their future, did nothing whatever to alter their identity. Their faces remained, as their portraits prove, practically the same.*
>
> *—Virginia Woolf,* Orlando[1]

If at first it seems a little incongruous to use an extract from Virginia Woolf's satiric novel to introduce a study of nineteenth-century tall tales, consider how equally incongruous it is to find that the archetypically masculine world of Davy Crockett is peopled with legendary women whose adventures and abilities are sometimes indistinguishable from those of their male counterparts. The novel and the tales do serve, however, to illuminate some broad points of common thematic concern. Both *Orlando* and the Crockett tall tales are works of fantasy and humor, and both Woolf and the anonymous authors of the tales comment, though with varying degrees of directness and with considerably different intent, upon traditional sexual stereotypes and roles.

Although there is no direct parallel between the story of Orlando—a young man of Elizabethan times who becomes a woman near the end of the seventeenth century and who is still only a thirty-six-year-old woman at the end of the book in 1928, the year of its publication—and the tall tales of legendary women, there is an uncanny similarity between the creation of these female characters. Replace "Orlando" with "Crockett" in the quoted passage and all the statements remain true. The physical change of sex does not alter the former male identity; the past personality remains constant as do the traditional male patterns of behavior. The "masculine" actions of Woolf's female Orlando, however, are heavily constrained by the mores of a civilization that expects and demands dependence; by comparison, the women of the Crockett almanacs are often as free as the wilderness that they inhabit. Unlike Orlando, they have no dual consciousness and instead are versions of Crockett that happen to be female. The issue of gender is seldom a major limitation for backwoods women like Davy's wife, Sally Ann Thunder Ann Whirlwind Crockett, or for his female friends and acquaintances such as Sal Fink, the Mississippi Screamer, Florinda Fury, or Zipporina, the hellion of the forest. Gender is simply a fact that sometimes places these women in different situations and somewhat different roles.

These slightly qualified descriptions are meant to indicate that although these tall-tale heroines often act as the equal of their men, they are more than heroes simply put into dresses. Women in the almanacs do not operate as agents who are completely independent of the cultural standards of the authors who pen the stories. Their fictional world still reflects the male-dominated society of antebellum America and the values that the authors accept or reject, applaud or satirize, all filtered through the exaggerated humor that is the hallmark of the tall tale. These female characters are primarily intended to entertain, but, in the way that fiction reveals truth, they also serve as barometers of the self-conceptions, ideals, prejudices, and taboos of the society that took their adventures, as well as those of Davy Crockett, to heart.

The popularity of the Crockett almanacs is uncontested. Their publication for the years 1835 to 1856 forms one of the longest continuous runs of early American comic almanacs.[2] When the death of the historical David Crockett at the Battle of the Alamo on March 6, 1836, invests the already mushrooming legend of the fictional Davy Crockett with even more vigor, the results are clearly epic. In the 1837 issue, for example, Davy expands the earlier newspaper stories of how he saved the United States from destruction by wringing the tail off Halley's comet by explaining what happened to him after the mighty deed:

> I was appointed by the President to stand on the Alleghany Mountains and wring the Comet's tail off. I did so, but got my hands most shockingly burnt, and the hair singed off my head, so that I was as bald as a trencher. I div right into the Waybosh river, and thus saved my best stone blue coat and grass green small clothes. With the help of Bear's grease, I have brought out a new crop, but the hair grows in bights and tufts, like hussuck grass in a meadow, and it keeps in such a snarl, that all the teeth will instantly snap out of an ivory comb when brought within ten feet of it.[3]

But by the end of his almanac career, Davy's creators have forced him into a series of roles, many of which provide a less flattering picture of America's history. The comic superman, who is still an attractive figure today, becomes an ardent warrior in the cause of territorial expansionism and a very dark comedic hero. He emerges as a sometimes cowardly, but more often harsh, crude, sexual, and racist protagonist, who pursues his adventures no matter what the cost to those around him who are nonwhite or too civilized. This side of the fictional Crockett, as well as that of the comic superhero, reflects what nineteenth-century writers, publishers, and readers regarded as funny and presents the modern audience with a view that simultaneously dismays and intrigues by offering a unique window on, or more accurately, a funhouse-like mirror of, a past world.

While the issues of states' rights and slavery are correctly cited as chief concerns of American society during the times of the Crockett almanacs, they receive little direct comment in those works. They are seemingly too volatile to include in publications designed to capture the widest possible readership.[4] Their political focus instead centers around the concept of Manifest Destiny, an idea to which most red-blooded Americans could eagerly subscribe. The social focus of the almanacs underwrites this belief by keying in on safe satiric targets, groups that are essentially powerless in nineteenth-century white America. Blacks, Indians, and Mexicans are caricatured as subhuman, ignorant wretches whose extermination could only benefit frontier society. But perhaps the most interesting social issue that the almanacs mirror involves the changing status of women. As one of the traditional subjects of satire, the writers of the tales also apparently view women as safe game and they further deflect criticism by emphasizing the "otherness" of these women as creatures, as backwoods screamers whose association with the wilderness has stripped them of nearly all of their femininity. Yet, on an unintentional or perhaps unconscious level, the writers do more than create extreme parodies of frontier life in the tall tales. On the one hand, they give the reader a clear subtext of the secondary status of women by praising traditional roles and, on the other, break women loose from those confining patterns to act out male adventures and fantasies with a freedom that only life in a wilderness state can allow.

No scholar has yet attempted to unravel the various levels of meaning in the fifty-eight stories that feature or include women in a significant way.[5] Indeed, except for the edited versions of twenty of the tales in Richard M. Dorson's *Davy Crockett: American Comic Legend* (1939) and a topical survey of extracts of various sizes in Mody C. Boatright's chapter on "Backwoods Belles" (1943), these sometimes delightful and sometimes outrageous portrayals of women have seldom been available to modern readers and have never received more than cursory critical comment.[6]

A substantial part of the problem lies in the fact that these depictions, like those of the "half-horse, half-alligator" male characters, are spun from the imagination of eastern writers who very likely never crossed the Appalachians and who, given the hiring practices of the printing trade, were also likely male. There is no attempt on their part to adopt a woman's point of view; they see a woman's world as only a man would see it, from the outside, from observation rather than shared experience. Starting in the first almanac (1835), these authors construct a supporting female mythology of the West that consciously flies in the face of the sentimental, genteel tradition of the nineteenth-century heroine. Although they proceed in fits and starts, with no apparent agenda, in their hands women nonetheless dive off the pedestal of romance and high culture into the mythic Mississippi to become one with the low comedy of the tall-tale frontier and often as not emerge as the near equal of their ranting, savage, brawling and bragging backwoods beaus.

As the term "shemale" makes abundantly clear, the Crockett almanacs offer an inversion of the then current ideal of femininity. The sentimental stereotype, particularly in eighteenth- and nineteenth-century literature, defines women as essentially emotional; they respond spontaneously to suffering, cry easily, depend upon men to solve their problems, are small of stature, weak, frail, sickly, and often the victims of unnamed fatal diseases.[7] Superior to men in sensitivity and matters of the heart, intellectually they are his inferior. In 1847, Dr. Charles Meigs describes this "natural" balance by explaining that a woman "has a head almost too small for intellect but just big enough for love."[8] They could feel love, but never passion. They could rule the home at least indirectly, but never involve themselves in the public sphere. And most conspicuously, although an emotional, and hence perhaps irrational creature, a woman is ironically never permitted to demonstrate any anger. Much the same view dominates women's popular literature in America from 1820 to 1860 and reinforces the then current cultural ideal of the "true" woman as one who is submissive, pure, pious, and domestic.[9]

While it would be desirable to present all the shemale stories of the Crockett almanacs in their entirety as the basis on which to evaluate the manipulation and satirization of the sentimental stereotype of the true woman, present restrictions of length make such a reprinting impossible.[10] What is possible, after establishing the authors' awareness of the sentimental tradition, is an examination of representative tales in major subject areas in which the tradition is parodied and, intentionally or unintentionally, reconstructed to create a new stereotype, the riproarious shemale of the American frontier.

The writers sometimes offer direct parodies to underscore their awareness of the sentimental tradition for the reader. In "Crockett's Account of the Concerts in Kansas," the teller of the tale has the refined female city dweller none too gently satirized by the backwoodsman.

> One of our extremely sentimental and musical ladies of New York, and who had long run mad after the Italian opera, with its foreign airs and foreign *hairs*, took a notion to emigrate with some of her agricultural relatives to Kansas, merely for the romance of the thing, and for some new sort of excitement. Like the fashionable belle who married an Indian, she put up with many privations and annoyances for the sake of the *romance*. She could get along without a street promenade, a fashionable gossip and scandal; "but," said she, "I shall positively expire from want of music and the dear opera. I am dying for the sounds and dulcet swells of a *concert*."
>
> "A consart!" cried Crockett, who happened to hear her; "a consart, Miss! Do you mean for to come for to go for to think that we've not consarts an' operas in Kansas, Ma'am? Jist you walk along with me to-night, an' you shall hear both, by as *hairy* a set of vocalists as Italian Opera-house can show."
>
> The lady was in raptures, and soon as the night came on she was in perfect readiness, when Crockett lifted her into his opera-cab, (a *farm-cart,*) and drove out to the neighboring forest, which was alive with all kinds of wild beasts and hideous birds of night. At first, a screech-owl opened the programme with a direful scream. — "Oh! what's that?" shrieked the trembling listener. "That," said Crockett; "oh, that's only Signorina Screech-Owl-ine." Next came forth the horrid howl of a hungry wolf, who was soon joined by the growls of a grizzly bear. "There, Ma'am," said Crockett, "you hear the two great *Bassos*, Signors Wolfini and Bearini." Next thing, a panther put in his most shrill and horrid scream. "That, Ma'am," said Davy, "is the great *tenore*, Signor Painterini." In a few moments more, the whole and intire natural *menagerie* all broke out together — wolves, bears, wild hogs, wild horses, panthers, owls, and Indians, in a mingled roar which made the whole forest tremble with the echo. At the same time, a huge bear walked out upon a fallen tree, with an Indian baby or papoose in his paws. "Thar, Ma'am," shouted Crockett, "thar's the chorus an' fine-alley; ain't it *fine*. An' thar's Signor Bearini come out for a bucket of flowers." The lady screamed, and fell into convulsions, and Crockett drove her home to the *symphony!*[11]

The tale is perhaps more biting in this case, because the satire has the two-fold target of both this type of woman and the ever-changing fashions of civilized life. Not surprisingly, the lady is shown as overly fond of romance

and the ornaments of civilization and responds to all situations emotion-
ally. And most damningly, she is displayed as a figure of little or no use
to a wilderness society that often ranks worth in terms of accomplishments,
and accomplishments in terms of survival.

The majority of the stories, however, are positive in their presentation
and use adaptation rather than straightforward mockery to produce humor.
Note the difference in tone in the following excerpt from "Crockett's Double-
Breasted Gal-lantry" when he, rather than a third-person narrator, gives the
reader both barrels of his backwoods sentimentality:

> My mother was a woman, an' so is my sister when she gets to be a mother,
> an' if she don't be a mother, then she aint no woman. Well women are Margaret-
> nificent creeturs – tha're angels without feathers: the werry sugar maple jelly o'
> creation, an' whenever I see them scandalized, or insulted, then the volcano
> o' my galantry begins to rumble for overwhelmen eruption.[12]

Although the passage has only a trace of the manufactured backwoods vernacular that typifies the tall-tale language of the most outrageous of his
tales, the final figure of speech leaves no doubt as to Davy's gallant commitment to defend the honor of those "Margaret-nificient creeturs" who evidently cannot and would not defend themselves. The author plays upon
two other commonplaces of the sentimental tradition in this light parody –
that a woman becomes a true woman only as a mother and that the ideal
woman is, to borrow the title of Coventry Patmore's best-selling poem of
the time, the angel in the house. The latter point is emphasized later in
the tale when Crockett goes on to describe the lady he is rescuing from an
Indian as a "splendacious angel" (1849, p. [20]).[13]

The ideal of the "true woman" undergoes major revisions in the fictional
wilderness of the tall tales. The purity of the shemales, whose total disregard
for the virtue of submissiveness generally eliminates them from the category of angels, is not raised directly as an issue in the almanacs, with the
authors evidently satisfied to allow the reader to determine the moral fiber
of the backwoods belles on the basis of their actions and demeanor. The
present body of stories reveals that their behavior ranges from active resistance to the amorous advances of unworthy suitors to active pursuit of
the flowers of frontier manhood. The language and the situations surrounding their actions, however, are clearly designed to parody the standards of
proper behavior even when the actions themselves are completely decorous
and appropriate.

An example of this type of inversion occurs as well in terms of both the ideals of piety and domesticity in the almanacs. Davy proudly tells the reader that

> My sister, Comfort, war one of the go to meetin gals' and one of the finest samples of Christianity, and womananity that I ever seed; I says it myself, she swallowed religion hull, and fed on that and do good-a-tiveness all the days of her life, till she war a parfect model of a natural saint; she could preach a few too; her pulpit was the rock, and her sacrament the pure nat'ral element of Adam; her words would make the coldest individuals heart open like a clam in dog dogs [days], and a reprobates hair stand straight up, an bow to her, and when she sung a psalm you'd a thought all the trees in creation war organ pipes, and a harrycane blowing the bellows; she has put her tracks and her tracts all the way from the Alleghany to the Rocky mountains; she is always on hand, with her heart, arms, an pockets open, an she has been the travellers sun, star, an salvation, for the last three years in the rocky mountains, and has worn out seven, out of her nine constitutions, used up four consumptions, an seven fever an agues in saving travellers from freezin, famine, wolves and vultures. The biggest heap of good she ever done was, when she walked the frozen banks of Columby river, for fifteen days, livin on nothin but pure hope to hunt up the fifteen lost men in Col. Fremont's caravan, that was scattered by a snow storm, an that are gal never rested head nor foot till she explored the hull country, rocks, ravines, an holler logs, an she stuck as true to the chase as an alligater, till she found 'em, an piloted 'em safe to Californy.[14]

Religious activism shemale-style intentionally explodes the bounds of even the most liberal interpretation of true womanhood, but does so while upholding the ideal of piety. The same artful manipulation is used to applaud domesticity while satirizing the backwoods model of such feminine virtuousness. The culmination of the image of the saint upon a pedestal, therefore, is still realized through the role of wife, mother, and homemaker, although the move from Boston to bear country necessitates certain modifications. Davy again serves as the narrator.

> Katy Whippoween war the gratest wife that ever lived in our cleering. Her husband war as proud of her as he war of his dog; for she would always put the two ends of every thing together, and help him git along in the world. She brot up a smart chance of children what want no axpense to him, only for thar eddikation. She cut down her husband's trowziz and leggins for the oldest boy, and maid him a jacket of the peases; then she cut 'em down for the nixt boy, and so on. When thar war no cloth in the house, she contrived to keep her boys kivvered. One of 'em had got nothing to ware to shoot but his skin, one cold day in winter. So her husband was as mad as a chimney o' fire, and swore for

"Davy's Sister [Comfort Crockett]. Rescuing Adventurers in the Rocky Mountains." From *Crockett's Almanac. 1851. Containing Life, Manners and Adventures in the Back Woods, and Rows, Sprees, and Scrapes on the Western Waters* (Philadelphia, New York, and Boston: Fisher & Brother), [24]. St. Louis Mercantile Library Special Collections Department.

haff an our. But Katy soon thort of sumthing to do. So she opened an old fether bed, and covered the boy with melted glue. She she rolled him in the fethers, and he cum out kivvered all over with all kinds o' fethers, and looked most beautiful. So she packed him off to skool, and the master vowed he would git himself sich a soot of close, and save the taylor's bills. One winter this woman tride to help her husband along by acting as a wet nuss. Thar war a lady what had took a young bear to bring up and to be treated as one of the family, and Katy offered to taik it to nuss till it got big enuff to feed. In this way she arned enuff to keep her husband in whiskey, and that is saying a good deal, for he was a ripsnorter over the keg. But she got nothing for her panes, for all her children turned out bad. One of 'em sallied off to the east, and sells out cloth and tape and pins, and won of 'em is a minister. They knowed nothing of life in the woods, and is a living disgrace to old Kaintuck.[15]

Comfort Crockett's exaggerated missionary work and Katy Whippoween's rejection of the value of sobriety by wet-nursing a bear to provide whiskey-money for her husband may reflect the authors' satiric awareness of the great impact of the proliferating number of volunteer societies that began in the 1830s and 1840s in terms of developing an alternative to the traditional passivity of the ideal woman.[16] While the writers toy with the new-fangled idea of a woman's role in moral reform, whether it be salvation or temperance, they also acknowledge the additional effect of the wilderness in encouraging and demanding that a woman become an energetic individual. They show that the reality of frontier life bears little relation to the romantic stereotype of women in literature and is, in fact, after due allowance is made for comic excess, a good deal closer to the four sections just quoted. A hostile environment thus requires different responses and fosters a new ideal—the woman of manly virtues and accomplishments, who is valued for her strength, independence, endurance, woodcraft, and vigor. In many ways, the more like a man she is, the more likely she, her husband, and family are to survive and prosper in the wilderness.

The anonymous authors of the Davy Crockett almanacs begin with a reasonable sense of these historical realities and then proceed to exploit the comic possibilities of the situation by creating and describing the riproarious looks and behavior of the shemales of the West in terms of reversals of the sentimental stereotype of the women of the East. Exaggeration and caricature abound in rollicking fashion in all five of the basic categories of the tales: wild description; battles with animals; battles with humans; courting stories; and stories with sentimental and religious overtones like those previously quoted. Many of the narratives cut across the five main topics and contain elements of two or more of the categories. They also often reveal a common structure of combining a wild, sometimes grotesque, description with a particular event or adventure usually dealing with combat or courtship.

The wild personal descriptions are the female counterpart of the roaring boasts of Davy Crockett and Ben Harding, the chief backwoods roosters of the almanacs. These women parade their ugliness as a singular virtue and see combativeness as a way of life. They are a direct inversion of the stereotype of the true woman. Since the fictional Davy prides himself on the fact that he could "walk like an ox; run like a fox, swim like an eel, yell like an Indian, fight like a devil, and spout like an earthquake, make love like a mad bull, and swallow a nigger whole without choking if you butter his head and pin his ears back" (1837, p. 40), it is only natural that he have an affinity for Lotty Ritchers, "The Flower of Gum Swamp":

> She stood six foot in her shoes; but as she hadn't 'em on very often, she war not quite so high. She used to brag that she war a streak of litenin set up edgeways, and buttered with quicksilver. She chased a crockodile one evening till his hide cum off, and one day I met her in the forrest just as she had killed a monstracious big bare, I seed it war too much for her great strength, so we laid holt together, she took the tail, and I the head part, and for this she treeted me to a slice of genuine steak. She still wears the shift that she made out of the varmint's skin. It is told on her that she carried twenty eyes in her work bag, at one time, that she had picked out of the heads of certain gals of her acquaintance. She always made them into a string of beads, when she went to church, and wore 'em round her neck. She never pared her nales, and had holes cut in her shoes, so that her toe nales could have room to grow. She war a real beauty; but the young fellers war shy of her, bekase she never wood kort long befour she wanted to box with her bo, and her thumb nale war grate for pullin out eyes. Finely she cort her death by standing two days up to her chin in the Massissippy to hale the steem botes as they past by.[17]

Davy narrates the tale for the reader; Lotty never gets to speak for herself. Herein lies a primary reason why even the most riproarious shemale never reaches the pinnacle of ring-tailed roarer status.[18] The major male protagonists of the almanacs almost always tell their stories in the first person and, in so doing, build a closer bond between the reader and themselves as well as heightening the tale in the reader's mind. None of the shemales ever tells her own story; these superwomen of the frontier are always described. Only in eleven sentences in the fifty-eight tales do the women speak directly to the reader using the first person and five of those statements involve parodies of the sentimental tradition rather than shemale characterizations. This "suppression" may provide indirect evidence of the male authorship of the tales.

Despite this slight diminution of effect, Lotty provides a shattering reversal of the sentimental stereotype of the true woman: instead of small, frail, submissive, domestic, and pious, she is a robust six-footer with her shoes on (a common fudge-factor among males who aspire to that benchmark of appropriate size), she chases a "crockodile," wears the skin of the "bare" she killed, has gouged out twenty eyes to provide some church-going finery and prefers to box and gouge rather than court.

Swamps, particularly Gum Swamp and its surrounding areas, breed some appropriately grotesque denizens for the almanac world, and the descriptions continually play against the ideal of the petite woman as the exemplar of the genteel tradition. In "Crockett's First Love," the reader meets Gum Hollow's Florinda Fury, who gives a certain support to the old dictum that you are what you eat:

> Every winter she fatted up on bear's meat, so that when she turned out in spring, she war bigger round than a whiskey barrel; and when I put my arms 'round the cretur, it war like hugging a bale of cotton. Her two legs war like a cupple of hemlock trees, and when she sneezed it shook the leaves from the trees, and skeered setting hens off thar eggs. She war a very varchus gal, too; for when a Yankee pedlar undertook to come the soft soap over her, she kotched him by the heels and poked him up the chimbly till his head come out the top.[19]

But the hands down, no-holds-barred winner of the shemale backwoods beauty pageant was Gum Swamp's own Jerusha Stubbs. According to Davy, this gal

> had only one eye, but that was pritty enough for two, and besides it had a grate advantage in our parts, where folks must rise arly, as she could wake up in haff the time that others could, as she had only one eye to open, while other folks had to open two. One of her legs was a little shorter than the other, but I tolled her I shouldn't make no fuss about that as the road to my house laid all along on the side of a hill, so that the short leg seemed as if 't was made a purpose for walking to my cabin. She had had two cancers cut out of her breast, so that she was as flat as a board up and down there, which I couldn't have got over no how, only she had a beautiful grate hump on her back, and that made up for having nothing of the kind in front. Enermost all her teeth had rotted out, but then she had a pesky grate swallow, so that she could take down her vittles without chawing. I forgot to say how she had a hare lip, but then she had a long nose, which almost covered the place from sight. There was a grate bunch on

"Gum Swamp Breeding." Davy discourages a rival suitor for the hand of
Jerusha Stubbs. From *The Crockett Almanac. 1840. Containing Adventures,
Exploits, Sprees & Scrapes in the West, & Life and Manners in the Backwoods*
(Nashville, Tennessee: Published by Ben Harding), 21. University of Tennessee
Library.

her left arm, but then she had a monstracious wen on the right side of her neck, that balanced that difficulty and made it all even agin.[20]

The eastern creators of the tales would have been hard pressed to concoct a more repulsive inversion of the ideal of beauty and of symmetry of form to depict their frontier fantasies.

Expectedly, Crockett's kin are also a formidable force in terms of the category of wild description. As Davy tells it, "My Aunt war the sister of Pine Rook, the most rantankerous fighter in the valley of the Massassippy. She war raised in Pine Clearing, and when she war a child, her pap war made of rattle-snake brains and maple sap, well peppered, and biled into a jelly" (1848, p. [5]). And Davy's aged mother does a bit more than warm a rocker on the front porch:

> Now I gin you a genuine portrait of my mammy, in her One-Hundredth and Forty-Eighth year, and an all-scream-glorious gal she is of her age. She can jump a seven rail fence backwards, dance a hole through a double oak floor, spin more wool than one of your steam mills, and smoke up a ton of Kentucky weed in a week. She can crack walnuts for her great grandchildren with her front teeth, and laugh a horse blind. She can cut down a gum tree ten feet around, and steer it across Salt River with her apron for a sail, and her left leg for a rudder.[21]

But Crockett notes that his frontier paradise has its problems. It seems that some of the shemales are affecting the latest fashions, albeit frontier fashions, and he laments the passing of the good old days when men were men and, more particularly, when women were men too.

> The gals about our plaice ar gettin' wonderful perlite and perticklar. They used to have combs with iron teeth, and do up thar hare with wooden skewers; but now they must have pewter combs, and do up thar hare with spike nales. If they puts on a crocodile-skin shift, they must have the ruff side outwards, and thar bear-skin pettykotes must be combed as offen as wunst a month. I have heered in kongress that Rome was ruined by luxuriousness and all that ar, and I'm afeered that old Kaintuck will be ruined by them ar gals that can't keep up the old ways of thar four-fathers. (1843, p. [21])

And just to show that Davy held no truck with such backsliding in his own family and that he passed on the proper riproarious genes to his own off-spring, examine the woodcut of "One of Crockett's Infant Children, Grinning Lightning at a Bear." You will note that his six-year-old daughter is rather well developed. A fairly explicit treatment of women's sexuality in the illustrations and occasionally in the texts of the tales is another forceful inversion of the romantic stereotype. Again, Davy tells it best. He begins with formulaic bragging that echoes his descriptions of himself.

I always had the praise o' raisin the tallest and fattest, and sassyest gals in all America. They can out run, out jump, out fight, and out scream any crittur in creation; an for scratchin, thar's not a hungry painter, or a patent horse-rake can hold a claw to 'em. The oldest one growed so etarnally tall that her head had got nearly out o' sight, when she got into an all storm fight with a thunder storm, that stunted her growth, an now I am afraid that she'll never reach her natural size; but still, it takes a hull winter's weavin to make her walkin and bed clothes; and when she goes to bed, she's so tarnal long, and sleeps so sound, that we can only waken her by degress, and that's by choppen fire wood on her shins; but the youngest one o' them takes arter me, and is of the regular airth-quake nater. Her body's flint rock, her soul's lightnin, and her fist is a thunder-bolt, an her teeth can out cut any steam mill saw in creation. She is a perfect infant prodigy, being only six years old; she has the biggest foot and widest mouth in all the west, and when she grins, she is splendifferous; she shows most beautiful intarnals, and can scare a flock o' wolves to total terrifications. Well, one day, this sweet little infant was walking in the woods, and amusin herself by picking up walnuts, and cracking them with her front grindstones, when sud-denaciously she stumbled over a thunderin great hungry he barr. The critter seein her fine red shoulders bare, showin an inviting feast, sprung at her as if determined to feast upon Crockett meat, he gin her a savaggerous hug, and was jist about bitin a regular buss out on her cheek, when the child resentin her insulted wartue, gin him a kick with her south fist, in his digestion, that made him buss the arth instanterly, and jist as he war a comin to her a second time, the little gal grinned sich a double streak o' blue lightnin into his mouth, that it cooked the critter to death as quick as think, an she brought him home for dinner. She'll be a thunderin fine gal when she gets her nateral growth, if her stock o' Crockett lightnin don't burst her biler, and blow her up. (1845, p. [33])

Davy's relation of the powers of his unnamed "perfect infant prodigy" is also an apt introduction to the category of battles with animals, numeri-cally by far the most popular of the genres with the almanac writers. In this group of stories, it is Davy's wife who appears most frequently; she has a prominent role in eight of the tales. Sally Ann Thunder Ann Whirl-wind Crockett, however, has an acute problem in the almanacs; she has to tread a narrow path between showing her "true grit" and not upstaging her screamer of a husband. To this end, she is fully named in only one of the tales and is otherwise referred to by Davy as "my wife" or as "Mrs. Crock-ett," is given only one line of dialog that reflects shemale domesticity rather than her active adventures,[22] and, in the category of wild description, never realizes her full riproarious potential as a backwoods grotesque. Her com-

"One of Crockett's Infant Children, Grinning Lightning at a Bear." From *Davy Crockett's Almanac. 1845* (Boston: James Fisher; Philadelphia and New York: Turner & Fisher), [33]. St. Louis Mercantile Library Special Collections Department.

paratively mild descriptions or lack of description may reveal another partial debt of the authors' to the sentimental tradition. In a sideways bow to the full realization of femininity through marriage and motherhood, they make the majority of their full-blown shemales single women.

Despite this diminution and the need for her tales not to have an adverse effect upon Davy's reputation, Mrs. Crockett is no shrinking violet. In "A Tongariferous Fight with an Alligator," she snares the gator and the next day Davy notes that the women take charge:

> my older darter took the tongs and jumped on his back, when she beat up the "devil's tattoo" on it, and gave his hide a real "rub a dub." He found it was sharp

work for the eyes, as the devil said, as a broad-wheeled waggon went over his nose. My wife threw a bucket of scalding suds down his throat, which made him thrash round as though he was sent for. She then cut his throat with my big butcher knife. He measured *thirty seven feet* in length. (1837, p. 10)[23]

On four occasions Mrs. Crockett pulls Davy's bacon out of the fire. Although in the first instance she is depicted in the woodcut only as the helpmate who acts as a prop for his rifle to steady Davy's aim (he is feverish and suffering from the ague), she then saves him from two other panthers by breaking one's back with an axe and shooting the other. The Crocketts then "dragged one home at a time, and skinned them; the largest weighed over four hundred pounds."[24] She also twice saves him from wild cats (1840, p. 10; 1842, p. [5]) and once from a huge bear. According to Davy in his "Perilous Adventure with a Black Bear," the beast chases him "snapping his teeth so near me, that I felt his breath warm on my face."

> My wife, although she could but just use her left hand as it was hardly healed, as she had lost her thumb and fore finger. They were bit off by a cat fish as she attempted to skin one alive. But she caught up a hickory rail, and as the bear rushed at her with his mouth wide open she ran it down his throat. He corfed as if he had swallowed something the wrong eend first. His attention was now taken from me, and although completely broken winded, I turned and jumped on to the varmint's back, when I reached his vitals with my big butcher; and after a most desperate contest, in which we were all more or less bitten and my wife had her gown torn nearly off of her, we succeeded in killing him. He was a real fat one and weighed six hundred lbs. (1837, p. 19)

Mrs. Crockett does pretty well on her own against wild animals. In "A Dangerous Situation," her only solo fight in this category of tales, she bests a hungry bear that has marked her as his next meal:

> she drawed out her two nitting needles, and while the bear war looking up at her she stuck 'em both into his eyes. He jumpt about three feet off the floor, and roared out like a stuck pig. He then tride to spring at her, but he couldn't see, and jumpt rite into the fire. Before he got fairly out of the fire, he had kicked the brands and coals all out upon the floor, and when he cum out, he sprawled round and kicked till he had put everything up in heeps, and broke the crockery; but my wife soon brought the rifle to bear upon his pesky carcase, and straitened him out like a corpse in December. The way she had pork stakes, for a month arterwards, its not worth while to explicitrize about. (1841, p. [17])

But her best tale in this group is the one in which she is outside the domestic setting of the previous story and is determined to have some eagle egg

"A Tongariferous Fight with an Alligator." From *Davy Crockett's Almanack, of Wild Sports in the West, And Life in the Backwoods, & Sketches of Texas, 1837* (Nashville: Published by the heirs of Col. Crockett), [9]. University of Tennessee Library.

"A Desperate Contest with a Great Black Bear." From *Davy Crockett's Almanack, of Wild Sports in the West, And Life in the Backwoods, & Sketches of Texas, 1837* (Nashville: Published by the heirs of Col. Crockett), [18]. University of Tennessee Library.

nog. This is the one tale that gives her name and serves well as a representative example of the tallest of the tales in this category. It falls short only in that Davy rescues her.

My wife, Mrs. Davy Crockett—whose maiden name war Sally Ann Thunder Ann Whirlwind—always had a nat'ral taste for Eagle's eggs: kase she war edicated to the idee that they give the blood the true sap o' freedom an' independence—made them that fed on 'em able to look the sun or lightenin' in the eye without winkin' or squintin'—an' likewise encouraged the growth o' that all daren disposition to stand no nonsense from man, woman, beast or Beelzebub, while they also hatched in the heart the spirit of fly-high-ativeness and go-ahead-ativeness.

W-a-l-l, the first Easter mornin' arter the annexation of our State that we licked out o' Mexico, Sal war determind to du honor to the occasion by havin' a drink o' *Eagle egg nog* from the top o' one o' the tallest trees in the country, whar thar happined to be a nest of a kind of a republic of eagles. So she took a bottle o' my blue lightnin', flogged a she Buffalo and milked her, and then walked up to the Eagles' nest to get the eggs to make her *nog*. But it happined that the hull Senate and House o' Representatives o' the eagle nation war then in session, and they met her with a deputation of *bills* and claws, that quite turned her hair out o' comb; but the gal went into 'em bite, smite an' claw, an' made the feathers fly like a snow storm or a geese picken; but arter she had flogged the wings off of about a dozen on 'em, her foot slipped, and havin' to use her hand to keep from fallin', two fresh cock eagles flew right at her eyes, an' would a made a week's provision of her if I had'nt a walked, and shot 'em both through with the same bullet. Arter that I walked up the tree, and we both drank to our victory in *Eagle egg nog!*[25]

Of the remaining top-notch she-screamers in this category, only Grace Peabody, "The Heroine of Kaintuck," ever needs rescuing. The illustration shows her escape from a pack of fifty wolves on the back of an unfriendly bear that happens to be in the tree she climbs for refuge and whose limbs she uses as ammunition against the wolves for "killing them off by degrees." She has almost given up when Davy and a friend come to the rescue (1840, p. 20). Among those others who need no help is the pious woman who tries to fulfill a Methodist preacher's desire for fresh eels. She thinks that "bush eels" are what he wants, and he soon sees her "with a big knotted club in her hand batterfanging a dozen rattle snakes that were squirming and twisting around her in all manner of shapes and fashions" (1836, pp. 12–13).

As a group these shemales are more than a match for any beast in the wilderness. Sal Fink, Mike's daughter, kicks some bear cubs like a "two-year old colt" to subue them and then beats the mother with "a succession

"Perilous Situation of Mrs. Crockett. Discovery of an Eagle's Nest." From the *Crockett Almanac 1854. Containing Life, Manners and Adventures in the Backwoods, and Rows, Sprees, and Scrapes on the Western Waters* (Philadelphia, New York, Baltimore, and Boston: Fisher & Brother; New York: Philip J. Cozans), [7]. St. Louis Mercantile Library Special Collections Department.

of ponderous thumps in the chest" with her "naked fists" before finishing the job off with a rock.[26] There is also no question that a large crocodile meets his match in Sappina Wing. She rams her mop down "his breathing hole" and he chokes to death.[27] Oak Wing's sister is a bit more basic in dealing with her foe; she skins the bear with her teeth and then makes "herself a good warm petticoat out of the pesky varmint's hide" (1847, p. [8]). Judy Finx, no relation to Mike Fink, uses a giant snake to thrash a catamount and involves both in a battle before continuing her ride home on the tame bear that her neighbor has provided as an escort since there are

"The Heroine of Kaintuck." From *The Crockett Almanac. 1840. Containing Adventures, Exploits, Sprees & Scrapes in the West, & Life and Manners in the Backwoods* (Nashville, Tennessee: Published by Ben Harding), 32. University of Tennessee Library.

"Judy Finx whipping a Catamount." From *The Crockett Alamanac. 1839. Containing Adventures, Exploits, Sprees & Scrapes in the West, & Life and Manners in the Backwoods* (Nashville, Tennessee: Published by Ben Harding). 5. University of Tennessee Library.

no beaus left to accompany her after the "tea squall."[28] And just as the "tea squall" is a parody of the polite tradition of a ladies' tea social, a lady of the frontier can take other hints from her well-to-do sisters to the East. Recognizing the difficulty of finding good servants, Nance Bowers, Davy's niece, solves the problem in a unique way; she tames a bear and trains it to do common household chores. Nance is such a fine teacher of domestic science that her bear graduates to additional duties: "when she wants to cross big muddy river, he takes her in his paws, as a nurse takes a baby, an carries her across as upright as a Yankee soldier, an brings her on shore, as dry as a smokin fire poker" (1851, p. [19]).

If one looks for a contender for the champion shemale outside of Davy's family, Katy Goodgrit is clearly one of the favorites. Crockett says that she "could grin a wild cat out of countenance" and, when wolves start dogging her trail,

> Sum gals wood have been skeered out of thar seven wits, but Katy always knowed it war the fust duty of a gal of Kaintuck to stand up to her lick log, salt or no salt. So she just squatted low for the present, and got up into a holler stump whar the wolves couldn't quite reach her, and they cum roaring around her, like the water boiling around Crocodile Rock, at Tumble Down Falls. They jumpt up evenmost to her face, and she spit at one so wiolent that it nocked his eye out. She cotch anuther by the scurf of his neck, and whipt his hed off agin the tree. So she kept stopping their wind, till the fust she knew thar war a pile of dead wolves around the tree, high enuff for the others to climb up on. Then she war obleeged to squat down, or they wood hav tore her hed off. She staid thar all nite; but early the nixt morning, she stuck up her head, and crowed, till she crowed and screamed all the wolves deff, and then they begun to cleer out, but she went arter 'em with a pole and killed haff of 'em before they got away. (1842, p. [19])

As one might expect, the group of narratives that are devoted to battles with humans are quite similar to those in the battles-with-animals section in regard to language and to the method of fighting. For example, a fine catch like Crockett's seagoing Tonto, Ben Harding, is worth a bit more than a normal hair-pull. Ben states that one of these beauties is "a fine gal, and as pretty as a figger head. She stood six foot without her shoes, and her waist was as big round as a windlass. So I couldn't help loving her, you know. But there was another craft about four feet long, from stem to stern. She was good what there was of her, but I take it that two hundred pounds of wife is better that [than] forty pound, and so I went with the majority as our bosun used to say." As the battle for his hand ensues, Ben has to be restrained from stopping the brawl. When the fight is over, the results and his conclusions are typical of the backwoods gallant: "The long one had lost her cloze and one nipple, and the short one lost an i and haff her nose. So I married the short one for the present, bekass she had suffered so much in my cause" (1842, p. [32]).

Some ring-tailed roarers evince less respect for shemales and often suffer for their lack of judgment. Even Mike Fink, who should know better, finds out the hard way that there is no scaring a Crockett. He bet Davy a dozen wildcats that he could scare Mrs. Crockett's teeth loose. But when Mike gets a little too close hidden inside an alligator skin, Davy's wife pulls out her knife "and with a single swing of it sent the hull head and neck flyin fifty feet off, the blade jist shavin the top of Mike's head." Recognizing the attempted trick, she then "battered poor Fink so that he fainted away in his alligator skin, an he war so all scaren mad, when he come too, that he swore he had been chawed up, an swallered by an alligator" (1851, p. [16]).[29]

Indians, as one would expect, are the main foe in many of the tales in this category. Davy's shemale kin hold up his family reputation in grand style in these encounters. Pictured here in her 129th year is his grand-mother, who has "a damned stubborn cough, and so echoaciously loud, that it used to set the cider barrels rolling about the cellar." Granny uses it to cough an Indian to death when he tries to scalp her.[30] The Crockett women are so attuned to the wilderness that the wild beasts help them to escape from their red-skinned adversaries. His daughter, Thebeann, for ex-ample, although a captive of and prospective meal for an Indian war party, is of such "true grit" that panthers gnaw loose her bonds, form a guard around her, and escort her halfway home (1851, p. [25]).

Mike Fink's wife could also best an Indian,[31] but it is his daughter, Sal, "The Mississippi Screamer," who takes the family honors in that department.

I dar say you've all on you, if not more, frequently heerd this great she human crittur boasted of, an' pointed out as *"one o' the gals"* — but I tell you what, stranger, you have never really set your eyes on *"one of the gals,"* till you have seen Sal Fink, the Mississippi screamer, whose miniature pictur I here give, about as nat'-ral as life, but not half as handsome — an' if thar ever was a gal that desarved to be christened *"one o' the gals,"* then this gal was that gal — and no mistake.

She fought a duel once with a thunderbolt, an' came off without a singe, while at the fust fire she split the thunderbolt all to flinders, an' gave the pieces to Uncle Sam's artillerymen, to touch off their cannon with. When a gal about six years old, she used to play see-saw on the Mississippi snags, and arter she war done she would snap 'em off, an' so cleared a large district of the river. She

"Sal Fink, the Mississippi Screamer." From the *Crockett Alamanac. 1854. Containing Life, Manners and Adventures in the Backwoods, and Rows, Sprees, and Scrapes on the Western Waters* (Philadelphia, New York, Baltimore, and Boston: Fisher & Brother; New York: Philip J. Cozans), [21]. St. Louis Mercantile Library Special Collections Department.

used to ride down the river on an alligator's back, standen upright, an' dancing *Yankee Doodle,* and could leave all the steamers behind. But the greatest feat she ever did, positively outdid anything that ever was did.

One day when she war out in the forest, making a collection o' wild cat skins for her family's winter beddin, she war captered in the most all-sneaken manner by about fifty Injuns, an' carried by 'em to Roast flesh Hollow, whar the blood drinkin wild varmints detarmined to skin her alive, sprinkle a leetle salt over her, an' devour her before her own eyes; so they took an' tied her to a tree, to keep till mornin' should bring the rest o' thar ring-nosed sarpints to enjoy the fun. Arter that, they lit a large fire in the Holler, turned the bottom o' thar feet towards the blaze, Injun fashion, and went to sleep to dream o' thar mornin's feast; well, after the critturs got into a somniferous snore, Sal got into an all-lightnin' of a temper, and burst all the ropes about her like an apron string! She then found a pile o' ropes, took and tied all the Injun's heels together all round the fire,—then fixin a cord to the shins of every two couple, she, with a suddenachous jerk, that made the intire woods tremble, pulled the intire lot o' sleepin' red-skins into that ar great fire, fast together, an' then sloped like a panther out of her pen, in the midst o' the tallest yellin, howlin, scramblin and singin', that war ever seen or heerd on, since the great burnin' o' Buffalo prairie! (1854, p. [21])

Davy's rendition of Sal's tale is typical in that it combines a number of the five essential categories of the stories, but places major emphasis upon one of the divisions, focusing in this instance upon her epic defeat of "about fifty Injuns." The only category, besides that of sentimental and religious stories, that is not alluded to in any way is that of the courting tales. The authors again seem to follow the sentimental view that causes them earlier to downplay the wild description of Davy's wife as a backwoods grotesque. Here, again by omission, they point ahead to the acceptance of the ameliorating influence of marriage and the dominance of the male in that union by excluding a number of their top-notch she-screamers from even the preliminaries of courtship. Shemales like Sal generally do not participate in the rituals that, given the necessity to find a proper match with a man who could equal or outdo them, would inevitably make them less male. The problem is less acute, but still present for the male screamer. He does not undergo a complete change in his station in life, but he too is less free to participate fully in the wilderness; he is constrained by the dependent relationship of wife and family and at least partially tied to home and hearth. The unmarried solitary hunter is simply a more appropriate role for a ring-tailed roarer of either gender.

Crockett gives some support to the significance of such role differentiation and their priority in his tall-tale world in the introduction to two of his tales. On the one hand he notes, using the civilized metaphor of cultivation, that "Every human in our clearing always thought it war thar duty to take a vartuous gal, and replenish the airth . . ." (1848, p. [29]). But contrast this "duty" with his preference: "I wonst had an old flame that I took sumthin of a shine to, bekase I had nothing else to do, and bekase other game war skarse at that seeson of the year. And she lived rite alongside of the path where I used to go to look for bears" (1840, p. 14). In his mind, the uncivilized act of hunting is clearly superior to courting, and even courting is conceived of in terms of the hunt.

Crockett reinforces the parallel between courting and hunting when he again refers to the prospective spouse as the "game" in his description of the "how tos" of backwoods courtship. According to Davy, males generally take the initiative and, he goes on to say, if the reader has

> any expereunce, he aut to kno as thar ar more kinds o' courting than won. Won kind ar where you shin up to a gal and give her a buss rite off, and take her by storm, as it wur; and then thar ar won kind whar you have a sneaking regard, and side up to her as if you war thinkin about sumthing else all the time, till

you git a fare chance to nab her, and then you cum out in good arnest. Thar ar one kind whar you ax the gal's pareints, and jine the church, and ar as steddy as a steembote, till arter marriage, when you may do as you like, seeing as how the game is run down, and you have nothing more to do. . . . (1841, p. [12])

Crockett goes on to tell of a fourth kind of courtship, one that he calls "larned courting," that is a parody of the polite traditions of civilized courtship and hinges on the clash of backwoods and "high" culture. A fine example of this type of story is "A Scienterifical Courtship." In it, Wicket Finney, a true ladies' man, feels he must master all the women in his clearing, so he naturally has to accept the challenge presented by the newly "citified" Meg Wadlow, whose behavior and language has cowed all the other bachelors. So Wicket "got him a soot-o-close that war bran new, and he made the shop keeper show him how to put 'em on. . . . He noed he war all in the hiter-fashion [height of fashion], and Meg wood have to own it, when she seed him." After Wicket's rough charms win her hand, however, he decides that she is too quick in her consent to suit him and rejects her. At this reversal, Meg "went into the high sterricks and the rumytiz, and the fainting fits, and all that sort o' thing, wich she had larnt at the boarding skools."[32] Davy's own attempt at landing a cultivated sweetheart, Kitty Cookins, is thwarted by his then present love, Rueliana Drinkwater, who scares her off by charging her like a panther and "would have chawed her up like a wad." Her display of true affection convinces Davy to stick "to Ruey like a chestnut burr" (1841, pp. [12–13]). Zipporina, an old flame of Crockett's, is less direct in ridding herself of the offensively civilized suitor who has taken a fancy to her. She pretends to give in to his entreaties and says that she will meet him in a dark section of the forest and would wear her bearskin cloak. The accountant for the mine falls for her trick and winds up hugging a bear. Davy notes that the "young spark" then tells all his friends "never to go up into our parts a courting, for the gals up that way loved so hard that they would have squeezed his bowels out if he hadn't got away from them" (1840, p. 14).

The actions of Rueliana and Zipporina undercut the universality of Davy's original unstated assumption in delineating the types of courtship — the male will not always take the initiative or dominate the courting relationship. Though the act of courtship diminishes the wild freedom of both participants by its domestic associations, shemales can take the lead in the romance and can act as the equal or near equal of their beaus. In part of one story that takes place at a camp meeting, "There was guards placed

"A Scienterifical Courtship." From *The Crockett Almanac. 1841. Containing Adventures, Exploits, Sprees & Scrapes in the West, & Life and Manners in the Backwoods* (Nashville, Tennessee: Published by Ben Harding), 27. Barker Texas History Center, University of Texas, Austin.

Zipporina's "Severe Courtship." From *The Crockett Almanac. 1840. Containing Adventures, Exploits, Sprees & Scrapes in the West, & Life and Manners in the Backwoods* (Nashville, Tennessee: Published by Ben Harding), 13. University of Tennessee Library.

all round to prevent the gals running after the fellers" (1836, p. 18). And as the actions of Rueliana and the two women who want to marry Ben Harding indicate, shemales are just as willing as their male counterparts to participate in a no-holds-barred backwoods brawl to win the hand of their intended.

In "A Pretty Predicament," the object of Davy's affections proves literally too rough for him to handle. The unnamed shemale has just rescued him and he falls in love and proposes marriage. She has strong feelings for Davy as well and agrees to try bundling first before consulting her father to see if she could marry. Davy states that when they are in the dark bedroom that

> She consented to haul off all but her under petticoat and so I thought I had a fine bargin. But I soon found my mistake. Her under petticoat was made of briar bushes woven together, and I could not come near her without getting stung most ridiculous. I would as soon have embraced a hedgehog. So I made an excuse to go out, and then I cut for home, leaving my coat and raccoon cap behind. I never went that way since. (1839, p. 14)[33]

Perhaps the best example of a courting tale between backwoods equals is one that gives all indications of culminating in a successful union. "Colonel Coon's Wife Judy" also includes material that falls into the categories of wild description and battles with animals, but its primary focus is to give the reader a taste of a backwoods match made in heaven.

> It's most likely my readers has all heered of Colonel Coon's wife Judy. She wore a bearskin petticoat, an alligator's hide for an overcoat, an eagle's nest for a hat, with a wild-cat's tail for a feather. When she was fourteen years old, she wrung off a snapping turtle's neck and made a comb of its shell which she wears to this day. When she was sixteen years old she ran down a four year old colt, and chased a bear three mile through the snow, because she wanted his hair to make a tooth brush. She out-screamed a catamount, on a wager, when she was just come of age; and sucked forty rattlesnake's eggs to g[i]ve her a sweet breath, the night she was married. It was not at all likely that Judy would throw herself away on any young feller that was a mind to set up a claim to her, and so, many of 'em found they were barking up the wrong tree and getting their fingers pricked with a chestnut burr. At last, one Tennessee roarer, that never backed out for any thing short of a mammouth, heard of Judy's accomplishments, and 'tarmined to try his flint agin her steel. So he got into a jumper on a cold winter night, and drove through the woods towards her father's house. He begun to

"Judy Coon stomping a Nest of Wild Kittens to Death." From *Davy Crockett's Almanack, of Wild Sports in the West, and Life in the Backwoods. 1836* (Nashville, Tenn.: Published for the Author), 33. University of Tennessee Library.

scream before he got within sight of the log hut where Judy lived, and his voice was heard five mile off. Judy's heart begun to beat when she heard him, for she knew whoever he was, he was a whole steamboat. When he got to the house, he give one leap from his jumper, dashed down the door, and bounced into the middle of the room. "Tom Coon, by Jingo!" cried every one in the house—for he was no stranger by fame, though they had never seen him before. Judy right away set down in a corner of the room to try his spunk, and said not a word, good or bad. He pulled half a dozen eyes out of his pocket, and flinging 'em down on the floor, swore with a round oath he'd place any man's eyes by the side of them that dared to say a word agin Judy! Judy than jumped up like a frog and said, "Tom Coon, I'm yours for life—I know what you've come for, and I'll be your wedded wife without any more fustification about it." So Tom got Judy and all her plunder. Tom took her into Tennessee with him right away, and begun to make a little clearing in the midst of the wood, when Judy soon gave him a speciment of her talents. For, being out one evening to a tea-squall, about ten mile off, in coming home through the wood, she found a nest of young wild-cats in the stump of a tree. She said nothing about it when she went home, but let her toe-nails grow till they were an inch long, when she started all alone, one morning, and went to the nest, and, jumping in upon the young wild-cats, stamped them to death with her feet. It was quite a tough job, and they bit her legs most ridiculously; but she stood up to the scratch, though they scratched her backsides so tarnaciously they've never itched since. (1836, p. 33)[34]

While these anonymous tales that are the work of many different hands do not conform to a single and unified theoretical framework for an easy explanation of their significance, they do again reveal certain mid-nineteenth-century cultural attitudes. In examining the last two stories quoted in their entirety, for example, very little difference exists between Sal Fink and Judy Coon in terms of how they are described. Sal, however, seems to exemplify more backwoods maleness in her exploits than Judy, perhaps because her actions are those of a single combatant fighting against overwhelming odds. If she fails to subdue "about fifty Indians," she will be their morning's meal. Judy's adventure with the "nest of young wild-cats" is not as life threatening and, perhaps more importantly, is partially eclipsed by the preceding impact of her future husband's entrance. She shares the stage in her story. It seems likely that courting stories like Judy's and those stories with sentimental and religious themes are too closely associated with the stereotypical views of femininity and the cult of true womanhood in the minds of the male authors to rise to the same outrageous heights of the tales that feature wild description, battles with animals, and battles with humans as their primary elements.

In evaluating the backwoods stature of the riproarious shemales, however, the most important comparison is not between individual characterizations or between categories or groups of categories of women, but between the shemales and the gamecocks of the wilderness like Davy Crockett. For despite the many similarities, they are not, like Woolf's Orlando, essentially equal in all matters except gender. Instead, the broad range of inception and depiction of the shemales diverges in several ways from that of their male counterparts. Although the reader is given parodies of the standard sentimental view and has it inverted and exaggerated to suit the wild and wooly backwoods until the women become the near equal of the savage males whose behavior and appearance are the stereotype for the frontier insofar as eastern readers are concerned, a number of these backwoods belles are kept from complete equality of action by the still operative associations of home, hearth, and gentility, no matter how bizarre a transformation of the ideal of the true woman that they represent. Their battles, for example, generally have less action and fewer vivid details than those of the men. They are often involved in housekeeping, but never involved in politics in the tales. They are always described, usually by Davy or Ben, and never get to tell their own stories. And most significantly, even though they rescue Crockett a number of times, they are never allowed to match his feats as a full-blown frontier legend who can tree a ghost, drink up the Gulf of Mexico, ride his pet alligator up the face of Niagara Falls, and save the universe from freezing to death by acting out the role of Prometheus.

These shemales then are at least in part the result of the projected comic fantasies of eastern male writers who saw the frontier as an almost equal opportunity experience regardless of the sexual stereotypes of the day, simply because the wilderness is freedom and no rules apply. But in so constructing their satire of traditional sexual stereotypes and roles in terms of these "she human critturs" that inhabit the mythic West, they give both indirect tribute to the achievements of pioneer women in conquering, not just civilizing, the real Trans-Appalachian West, and direct support to the early stages of the formation of a liberating new feminine ethos in this type of popular fiction. It is no great step from Sally Ann Thunder Anne Whirlwind Crockett and Sal Fink in the Crockett almanacs to Calamity Jane and other heroines of the dime novels like Hurricane Nell, Rowdy Kate, Katrina Hartstein ("The Jaguar Queen"), and Mountain Kate in the last three deades of the nineteenth century.[35] By this time, it is even possible for this new generation of shemales to be villains. Neither would it be stretching the point too far to cast a net over the wider range of media in the twentieth century and point to a catch that includes such diverse characters as Tugboat Annie Brennan, Mammy Yokum, Granny on "The Beverly Hillbillies," Sheena, Queen of the Jungle, Wonder Woman and similar superheroine clones, and Sigourney Weaver's portrayal of Ripley, an example of the shemale in outer space, in the movie *Aliens*. All operate on a level that shows that they are better at being men than the men in each of their particular worlds, and yet they are still able to retain some degree of their feminine sense of self as well.

The legendary connection reaches backward in time as well as forward. Remember that Wonder Woman, as she is introduced in comic books in 1941, is an Amazon princess who is as wise as Athena, as lovely as Aphrodite, and has the speed of Mercury and the strength of Hercules. Recall that the name Amazon comes from the ancient Greek and means "without a breast."[36] Is it really so far from these fierce warriors who cut away one of their breasts to improve their accuracy as archers to the shemales who grow their toenails to stomp a nest of young wild cats or grow their thumbnails to pluck out eyes? Like Davy Crockett, who resonates with the tradition of the wild man as far back as Enkidu in *The Epic of Gilgamesh*[37] and is also a nineteenth-century incendiary spokesman for Manifest Destiny in the Mexican War and the Oregon question, the shemales of the Crockett almanacs are at once very old and very new. They are, in one sense, the long-term loyal opposition to male-dominated societies.

In the final analysis, the riproarious women of the Crockett almanacs offer much more than the casual enjoyment of the fanciful, exaggerated language and the unbelievable deeds in their tall tales. For just as these "rantankerous" women provide an immediate insight into the social beliefs of nineteenth-century writers, publishers, and readers through the double-edged satire of the stories, so too do they place before the modern reader the means, both humorous and serious, to forge an intriguing and revealing chain between fiction and history that links the depictions of the Amazons of Greek mythology, the new women of the westering frontier of the nineteenth century, and the participants in the women's movement of the last three decades together as legendary shemales.

NOTES

1. Virginia Woolf, *Orlando: A Biography* (New York: Harcourt, Brace and Company, 1928), 138.

2. For a recent overview of the content and significance of the almanacs, see Michael A. Lofaro, "Davy Crockett, Tall Tales, and the Second Nashville Series of Crockett Almanacs" in his edition, *The Tall Tales of Davy Crockett: The Second Nashville Series of Crockett Almanacs, 1839–1841* (Knoxville: University of Tennessee Press, 1987). See also, in Michael A. Lofaro, ed., *Davy Crockett: The Man, The Legend, The Legacy, 1786–1986* (Knoxville: University of Tennessee Press, 1985), John Seelye's "A Well-Wrought Crockett: Or, How the Fakelorists Passed through the Credibility Gap and Discovered Kentucky," 21–45; Michael A. Lofaro's "The Hidden 'Hero' of the Nashville Crockett Almanacs," 46–79; and Catherine L. Albanese's "Davy Crockett and the Wild Man; Or, The Metaphysics of the *Longue Durée*," 80–101. Two fine articles to pair with that of Albanese on the development of Crockett from Old World forms are Walter Blair's "Americanized Comic Braggarts," *Critical Inquiry* 4 (Winter, 1977): 331–49, and John Seelye's article in the present volume.

3. *Davy Crockett's Almanack, of Wild Sports in the West, And Life in the Backwoods, & Sketches of Texas, 1837* (Nashville: Published by the heirs of Col. Crockett), 2. After the initial full reference, each subsequent citation to a particular Crockett almanac will be listed parenthetically in the text of this essay. Each full citation will contain the description of known variant imprints for the otherwise identical almanacs.

4. Lofaro, "The Hidden 'Hero,'" 46–48.

5. The total number of tales proper to include in the study will of course vary depending upon the criteria each reader uses to determine that a role is significant. The major criterion for this investigation is how large a part a woman has in a tale. In all but fifteen of the stories, women are judged to play full rather than partial roles. Other factors include the tallness of the tale, the level of the character's activity in the story, and the presence of backwoods dialect and first person statements.

6. Richard M. Dorson, ed., *Davy Crockett: American Comic Legend* (New York: Spiral Press for Rockland Editions, 1939). For some of the problems with using Dorson's edition, see Lofaro, "The Hidden 'Hero,'" 49 and 77–78, notes 10, 11. The rarity of the almanacs themselves and the complexities of their origins (see Seelye, "A Well-Wrought Crockett," 21–45) have further discouraged investigation until the last few years. Mody C. Boatright, "Backwoods Belles," in *Backwoods to Border*, eds. Mody C. Boatright and Donald Day (1943; reprint Dallas: Southern Methodist University Press, 1967), 61–78. Walter Blair drew attention to one of the best tales by reprinting "Sal Fink, The Mississippi Screamer" in his seminal collection *Native American Humor 1800–1900)* (New York: American Book Company, 1937), 284–85. Constance Rourke summarized two of the stories in *American Humor: A Study of the National Character* (New York: Harcourt, Brace and Company,

1931), 65, and one in her *Davy Crockett* (New York: Harcourt, Brace and Company, 1934), 236. Few recent works treat these tales. Those that do are derived from the sources cited above rather than from the original texts and tend to use the material briefly as part of a large overview. See, for example, Jane Curry, "The Ring-Tailed Roarers Rarely Sang Soprano," *Frontiers* 2 (1977): 136–37, 140 n. 20, and Beverly J. Stoeltje, "'A Helpmate for Man Indeed': The Image of Frontier Women" in *Women and Folklore*, ed. Claire R. Farrer (Austin: University of Texas Press, 1975), 32–33.

7. Cynthia Griffin Wolff, "A Mirror for Men: Stereotypes of Women in Literature," *Massachusetts Review* 13 (Winter–Spring 1972): 210–12.

8. Charles D. Meigs, M.D., *Lecture on Some of the Distinctive Characteristics of the Female* (Philadelphia: T. K. and P. G. Collins, 1847) 16–17. See also Susan Phinney Conrad, *Perish the Thought: Intellectual Women in Romantic America, 1830–1860* (New York: Oxford University Press, 1976). For more on Meigs's views set into the context of many other similar statements, see Barbara Welter, "The Cult of True Womanhood," *American Quarterly* 18 (Summer 1966): 151–74.

9. Welter, 152. See also Wolff, 210–12. Although recent critics have taken issue with the historical accuracy of submissiveness as one of the cardinal virtues enumerated by Welter, it seems clear that this concept remained a central part of the stereotype of the true woman, at least insofar as most men were concerned. For two examples of this qualifying view, see Mary P. Ryan, *The Empire of the Mother: American Writing about Domesticity, 1830–1860* (New York: The Haworth Press, 1982), 2ff.; Gerda Lerner, "The Lady and the Millgirl: Changes in the Status of Women in the Age of Jackson," *Midcontinent American Studies Journal* 10 (Autumn–Winter 1971): 11–14.

Other works not cited elsewhere in these notes, but to which this very brief summary paragraph on the feminine ideal is indebted, include: Ann Douglas, *The Feminization of American Culture* (New York: Alfred A. Knopf, 1977); Ernest Earnest, *The American Eve in Fact and Fiction, 1775–1914* (Urbana: University of Illinois Press, 1974); Daniel Walker Howe, "American Victorianism as a Culture," *American Quarterly* 27 (December, 1975): 507–32; Madonna Kolbenschlag, *Kiss Sleeping Beauty Good-Bye: Breaking the Spell of Feminine Myths and Models* (Garden City, N.Y.: Doubleday & Company, Inc., 1979); David S. Reynolds, "The Feminization Controversy: Sexual Stereotypes and the Paradoxes of Piety in Nineteenth-Century America," *New England Quarterly* 53 (March, 1980): 96–106; Carroll Smith Rosenberg, "Beauty, the Beast and the Militant Woman: A Case Study in Sex Roles and Social Stress in Jacksonian America," *American Quarterly* 23 (October 1971): 562–84; Nancy Walker, "Wit, Sentimentality and the Image of the Woman in the Nineteenth-Century," *American Studies* 22 (Fall 1981): 5–22; and Joyce W. Warren, *The American Narcissus: Individualism and Women in Nineteenth-Century American Fiction* (New Brunswick, N.J.: Rutgers University Press, 1984).

10. An edition of all of the tales is being completed by the present author.

11. *Crockett Almanac, 1856* (Philadelphia, New York, Boston, and Baltimore: Fisher & Brother), [33].

12. *Crockett Almanac, 1849* (Philadelphia and New York: Turner & Fisher; Boston: James Fisher), [20].

13. For more on tall-tale language, see "Appendix: The Tall Talk Tradition" in Michael Montgomery's "David Crockett and the Rhetoric of Tennessee Politics" in this volume. For general background on the notion of the angel in the house, see Marlene Springer, "Angels and Other Women in Victorian Literature," in *What Manner of Woman: Essays on English and American Life and Literature,* ed. Marlene Springer (New York: New York University Press, 1977), 124–31.

14. "Davy's Sister. Rescuing Adventurers in the Rocky Mountains." Published in *Crockett's Almanac. 1851. Containing Life, Manners and Adventures in the Back Woods, and Rows, Sprees, and Scrapes on the Western Waters* (Philadelphia, New York, and Boston: Fisher & Brother), [24]. I wish to thank John N. Hoover of the St. Louis Mercantile Library Association and D. Strong Wyman of the University of Tennessee Library for their assistance in providing the illustrations for this study.

15. Taken from "A Good Wife" in *Ben Hardin's Crockett Almanac. 1842. Rows – Sprees and Scrapes in the West; Life and Manners in the Backwoods; and Terrible Adventures on the Ocean* (New York and Philadelphia: Turner and Fisher; Baltimore: Turner), [8–9].

16. Ryan, 71–72, 98–99; Stoeltje, 25–41; Gail Parker, ed., *The Oven Birds: American Women on Womenhood, 1820–1900* (Garden City, N.Y.: Doubleday & Company, Inc., 1972), 4–15.

17. *The Crockett Almanac, 1841. Containing Sprees and Scrapes in the West; Life and Manners in the Backwoods; and Exploits and Adventures on the Prairies* (Boston: J. Fisher), [21]. There is a Louisville, Ky., variant published by Joseph T. Clark, but Clark deletes page [21] and replaces it with the final woodcut from page [36] to free that back cover for an advertisement for his business. Clark may have thought the tale offensive, since there were five other tales that could have been just as easily deleted.

18. Curry, 136–37, is in error in assuming that these "female supermen are just that – identical models of their superhuman counterparts."

19. *Crockett's Almanac. 1848* (Boston: James Fisher; Philadelphia: Philip Borbeck), [21]. A significant textual variant published by Magee & Kneass in New Orleans omits the story, along with several others, to include advertisements, anecdotes, jokes, etc.

Sal Tuig of Green Swamp, the occasion of Davy's "fust disappointment in love," is as memorable as Florinda Fury.

> She stood six foot and two inches without her shoes; she had a fist like a rock, and the biggest feet in the whole cleering. Besides all this she had lost a eye at a tea-squall, and one ear had been bit off in a fite with two wolves.

The description is taken from "Crockett's Disappointment" in *Fisher's Crockett Almanac. 1843. With Rows, Sprees and Scrapes in the West: Life and Manners in the*

Backwoods: Terrible Battles and Adventures on Sea and Land (New York: Turner & Fisher), [8].

20. Extracted from "Gum Swamp Breeding" in *The Crockett Almanac. 1840. Containing Adventures, Exploits, Sprees & Scrapes in the West, & Life and Manners in the Backwoods* (Nashville, Tenn.: Published by Ben Harding), 21.

21. *Davy Crockett's Almanac. 1845* (Boston: James Fisher; Philadelphia and New York: Turner & Fisher), [5]. A significant textual variant published in New Orleans by Magee, Kneass & Co. includes this tale, but places it on page [35]. See also n. 19.

22. *Davy Crockett's Almanack, of Wild Sports in the West, and Life in the Backwoods. 1836* (Nashville, Tenn.: Published for the Author), 44.

23. Davy's wife has another roughly similar adventure in "A Thief of an Alligator" (1836, 44).

24. *Davy Crockett's Almanack, of Wild Sports of the West, And Life in the Backwoods. 1835* (Nashville, Tenn.: Published by Snag & Sawyer), 8.

25. "Perilous Situation of Mrs. Crockett." Published in *Crockett Almanac 1854. Containing Life, Manners and Adventures in the Backwoods, and Rows, Sprees, and Scrapes on the Western Waters* (Philadelphia, New York, Baltimore, and Boston: Fisher & Brother; New York: Philip J. Cozans), [7]. The story also provides a mild taste of the nationalistic and expansionistic bias of some of the tales.

26. *Crockett Almanac 1853. Containing Life, Manners, and Adventures in the Back Woods, and Rows, Sprees, and Scrapes on the Western Waters* (Philadelphia, New York, Boston, and Baltimore: Fisher & Brother), [19].

27. *Davy Crockett's Almanac. 1847. Daring Adventures in the Back Woods; Wonderful Scenes in River Life; Manners of Warfare in the West; Feats on the Prairies, in Texas and Oregon* (Boston: James Fisher; New York and Philadelphia: Turner & Fisher), [23].

28. *The Crockett Almanac. 1839. Containing Adventures, Exploits, Sprees & Scrapes in the West, & Life and Manners in the Backwoods* (Nashville, Tenn.: Published by Ben Harding), 10.

29. This tale forms the central episode of a recent children's book. See *Sally Ann Thunder Ann Whirlwind Crockett*, retold by Caron Lee Cohen, illustrated by Ariane Dewey (New York: Greenwillow Books, 1985).

30. *Davy Crockett's Almanac. 1844. Life and Manners in the Backwoods: Terrible Battles and Adventures of Border Life: With Rows, Sprees, And Scrapes in the West* (Boston: James Fisher; Boston: J. Fisher; Philadelphia and New York: Turner & Fisher; Philadelphia: Turner & Fisher; New York: Turner & Fisher; New York: Charles Small), [4].

31. *Crockett Almanac 1852. Containing Life, Manners, and Adventures in the Back Woods, and Rows, Sprees, and Scrapes on the Western Waters* (Philadelphia, New York, Boston, and Baltimore: Fisher & Brother; Boston: G. W. Cottrell & Co.), [24]).

32. *The Crockett Almanac. 1841. Containing Adventures, Exploits, Sprees & Scrapes in the West, & Life and Manners in the Backwoods* (Nashville, Tenn.: Published by

Ben Harding), 23–24. Further parenthetical references to this almanac in the text will be cited as "1841 N" to distinguish it from the almanac published by J. Fisher in the same year.

33. The story also includes an ironic aside to "larned courting" and the value of civilized accomplishments: "She said she could not play on the piane nor sing like a nightingale, but she could outscream a catamount and jump over her own shadow; she had good strong horse sense and knew a woodchuck from a skunk" (14).

34. For another descriptive courtship, see "Crockett Popping the Question" (1848, [29], [32]).

35. See, for example: Edward L. Wheeler, *Deadwood Dick on Deck; Or, Calamity Jane, The Heroine of Whoop-Up* (New York: Beadle and Adams, Feb. 11, 1885); Edward L. Wheeler, *Bob Woolf, The Border Ruffian. Or, The Girl Dead-Shot* [Hurricane Nell] (New York: Beadle and Adams, Aug. 6, 1884); Edward L. Wheeler, *Apollo Bill, The Trail Tornado; Or, Rowdy Kate from Right Bower* (New York: Beadle and Adams, Jan. 31, 1882); Frederick Whittaker, *The Jaguar Queen; Or, The Outlaws of the Sierra Madre* (New York: Beadle and Adams, October 22, 1872); Joseph E. Badger, *Mountain Kate: Or, Love in the Trapping Grounds. A Tale of the Powder River Country* (New York: Beadle and Adams, September 10, 1872).

36. See the introductory essays by Gloria Steinem and Phyllis Chesler to *Wonder Woman* (New York: Holt, Rinehart and Winston and Warner, 1972), and Jeannette Mirsky's foreword to Emily James Putnam's *The Lady: Studies of Certain Significant Phases of her History* (1910; reprint, Chicago: University of Chicago Press, 1970).

37. Again see Albanese's "Davy Crockett and the Wild Man; Or, The Metaphysics of the *Longue Durée*," 80–101; Blair's "Americanized Comic Braggarts," *Critical Inquiry* 4 (Winter 1977): 331–49; and John Seelye's article in the present volume for the ancient origins of Davy Crockett.

Cats, Coons, Crocketts, and Other Furry Critters —

OR, WHY DAVY WEARS AN ANIMAL FOR A HAT

John Seelye

When you talk about Crockett, most particularly in Tennessee, you want to make clear just which Crockett you are talking about. There is first of all the historic *David* Crockett, pioneer, legislator, martyr at the Alamo. I am not interested here in discussing David Crockett. Next, there is *Davy* Crockett, frontiersman, hunter, and folk hero, who figures in several fictionalized autobiographies that were inspired and probably in part written by the historic David Crockett. I'm not going to discuss that Crockett, either. Then there is *Davy Crockett II: The Sekwel*, racist bigot, rabid expansionist, and an otherwise objectionable low-life who figures as the narrator and chief exhibitionist in dozens of comic almanacs published over his name but who has only the most remote connection with the historical David Crockett. I ain't a-goin' to touch that Crockett with a ten-foot pole. No, the Davy Crockett I am going to be discussing is a fairly rare animal, seldom exhibited under one tent before now.

"In the theater," writes Richard Boyd Hauck, "Davy Crockett has consistently been portrayed as an American hero, the straight-shooting backwoodsman."[1] Where in the almanacs, Davy is generally portrayed as a *Yahoous Americanus,* having bodaciously bad-mannered adventures with the likes of Mike Fink, beating up Negroes and killing Indians and Mexicans, all in the name of Mississippian manhood and American expansion, the stage Crockett is an amusing but relatively pacific frontiersman, strong of heart and hard of hand, but gentle as a turtledove in the presence of ladies and other minorities. He is an American hero who may be placed in a direct line that begins with Cooper's Leatherstocking and ends with John Wayne. In that line, moreover, appears Owen Wister's Virginian, a soft-spoken, straight-shooting, somewhat woolly, if not entirely wild, cowboy, who perhaps owes as much to the Crockett stage tradition as he does to the idealization of American western types by Theodore Roosevelt and Frederic Remington.

I intend to determine here the extent of Wister's debt to the stage Crockett, but first I want to demonstrate Davy's French connection, a contingency that begins with the coincidence of the centennial of the arrival in America of Bartholdi's Statue of Liberty and the bicentennial of the birth of the historic David Crockett. For Davy too is something of an immigrant, whose emergence as a "native American" hero sheds clouds of a distinctly European glory, an iconographic, as well as a literary, genesis that can be traced to Old World origins. Having earlier demonstrated that the Davy Crockett of the almanacs originated in a city somewhat to the east of Nashville, I want here to show that Davy's ultimate origins were in a range of mountains considerably to the east of the Appalachians, and that his translation westward was an iconographic equivalent to the melting-pot process. We can then go on to verify that the Virginian (as an idea) originated also in mountains well to the east of the Grand Teton range.[2]

Let us start at the magical moment when the Crockett iconography began, with the engraving depicting the actor James Hackett as Nimrod Wildfire, the character in James Kirke Paulding's play *The Lion of the West*, who was inspired in part by the real-life David Crockett. As Joseph Arpad has shown us, it was this picture that inspired the woodcut portrait of Davy Crockett that appeared on the cover of the "Tennessee" almanac of 1837, the year in which the historic Crockett attained political apotheosis following his death at the Alamo.[3] In both versions, Davy is portrayed in a hunter's fringed-leather jacket, trimmed with fur, and wearing a hat made from a wildcat, its head and tail intact. In subsequent depictions, Davy will be given a raccoon for a cap, a transmogrification that I shall discuss presently. But let us begin with the wildcat, and with the general question concerning what has become so familiar an accoutrement as to pass by unobserved. Why does Davy wear an animal for a hat?

The question is answered in part by the familiar image of Robinson Crusoe, posed with musket and dog and clothed in his homemade costume of goatskins, including the impossible shako fashioned from the same shaggy material. Part of the answer may be found at the other end of the chronological spectrum, in the image of Tarzan, his privates concealed by a loincloth made from the skin of a lion or leopard. But perhaps the strongest clue may be found in a famous French portrait of Ben Franklin in a fur hat, for Doctor Franklin was regarded by European savants as a premier wonder of the New World, a self-made and thereby "natural" philosopher, whose arrival in the Old World conveniently coincided with the emergence

Robinson Crusoe by Grandville. From *The Life and Adventures of Robinson Crusoe . . . Illustrated with two hundred engravings by [Jean Ignace Isidore Gerard] Grandville* (New York: Appleton, 1852 et seq.). Courtesy, American Antiquarian Society.

Benjamin Franklin by Cochin. Courtesy, American Antiquarian Society.

of Rousseau's notions about the benign effect of life lived in the world of
pure Nature undefiled. We know, of course, that Ben lived much of his life
in Philadelphia, but for the French his home was Pennsylvania, Penn's
Woods, a pastoral asylum filled with the pacific spirit of Quaker Oats.
Educated by Moravian missionaries, boon companion of Delaware Indians,
Fenimore Cooper's Leatherstocking originated in the same Rousseauean
neighborhood, and likewise wore a fur hat, to which he added buckskins
borrowed from Daniel Boone. That is to say, Leatherstocking's nether parts
were covered with Boone's buckskins, but his head, that seat of common-
sense sapience, was kept warm by Ben Franklin's fur hat, a distinction to
which we shall return.

For the present, it suffices to point out that to wear the skins of animals
with the fur (or fringe) showing attests that the wearer is a true Child of
Nature, a tradition that emerges from an ancient European archetype, the
"Wild Man." A shaggy figure that flits through the iconographic forests of
the Middle Ages, the Wild Man finally emerges, definitively, if antithetic-
ally, as Satyrane in Spenser's *Faerie Queene* and as Caliban in Shakespeare's
The Tempest. The literary and artistic heritage of the Wild Man has been
thoroughly traced by Richard Bernheimer, who shows us that by the time
of the English Renaissance the archetype had taken two divergent direc-
tions: the one version, as in the case of Caliban, was identified with bestial,
degenerate humanoid forms, associated with violence, rape, even cannibalism, inspiring Swift's Yahoos on the one side of the ocean and accounts
of American Indians by Cotton Mather on the other.[4] Spenser's Satyrane,
by contrast, evokes a gentler version, one in which the Wild Man is adapted
to the larger myth of Chivalry.

Taken captive by a knight, the Wild Man is brought to understand the
beauties of civilization, often through the agency of one such beauty, usually a young maiden, with whom the Wild Man falls in love. Occasionally,
according to Bernheimer, it is the maiden and not a knight who leads the
Wild Man on a chain out of the woods and into her bower, for the Wild
Man is also associated with the Unicorn, over whom maidens have similar
powers. It is this shaggy tale that nourished Rousseau's theories about
noble savagery and children of nature, and that resulted in America in both
Uncas and Hawkeye in *Last of the Mohicans*, domestic versions of that
romance pairing very popular in the Middle Ages, Valentine and Orson,
who for some reason experienced a revival of interest in England and the
United States during the early years of the nineteenth century, largely

through the agency of children's books and a popular play by Thomas Dibden.[5] Early on, in the medieval version, Valentine leads his brother back to civilization, shaves off his fur, and the two have howling adventures among the Saracens.

Catherine Albanese has recently demonstrated the extent to which the almanac Crockett is indebted to the dark half of the Wild-Man myth, Davy's "comic" adventures being characterized by the same violence and bloodshed, even the cannibalism associated with the image of the American Indian as promoted by Cotton Mather.[6] What remains is to show the extent to which the "other" Crockett, the straight-shooting "American" hero of the stage is indebted to the "other" version of the Wild Man, the one filtered through a chivalric sieve. Which brings me back once again to the wildcat hat, an article of apparel whose meaning far transcends the obvious humor in such an outlandish notion of fashion. To begin with, a hat can be a highly charged symbol, associated as it is with the head, the traditional seat of intellect or the absence of same: thus Mercury (and Charlie Chaplin) wear a helmet, and Happy Hooligan a tin can. As we have seen, by donning a fur hat, Ben Franklin encouraged associations with the wild idea, much as in his writings he put forth the appearance of a simple Socratic inquirer after truth. But why a wildcat hat?

In his study of the origins of Liberty as an emblematic figure standing for Republican France, Maurice Agulon has shown that a lion is often depicted as a symbolic companion of Liberty, most particularly when that icon also stands for the French nation, for the lion is a traditional symbol of political power—the might of the People.[7] But the cat, likewise, is occasionally found as a companion to Liberty, standing for "enmity to restraint," i.e., Independence.[8] Agulon also discusses the various kinds of headgear worn by Liberty, from the Phrygian Cap to helmets, occasionally adorned by a griffin or a lion's head. Davy Crockett therefore wears a wildcat hat because he stands for a populist notion of Independence, the wildcat being a smaller version of the lion and a wilder version of the familiar house pet. Remember, Paulding's play was entitled *The Lion of the West*, as was one of the first canal boats to pass from Lake Erie en route to New York harbor during the great Canal Celebration of 1825, a self-consciously symbolic "ark" that carried a wild cargo of animals from western regions.[9]

The point to be made here is that, though we may associate Davy Crockett on the stage with simple, democratic virtues, his creators were sophisticated writers well aware of European iconographic lore. This extends even to the coonskin hat, the comic counterpart to the more heroic wildcat helmet, and associated with the make-do and raffish spirit of the Mississippi frontier. The raccoon is a native American species, but the block on which Davy's hat was fashioned had been imported from Europe, for like the cat and the lion, the raccoon has traditional characteristics that lend themselves to symbolism. An animal known more for cunning than courage, the raccoon suits the almanac Crockett most particularly, since that version is something of a trickster figure, engaged in outwitting (as well as outfighting) a wide range of trans-Mississippi types. Moreover, the coon, as a "ringtailed roarer," is associated with the wild feats of boasting that the almanacs attribute to the rivermen and hunters of the Mississippi Valley, of whom Davy Crockett is both the chief and the champion.

Therefore, we may conclude that at the same time the classical figure of Liberty was undergoing a complex metamorphosis in the hands of European sculptors, Davy Crockett, by means of the bifurcated stage and almanac evolution, was coming to stand for two disjunctive versions of western American hero, the straight-shooting, high-minded prototype traceable to Rousseauean origins, and the bragging, knock-down-and-drag-out ruffian that is an avatar of a much less diluted Wild-Man spirit. Thanks to Bartholdi, the French conception of Liberty-as-the-Republic would eventually come to stand for America also, not so much as "Liberty Enlightening the World," however, but more as the United States guiding the world to these shores, there to share the benefits of political freedom and economic opportunity. Davy Crockett, by contrast, was never intended as a national symbol, but stood instead for the regional and political aspects of this country generated by frontier life. They were more "American" perhaps than the qualities associated with eastern heroes, like the Caesar-shaped George Washington, but they were representative chiefly of the regional part rather than the national whole.

Along with his animal hat, Davy is generally figured as holding a rifle, the western counterpart to the Liberty Pole or Sword that is associated with the emblematic European figures of national significance. This, too, is symbolic of his independence, as both weapon and hunting tool, on which Davy depends both for defense and subsistence. But the rifle takes further meaning from the notion of "straight-shooting," the kind of personal integrity that "calls the shots" as they are seen, much as Davy Crockett on the stage is a latter-day descendant of the "plain speaker" of Shakespeare's theater. "Straight-shooting" as a register of moral superiority is likewise associated with Leatherstocking, who in *The Pioneers,* especially, demonstrates incredible skill at marksmanship and stands for the kind of truth associated with Higher Laws. Behind both Leatherstocking and the stage version of Davy Crockett, there stands that ancient European mythic hero, William Tell, piercing with an arrow the apple perched on the head of his young son. Coincidentally, it is Mike Fink, associated also with feats of marksmanship, who liked to shoot a tin cup off the heads of his friends, and whose death, it is said, resulted from an undersight that killed one such friend, whose friend killed Mike Fink. Crockett is associated with no such feat—or fate—merely with epical hunting exploits, but a brief review of William Tell's legend suggests a number of interesting parallels, and strengthens the Wild-Man connection, to which we shall be returning shortly.

As told by Jean Pierre Claris de Florian, who created the version of Tell's legend perhaps best known to early nineteenth-century readers, the story of the Swiss patriot has complex political implications. Written while the author was imprisoned during the French Revolution, the book was presented by Florian as proof of his sympathy for the radical cause of Republicanism, for Tell is portrayed as a champion of his people, who takes up his bow against cruel oppression. But the act for which Tell is arrested is his refusal to make obeisance to a hat set upon a pole in the marketplace by the dictatorial bailiff, Gessler, a situation that may be traced back to the Old Testament story of Haman, but that during the French Revolution had a much more contemporary connotation. For the Phrygian Cap set upon a Liberty Pole was a common symbol associated with both Liberty and Revolution and, by means of the Reign of Terror, with tyranny as well.

More pertinent to our discussion here is Tell's costume, for he is described by Florian as wearing a wolfskin cloak, with the head intact as a helmet: "William . . . clad himself in the wolf-skin which he always wore when he hunted wild animals at a distance from home. This skin, fastened to his body by a broad girdle, covered even his head, and the animal's teeth shone brightly upon his forehead. His legs were partly covered with bearskin trowsers; on his shoulders he bore a quiver full of the brightest arrows, and on his arm that terrible bow which he had never bent in vain."[10] When he confronts Gessler, Tell has on his hairy outfit, symbolic of his courage as a hunter and his origins in the wild mountain region of Switzerland. Florian in an opening apostrophe to the reader makes this complex connotation clear:

William Tell by Butler. From *William Tell, the Patriot of Switzerland. . . . To which is added, Andreas Hofer, the Tell of the Tyrol. Illustrated with Engravings on Wood, by Butler* (New York: Wiley and Putnam, 1842). Courtesy, American Antiquarian Society.

Listen to me, friends of Liberty! you whose lofty souls and feeling hearts would teach you to die for your independence, or to live for the happiness of your country! Come, and I will tell you how a man, born in a barbarous country, in the midst of a people enslaved under the rod of an oppressor, alone, with no other aid than his own courage and magnanimity, gave to his desponding countrymen Liberty and a new existence, and taught them to know their birthright.

This man, whom nature called her son, and armed to maintain her laws, roused up [with] his powerful voice the slumbering spirit of his countrymen, groaning under the weight of their chains; taught them to change their ploughshares for the sword of the hero, conquered the armed bands which tyrants sent to oppose him, and founded in a barbarous age, upon barren rocks, a retreat for Reason and Virtue, the daughters of Heaven, who descended to console mankind (5–6).

Richard Bernheimer, in his study of the Wild Man, tells us that one of the richest sources of legends and lore is found in the Alps, and though another scholar has specifically excluded William Tell from the ranks of Wild Men, the wolfskin cap and the identification of the spirit of Liberty with the mountain sanctuaries suggests otherwise.[11] As Bernheimer shows us, the transition of the Wild Man from a fur-bearing creature to one wearing symbolic furs marks the transformation of a mythic archetype into an allegorical symbol. There is in this regard an important iconographic display found in a French engraving of 1727, in which William Tell appears naked save for a lion's pelt, presenting his bow and arrows to a panoply of figures standing for Switzerland, Liberty, Concord, etc. Thus clothed (or naked), Tell evokes Hercules, identified by Bernheimer as one of the classical analogues of the Wild Man, whose traditional weapon is a club. The source of this print, Franz Heinemann's *Tell Iconographie* (Lucerne, 1902), which reproduces pictures of William Tell dating back to the Middle Ages, suggests that an animal skin was not Tell's customary garment, and the earliest nineteenth-century depiction of Tell in his wolfskin I have thus far found dates from 1842, by which time the American illustrator may well have been inspired by stage or almanac versions of Davy Crockett! But even this possibility serves to underline the contingency, suggesting that Americans were conscious of the parallels between the two straight-shooters born in the midst of wild Nature.[12]

True, Davy Crockett is seldom conceived of as a champion of Liberty — though Whigs might have seen his standing up to "King" Andrew Jackson as equivalent to Tell's refusal to bow down to Gessler. Instead, Crockett devotes his marksmanship to killing wild game and the wild men whom he

William Tell from Franz Heinemann, *Tell Iconographie* (Lucerne: J. Eisenring, 1902). Courtesy of the Trustees of the Boston Public Library.

so closely, in the almanacs, resembles. Still, his legend ends at the Alamo, where he enlists his rifle in the patriotic cause of national expansion, to which he dies a martyr. In Paulding's play, likewise, Davy is allowed to draw a heroic bead on one occasion, but his "straight-shooting" is mostly in the metaphoric vein. Still, the popularity of Schiller's drama and the play *William Tell*, by the British dramatist James Sheridan Knowles (which had a successful run in New York in 1828), may have suggested to Paulding in 1831 the dramatic possibilities of the American marksman Davy Crockett. But even if we see the similarities as matters of mere coincidence, the analogy helps define Paulding's creation as a native American version of a European archetype, and that such was the intention of the drama, we shall now discover.

The version of Paulding's play available to us is one that was considerably revised and rewritten for production in Great Britain by the British dramatist William Bayle Bernard, a writer of farces, who added the important character of Mrs. Wollope, a satiric portrait of the English travel writer Mrs. Frances Trollope, whose unfavorable description of manners in the United States had scandalized Americans when it was published in 1832, just in time to be incorporated in Bernard's improved play of 1833.[13] Bernard was a skillful and sophisticated man of the theater, and given the context within which the most important allusion to the Wild Man appears, we must credit him, not Paulding, with the reference. But the drama as revised by Bernard returned to the United States, where it became a standard vehicle for the talents of James H. Hackett, who originally commissioned the play and who created the role of Nimrod Wildfire. It thereby conveyed the Wild-Man idea to the American scene once again, much as the myth had earlier migrated westward during the English Renaissance by association with the American Indian.

Much of the humor in the farce results from a misunderstanding between Wildfire, a Kentuckian visiting relatives in New York, and Mrs. Amelia Wollope, who proposes setting up an academy that will "ameliorate" the uncouth manners of Americans. She solicits Colonel Wildfire for funds in a manner that he confuses with a proposal of marriage, and he makes plans to carry her off in his covered wagon to Kentucky. The situation has its analogue in Irving's "Legend of Sleepy Hollow," where Ichabod Crane, the comic Yankee, likewise dreams of loading Katrina Van Tassel in his wagon and heading westward, but in the Paulding/Bernard play the tables are turned, not on Wildfire, but on Mrs. Wollope and her brother, Jenkins, who has been posing as a wealthy English lord in the hope of marrying an American heiress. Jenkins imagines that by challenging Wildfire to a duel he has "scared him back to the woods. . . . I can imagine him on the back of a rough colt without saddle or bridle, belaboring the poor beast with a thick stick and fearing to turn his head least he should perceive . . . Death and the Devil!" This is an obvious allusion to the violent denouement of Irving's tale, though the final exclamation is cued by Wildfire's entrance "in his hunter's dress with a rifle on each shoulder," ready to duel on his own rough-and-ready terms.[14]

The parallels with Irving serve chiefly to illustrate the impact of his American stories on English readers—though we must not discount the intermediary influence of his friend Paulding—for Bernard, in attempting to structure an "American" situation, drew upon Irving's Hudson-River story for his Kentuckian-in-Manhattan situation. By his agency, the Dutch-versus-Yankee conflict mounted by Irving was transferred to a western frame, where the conflict between the "Dandy and the Squatter" – to evoke one of Mark Twain's earliest sketches – would become a standard situation. When Wildfire enters carrying two rifles on his shoulders, it is both a naive reaction to the European notion of dueling and an effective American rebuff to the snobbish Jenkins. Of a similar sort is Wildfire's misunderstanding of Mrs. Wollope's solicitation of funds, which once again takes the form of a direct and (to the European sensibility) a frightening response, her fear enhanced by the matter of the Wild Man, evoked by Wildfire in his wildcat costume. "This savage," laments Mrs. Wollope, "will marry me by main force, thrust me into his covered wagon, and then – –" "La, Ma'am," cries her maid, "don't think of it!" (47). But we the audience *do* think of it, and the implication is that Mrs. Wollope will be ravished by Wildfire in his western wilderness. Likewise, the Wild Man in medieval art is often depicted carrying away a young maiden to his forest lair, with obviously sexual intentions, a threatening image providing counterpoint to Jenkins's picture of a Wildfire riding a "rough colt" whom he beats with a "thick stick," in effect, the Wild Man in retreat.[15]

That Wildfire is to be taken as a modern Wild Man is certified by an important literary allusion, a punning bit of dialogue that occurs when the Kentuckian serenades Mrs. Wollope by singing "Yankee Doodle" outside her window. "There's a Valentine for you!" declares her maid, to which Mrs. Wollope responds: "A Valentine! An orison!" (42). The rejoinder evokes the story of Valentine and Orson, as does another remark by Mrs. Wollope a few lines earlier, when she makes fun of the possibility of being courted by such an uncouth specimen of American manhood as the "Alligator Colonel," as she calls him: "The brute! a flattering conquest – the alligator caught. Ha, ha! Can this be possible? I attributed his familiarity last night to any *spirit* but that of *love*, and yet who but that powerful enchanter could tame such a modern centaur?" (42). At face value, Mrs. Wollope's remark seems an open allusion to Wildfire's boasted "half-horse, half-alligator" nature, hence "modern centaur." But the half-man, half-horse familiar to ancient mythology, according to Bernheimer, is another classical avatar of the Wild-Man idea. Finally, when asked to produce his calling card, Wildfire produces "The King of Clubs," at once a signature of his naiveté and another link to the Herculean prototype.

Though averse to the notion of marrying the uncouth colonel, Mrs. Wollope determines that the Kentuckian is a suitable subject for "amelioration," and she plans through a flirtation to obtain a contribution for her projected academy: "By thus flattering his vanity, I shall rivet his chain and lead him as I please," she boasts, yet another image warranted by the iconography of the Wild Man, often depicted according to Bernheimer as being led out of the forest by a maiden on a leash-like chain (43).[16] Ironically, Mrs. Wollope's would-be captive is inspired by her overtures to make his own plans, as we have already seen, and in returning to that Irvingesque situation, we can now recall the extent to which Irving, in concocting his "Hudson-River tales," was dependent himself on European folk material. It is out of this highly cosmopolitan, cross-Atlantic mix that Davy Crockett emerges — as American, once again, as the Statue of Liberty.

The pedantic puns assembled by Bernard may not have been intended for popular comprehension, and they have remained undetected until now even by scholars. They may not improve the quality of Bernard's farce, but they do attest to the dramatist's sophistication and demonstrate that he was able to see and embroider upon the connection between Paulding's original creation — inspired by the stories circulating about Congressman Crockett — and an ancient archetype, that "child of chivalry" as Mrs. Wollope refers to Wildfire, the American Satyrane. Equally important, the notion of a Wollope/Wildfire nuptials, which is taken seriously by the Kentuckian only, will have a long reach in subsequent American literature, as will Mrs. Wollope's plan to "ameliorate" the Alligator Colonel. For, as Annette Kolodny has shown us, the presence of women on the frontier was early associated in America with the process of domestication, hence civilization.[17]

As early as 1792, Gilbert Imlay, in his novel *The Emigrants*, showed how the genteel hand of an immigrant British belle could make the Kentucky desert bloom like an English garden. The idea, once again, is generic to the medieval myth of the Wild Man tamed by a Virgin, but it is also intimate with the equivalent nineteenth-century notion of the benign influence of femininity, the reforming power of women, which Ann Douglas discusses in *The Feminization of American Culture*.[18] By the time Paulding's play was written, the notion of female "influence" was already sufficiently prevalent to be made fun of by Bernard, and by 1872, forty years later, the sentimentalization of American culture, assisted by the example of Victorian England, had increased to such a degree that when Frank Murdock wrote his play *Davy Crockett: Or, Be Sure You're Right, Then Go Ahead*, the theme of "amelioration" was a serious matter sustaining Murdock's plot. In Murdock's version of "Crockett in Love," the frontiersman's courtship is both seriously conceived (if often comically conducted) and successful, in terms that place the idea of feminine "influence" and the Wild-Man archetype in a context quite different from what we have found in *The Lion of the West*.

In Murdock's play, the Wild-Man theme is thoroughly subsumed to conventional, sentimental formulas, without the subtle literary allusions used by Bernard. Murdock's Davy, though conceived in a humorous vein, is the hero of a melodrama, not a figure of fun in a roaring farce, and his sterling character is set off against the wicked machinations of a villain who hopes to win a maiden's fortune by marrying her to a weak dupe. As in the Paulding/Bernard play, the marriage theme is associated with an imposter, but here Davy is himself in active contest for the hand of the girl (again a rich heiress), instead of being paired off with a comic counterpart in a subplot. Once again, the story line resembles Irving's "Legend" (reminding us that Joseph Jefferson in 1865 had made Boucicault's *Rip Van Winkle* one of the most popular of all American plays), but Crockett is more than ever a western Brom Bones, seeking to drive off an eastern interloper and marry the girl himself. Though the heroine, like Katrina Van Tassel, is a local heiress, she has been long absent from her home in the Tennessee mountains and has been educated in sophisticated manners by a guardian, who is also involved in the plot to marry her to an unsuitable mate, in order to pay off his gambling debts. But, like Brom Bones, Davy Crockett has a prior claim to the hand of Eleanor Vaughan ("Nellie" to her Tennessee friends), the two having been sweethearts since childhood. The turning point of the plot comes when Eleanor reads Scott's poem "The Young Lochinvar" to the illiterate Davy, an intensely literary moment (made possible by her education) that will trigger his innate chivalry.

Scott's stirring ballad from *Marmion* has a determining effect on Murdock's hero: "There's something in this rough breast of mine that leaps at the telling of a yarn like that. There's a fire—a smouldering fire that the breath of your voice has just kindled up into a blaze—a blaze that will sweep me down and leave my life a bed of ashes—of chilled and scattered ashes."[19] Davy, though smitten by both the tale and the teller, recognizes that Nellie's education and wealth places her far beyond his reach: "I ain't fit to breathe the same air with you. You are scholared and dainty, and what am I, nothing but an ignorant backwoodsman, fit only for the forests and the fields where I'm myself hand to hand with nature and her teachings, knowing no better" (122). At this point, Davy resembles Leatherstocking in love with Mabel Dunham in *The Pathfinder*, a love that cannot possibly result in marriage, for as Henry Nash Smith has shown us, Cooper's hero as a symbol of uncivilized Nature cannot marry, because marriage would change his emblematic meaning.[20]

Even on the level of realism, a union between Davy Crockett and Eleanor Vaughan would seem highly unlikely; given the wide cultural disparity, Mrs. Wollope's derisive rejection seems closer to the mark. But Murdock's play obeys a sentimental imperative, and Davy Crockett eventually marries his darling Nellie: inspired by the poem, he emulates Lochinvar by carrying her off on a borrowed horse just before she is to be married to the undeserving suitor, an act, incidentally, that echoes the fate narrowly escaped by Mrs. Wollope. It is not, however, that Davy has been transformed to a knight from a Wild Man of the Woods by Scott's poem; instead, he has been inspired by the poem to prove himself the natural knight he already is. Notably, at one point he "translates" Scott's poem into homely, backwoods terms: "There was once a game young knight, I think that is what they called him. He was a scout—a trapper, a man who forded rivers in his buckskins with nary a friend but his horse and his rifle. Away he went, caring for nothing, stopping at nothing, until he reached the house that held the gal of his heart. 'What do you want here?' says the dad—'I want my bride,' says the knight—'Get out,' says the dad—'Whoop,' says the knight, 'I'm Lochinvar. Who dares to follow?'" (143–44).

It is Davy's natural nobility that awakens in Nellie her own mountain values, leading to a realization that his simple but virtuous life is far superior to her rich and sophisticated, but essentially empty, existence: "Gaudy jewels that please the eye when the heart is empty. Oh, I have been so lonely amidst all these splendors" (146). She gives away her money so as to relieve her guardian of his debts, planning to find true happiness in "my new resting place—the heart and home of Davy Crockett," as the penultimate line of the play has it, the strains of "Home, Sweet Home" sealing the moral. The Maiden does not put a leash on this Wild Man; instead, he carries her off to his forest sanctuary with her willing cooperation. There, in the Tennessee mountains, as Davy explains to Nellie's wicked oppressor, "We of the hills and mountains band ourselves together, and form a court of law where there's mighty little learning, maybe, but where there's a heap of justice, and where a judge sits that renders a sentence— strikes terror to the boldest heart. Do you know his name? It's Lynch— Judge Lynch" (147).

Where Paulding and Bernard have farcical fun with the Wild-Man idea, mounting it as a burlesque encounter between bold, plain-speaking America and sophisticated but silly Europe—a contrast as old as Royall Tyler's 1787 comedy of that title—Murdock reverses the chivalric formula. Crockett the Wild Man is inspired by a tale of knightly derring-do, but he is not reformed in any way by it, nor does Eleanor's "influence" have any transforming effect on him, save to inspire him to thoughts of love and deeds of courage. Instead, it is she who is changed, for, recovering her Tennessee mountain values, she willingly gives up her received culture and the useless jewels of wealth for a simple life as the wife of a good man. Written thirty years apart, a periodicity that brackets the rise of the Victorian notion that woman's influence can affect moral reform, both *The Lion of the West* and *Davy Crockett*, utilizing contrasting genres (farce and melodrama) and points of view (country in city, city in country), reject the idea that the naive, even illiterate, frontiersman is in need of reformation. Exposing a crude primitivism, the authors express an ideology essential to American nativist radicalism, which holds that the pastoral zone and its inhabitants are avatars of a fearless, even militant, virtue that traditionally assumes not a female, but a manly, guise: In Davy Crockett both the Wild Man and the Knight are combined.

Of the two dramas, Murdock's seems to have enjoyed the greater popularity, remaining a standard in the repertoire of Frank Mayo, who originated the role of Davy Crockett and played the part (now in a coonskin cap) until he died in 1896. The mixture of frontier heroics and feminine surrender to masculine supremacy seems to have appealed to a broad American audience, so that by the turn of the century Davy Crockett was firmly associated with courtship and marriage, reversing Cooper's Leatherstocking formula. I do not know if Owen Wister ever saw Murdock's play, but, for whatever reason, when Wister turned from writing realistic stories about the life led by cowboys and cavalrymen to framing a novel that would have a wider readership, he seems to have borrowed certain elements from Murdock's formulaic encounter between the Wild Man and his genteel damsel. *The Virginian* is not customarily thought of as a latter-day revival of the adventures of Davy Crockett, but the ideal Cowboy in his "broad, soft hat," scarlet kerchief, and dusty overalls, has much in common with the Rousseauean hunter in his animal-skin costume.

First of all, the recent discovery and publication of Wister's early, unfinished attempt at a cowboy novel, with the working title *Chalkeye,* suggests that his subsequent best-seller sprang from a wild seed.[21] Chalkeye, as his name suggests, is a somewhat more picaresque—and picturesque—hero than the Virginian, starting with his dog, a former circus performer named Skunk. Chalkeye, whose last name is Hilary, lives in an isolated mountain cabin, is pointedly womanless, and keeps as pets an eagle and an elk calf. As a signature of his wildness he wears a rattlesnake skin around his broad-brim hat and evinces the sense of humor revealed in his name by hazing tenderfoot intruders: one such, an apothecary from Omaha dubbed the "Turkish Delight," is stripped naked and "branded" all over with rubber cement. Wister's Virginian likewise has a penchant for practical jokes, as when he stages a shivaree in order to discomfit some traveling salesmen whose familiarity has insulted his sense of decorum, or, later, when he and a fellow cowboy switch babies during a dance, a bachelor gesture of defiance against the encroachments of marriage upon the free life of the cattle country. Both the shivaree (charivari) and baby "switching" are rituals of misrule associated with the Wild-Man myth as defined by Bernheimer, tricks aimed at upsetting civilized modes of behavior. Though the Virginian lacks Chalkeye's animal companions, and wears no snakeskin around his hat, he is compared throughout the novel to a Bengal tiger because of the animal grace of his physical presence. He is, therefore, a Wyoming equivalent to the "Lion of the West," and even his nickname (we never learn his real one) suggests a kind of chivalric caste, relating him to the rural gentry of which Washington was the noblest example.

At the same country dance where he switched babies around, the Virginian is teased and humiliated by Molly Wood, the Vermont-born schoolteacher who has recently arrived in town and whom the Virginian will eventually marry. He has earlier rescued her from a swamped stagecoach, and accepting her rebuff as a challenge, he begins his courtship the day after the dance, resolving to improve himself so as to meet her civilized measure: "'I ain't too old for education. Maybe she will lend me books. And I'll watch her ways and learn. . . .'"[22] In her turn, Molly dreams that night "that the Virginian had ridden his horse into [a] railroad car, and sat down beside her," a fantasy in a class (albeit a Freudian subset) with that of Lochinvar's riding boldly into the hall to claim his bride. Much as Amelia Wollope schemes to "ameliorate" Nimrod Wildfire, so Molly Wood will "mollify" the wild Virginian, and, as in Murdock's play, the instrument will be literature.

Among the books she provides her lover, Molly includes Scott's *Kenilworth* (which Wister as well as his hero admired), but, as if to show that the schoolteacher is an up-to-date (if not exactly "new") woman, she also provides novels and poetry that were thoroughly modern reading matter in 1885, the date when the action takes place, including authors like George Eliot and Robert Browning, and even a Russian novel.[23] But Molly's favorite is Jane Austen, whose *Emma* she gives the Virginian and to which he applies himself manfully but unsuccessfully. His preference is for Shakespeare's plays, most particularly *Henry IV*, for he feels naturally drawn to the fun-loving yet heroic young prince and is amused by Falstaff's antics. Much as Molly very nearly makes the kind of wrong decision very nearly made by Austen heroines—rejecting the right man for the wrong reasons—so the Virginian's transformation parallels that of Shakespeare's Prince of Wales, and he too turns away his Falstaff, leading a lynching party that hangs his former buddy, Steve—the one man who can call the Virginian a "son-of-a-bitch," familiarity which, like Falstaff's, fails to save him from justice—who has turned cattle rustler and outlaw. Both Falstaff and Steve stand for the wild life a man must set behind him if he is to advance to a position of mature leadership: the Virginian has already been promoted to the position of foreman on Judge Henry's ranch, and he will eventually become a partner.

The lynching incident almost causes a permanent break between the Virginian and Molly, which is averted when Judge Henry delivers a long apologia for the use of Lynch Law, necessary in a wild country that does not have the adequate support of authority by its citizens. Lynch Law, as we have seen, likewise provides an important speech in Murdock's play, evoked by Davy Crockett as necessary "when a man wearing the image of the Almighty Maker shames nature and changes off with the wolf," becoming thereby truly wild (147). Molly Wood does not openly accept the judge's argument—she feels that hanging is too severe a penalty for cattle rustling—but it is a major step in her own education, which eventually brings her to an acceptance of the necessity that her fiancé must kill Trampas in defense, not of his life, but his honor. Much as she has introduced the Virginian to the finer things in life, so he and his western cohort have instructed her in the Code of the West, of which he is the finest exemplar, a Knight Exemplar, if you will.

Still, the question remains as to the real extent of the Virginian's reformation. Molly most certainly is transformed, not by literature, but by encounter with the realities of western life, but like Murdock's Crockett, Wister's Virginian is a diamond in the rough, being a knight in overalls who acts by a code that suffices for all occasions. Like Murdock's Crockett, he translates chivalric matter into his own language, but the spirit remains true: "'The British king (Henry the Fourth) is fighting, and there is his son the prince. He cer'nly must have been a jim-dandy boy if that is all true. Only he would go around town with a mighty triflin' gang. They sported and held up citizens. And his father hated his travelling with trash like them. It was right natural—the boy and the old man! But the boy showed himself a man too. He killed a big fighter on the other side who was another jim-dandy—and he was sorry for having it to do. . . . That play is bed-rock, ma'am!'" (270). And so, we must conclude, is the Virginian. It is Molly Wood who, like Murdock's Nellie Vaughan, is brought around, who finally realizes that her cowboy is both morally and physically superior, and who ends by acknowledging her preference for life on the western frontier to a civilized and snobbish existence in the East.

True, the Virginian does put aside his mischievous ways, so disruptive to orderly, civilized rituals and routines, and his rise, first from the cowpuncher to a foreman and then to a part-owner of Judge Henry's ranch, is, as John Cawelti has pointed out, an Alger-like story of success that is paralleled by his mastery of genteel manners and correct spelling and grammar.[24] By the end of the book, the Virginian's discourse can at times be completely free of dialect and grammatical faults. And yet, even at the beginning of his transformation, his spelling, as the narrator observes, is no worse than that of the greatest Virginian of all, George Washington, and he remains the same essential Tiger he was compared to at the start of the novel.[25] There, he demonstrated his superior skill with a lariat in bringing to harness a cunning, recalcitrant pony, and the subsequent contest between the Lady and the Tiger ends with the Lady, as the poem has it, subsumed to the Tiger, led by a western leash (a lariat) to her new western home. This "wild man," as the wife of Judge Henry observes, has "subtle traits" (346), and like Prince Hal (and Davy Crockett) he goes ahead once he knows that he is right. Unlike Molly Wood, he is always right if not inevitably correct.

Having been joined to her in marriage, the Virginian takes his bride into "the solitudes where only the wild animals would be," for like the mythic Wild Man he carries his prize to his secret lair in the forest, within view of the remote, untenanted Grand Tetons, the nursery of the spirit of western independence. "'This is how I have dreamed it would happen,'" he tells his bride, "'only it is better than my dreams,'" but about Molly's dreams we hear no more (352, 380). They spend the first week camping on an island in the middle of a symbolic stream that divides the pine forests above from the cattle country below, a type of Jordan that serves as a threshold to the "promised land" beyond. Here, "deep in the unsurveyed and virgin wilderness," in a secret spot known only to the Virginian, the cowboy will instruct his bride in the ways of the trail, teaching her "how to loop and draw the pack ropes, and the swing ropes on the packsaddles, and how to pitch a tent," the freemasonic mysteries of the Wild Man's world (378, 380). These matters, presumably, will make Molly's education complete. Of *Emma* we hear no more, either.

Starting with *The Lion of the West*, we have seen how the Davy Crockett stage tradition involves — in both a farcical and a seriously (if humorous) romantic setting — the wooing and capture of an essentially civilized woman by a man who represents the wild yet admirable qualities nurtured by frontier conditions. Virtuous, wise, and independent — if naive concerning sophisticated culture — the Davy Crockett of the stage is a true Child of Nature in the Rousseauean vein, a lineal descendant of the mythic Wild Man of the Woods. As such, he recognizes his need for a mate who will bring into his life the necessary gentling, feminine touch, illustrating the Victorian notion of female "influence," but in all instances the transformation is at best imperfect. As in Cooper's Leatherstocking Tales, there seems to be a perception in America that the integrity of frontier virtue will remain both superior and impervious to civilized "improvements." This idea is backed by an erotic geopolitics, moreover, commencing with the British/American division in Paulding's play (which is reinforced by the traditional city/country dichotomy), continuing with the eastern/western dualism in *Davy Crockett*, and culminating with Wister's self-conscious nod toward the spirit of Reconstruction and reunion that is reflected in the northern/southern origin of his heroine and hero.[26] Notably, however, it is the Yankee who is reconstructed, not the Rebel, led by love to accept two institutions firmly (by 1900) associated with the darker aspects of southern life — dueling and lynching. Under the Virginian's chivalric armor can be found the hairy man of the Crockett almanacs, the Hawkeye/Chalkeye who lives where the wild things are, and wears an animal for a hat.

The Wild-Man idea would surface again, more visibly, in the Tarzan novels by Edgar Rice Burroughs, where an "Ape Man" is captivated by a highborn Englishwoman, who eventually abandons her civilized life to find happiness in the African treetops. Other instances (albeit tragic) include

Eugene O'Neill's *The Hairy Ape* and the movie *King Kong*, but it is the man in the leonine leotard, immortalized by Johnny Weismuller and Carol Burnett, who serves chiefly here to point back toward the man in the wildcat helmet, by way of the man in the wide-brimmed hat who has the grace and power of a Bengal tiger. I began by demonstrating that Davy Crockett as a literary idea is a complex amalgam of European themes. Let me end by stating that the line between Paulding and Wister carries those themes into a further range, demonstrating that Davy Crockett from Tennessee had a long afterlife, that like Cooper's Leatherstocking he migrated westward to the prairies, there to surface as the Cowboy, the American Centaur, the "Horseman of the Plains," and the prototype for courtly cow punchers and bear-killing presidents yet to come. And yet, when it is all said, what we have is a story if immigration, for whether he wears the coonskin of Davy Crockett or the ten-gallon hat of the Virginian, the "native American hero" is a wild man from the forests of Europe under it all.

NOTES

1. Richard Boyd Hauck, "Making It All Up: Davy Crockett in the Theater," in *Davy Crockett: The Man, the Legend, the Legacy, 1786–1986*, ed. Michael A. Lofaro, (Knoxville: University of Tennessee Press, 1985), 103. Hauck provides an extended examination of the theatrical "Crockett," which I have drawn on in making my own summary discussion below.

2. John Seelye, "A Well-Wrought Crockett: Or, How the Fakelorists Passed Through the Credibility Gap and Discovered Kentucky," in Lofaro, *Davy Crockett*, 21–45.

3. Joseph Arpad, "John Wesley Jarvis, James Kirke Paulding, and Colonel Nimrod Wildfire," *New York Folklore Quarterly* 21 (1965): 92–106. Hauck alludes to this important essay, from which much revisionist research has dated, as a check of the index to Lofaro's collection will reveal. The engraving and the woodcut are reproduced in Hauck's article, 106–7.

4. Richard Bernheimer, *Wild Men in the Middle Ages: A Study in Art, Sentiment, and Demonology*, (Cambridge, Mass.: Harvard University Press, 1952). See also Edward Dudley and Maximillian E. Novak, eds., *The Wild Man Within: An Image in Western Thought from the Renaissance to Romanticism* (Pittsburgh: University of Pittsburgh Press, 1972), a collection of essays built on Bernheimer's book, to which the present effort is much indebted.

5. Arthur Dickson, *Valentine and Orson: A Study in Late Medieval Romance* (New York: Columbia University Press, 1929), especially Appendix 2, "*Valentine and Orson* in English," which reveals that Dibden's play, first published in 1804,

Robinson Crusoe by Grandville. This fanciful monument brings together
Crusoe, his wild-man costume, dog, and parrot, with the two conceptions of
the American Indian as cannibal and incipient Christian, contraries that match
the two versions of the wild man as defined by Bernheimer. Why the statue is
inscribed "Fernand Suez" remains an iconographic puzzle, but the congruency
of the symbols (including the goats with their Pan-like faces) otherwise
confirms the genesis of the Wild Man in Europe and America. Courtesy,
American Antiquarian Society.

had gone through five editions by 1830, and seems to have inspired an equal number of chapbooks. According to Dickson, "Professor R. H. Rusk has notes of nine performances [of Dibden's play] in Louisville, Cincinnati, and Detroit, between 1831 and 1838" (292). Thus Dibden's *Orson* seems to have played John the Baptist for American versions of the myth soon to burst on the western scene.

6. Catherine Albanese, "Davy Crockett and the Wild Man; Or, The Metaphysics of the *Longue Durée*," in Lofaro, 80–101. See also Carroll Smith-Rosenberg, "Davy Crockett as Trickster: Pornography, Liminality, and Symbolic Inversion in Victorian America," in *Disorderly Conduct: Visions of Gender in Victorian America*, ed. Carroll Smith-Rosenberg, (New York: Alfred A. Knopf, 1985), 90–108. Smith-Rosenberg's "Crockett" is derived from the most violent of the almanacs.

7. Maurice Agulon, *Marianne into Battle: Republican Imagery and Symbolism in France, 1789–1880*, (Cambridge: Cambridge University Press, 1981), 44–45. See also Marvin Trachtenberg, *The Statue of Liberty*, (New York: Viking, 1976), especially Chapter 3, "Liberty."

8. Agulon, 11, quoting "the great treatise *Iconologie*, illustrated with the engravings of Gravelot and Cochin." On page 20 there appears an "allegory of the Republic" by Prudhon, showing Liberty in the company of both a cat *and* a lion, as well as a sheep.

9. In "'Rational Exultation': The Erie Canal Celebration," I allude to this peculiar craft as one element in a carefully contrived iconographic display by means of which New Yorkers asserted the complex meaning of the canal's completion, worth mentioning here as a prolonged demonstration of the sophisticated symbolism Americans were capable of mounting during the years when Davy Crockett emerged as a popular icon (*Proceedings of the American Antiquarian Society*, 94 [October 1984], 256–57). It should also be noted here that the transformation of the historic David to the "mythic" Davy Crockett was to a very large extent the work of the Whig Party, who brought considerable iconographic ingenuity to the American political process.

10. *William Tell, the Patriot of Switzerland. . . . To which is added, Andreas Hofer, the "Tell" of the Tyrol. Illustrated with Engravings on Wood, by Butler* (New York: Wiley and Putnam, 1845), 39. Further page citations will appear parenthetically in the text.

11. Bernheimer, *passim* in cf. Erhard Bahr, "Papageno: The Unenlightened Wild Man in Eighteenth-Century Germany," in *The Wild Man Within*, 249. To be fair to Bahr, his specific reference is to Schiller's hero, not the legendary original.

12. Another possible model was William Dunlap's drama *The Archers* (1798), a play about William Tell based very closely on the story as told by Florian. In *Prodigals & Pilgrims: The American Revolution Against Patriarchal Authority, 1759–1800*, (Cambridge: Cambridge University Press, 1982), Jay Fliegelman discusses Dunlap's play in relation to the emerging myth of George Washington, but in a note he points out "Tell's association with the forest (and its values), his marksmanship, and his commitment to freedom. The figure of Tell may thus lie somewhere behind Fenimore Cooper's Natty Bumppo, a figure whose European ancestry has been insufficiently investigated" (307). Equally worth investigation is the European ances-

try of Daniel Boone, as the "legendary" creation of myth-makers like schoolteacher John Filson, writers of considerable sophistication. But behind both Tell and Boone (as well as Bumppo and Davy Crockett) stands the archetypal Wild Man, with implications to the genesis of our folk heroes and popular literature that I intend to develop further in another place.

13. See the introduction by James N. Tidwell to his edition of *The Lion of the West*, (Stanford, Calif.: Standford University Press, 1954), 7–14. A photocopy reprint of Tidwell's edition is now available through the Multimedia Studies in American Drama, Humanities Institute, Brooklyn College. Professor Vera Jiji, program director for the Program for Culture at Play at Brooklyn College, has also prepared a valuable collection of background information concerning Paulding's play, including contemporary reviews of the several versions, entitled *Showcasing American Drama: A Handbook of Source Materials on "The Lion of the West" by J. K. Paulding* (Brooklyn: Humanities Institute, 1983).

14. *Lion of the West*, Tidwell edition, 57. Further page citations to this edition will appear parenthetically in the text.

15. See Bernheimer, Chapter 5, "The Erotic Connotations," but especially pages 122–26. Bernheimer concludes that the abduction motif is not primarily erotic: "When whisking the lady away to his residence beyond the great divide, the wild man acts . . . as a demon of death" (126). The burden of his evidence suggests otherwise.

16. Bernheimer, 112–25: "She has, to use the medieval term, captured him to subject him to her quieting and civilizing influence."

17. Annette Kolodny, *The Land Before Her: Fantasy and Experience of the American Frontiers, 1630–1860*, (Chapel Hill: University of North Carolina Press, 1984), especially "Book Three: Repossessing Eden, 1850–1860."

18. Ann Douglas, *The Feminization of American Culture* (New York: Knopf, 1977): "Between 1820 and 1875, in the midst of the transformation of the American economy into the most powerfully aggressive capitalist system in the world, American culture seemed bent on establishing a perpetual Mother's Day" (6).

19. Barrett H. Clark, ed., *Davy Crockett & Other Plays, America's Lost Plays*, (Bloomington: Indiana University Press, 1963), 4:122. Further page citations to this edition will appear parenthetically in the text.

20. Henry Nash Smith, *Virgin Land: The American West as Symbol and Myth*, (Cambridge, Mass.: Harvard University Press, 1950), 64–70.

21. Owen Wister, "The Story of Chalkeye: A Wind River Romance," *American West* (January/February, 1984): 38–47. Of two chapters and an unfinished third, only the completed chapters are published, with an accompanying essay by Wallace Stegner.

22. Owen, Wister, *The Virginian: A Horseman of the Plains*, edited by John Seelye (New York and London: Penguin Books, 1988), 105. Relevant discussion of the Wild Man theme may be found in the introduction to this edition. Further citations will appear parenthetically in the text.

23. In "'When You Call Me That . . . ': Tall Talk and Male Hegemony in *The Virginian*," Lee Clark Mitchell sets Wister's novel against the women's rights issue,

Wyoming having passed women's suffrage legislation as early as 1869, and sees *The Virginian* as a negative response, for Wister not only ignores Wyoming's reputation as "The Equality State," but overrides it by mounting a defense of male hegemony (*PMLA* 102 [1987], 66–77). Mitchell provides an extended discussion of the literature urged on the Virginian by the schoolteacher, part of his emphasis on the importance of "talk" (whether "tall" or sophisticated word-play) to the novel, with conclusions similar to my own. I am indebted to my colleague, David Leverenz, for showing me a manuscript copy of Mitchell's article prior to its publication, as well as for other help at a late stage in the composition of my own essay.

24. John Cawelti, *Adventure, Mystery, and Romance: Formula Stories as Art and Popular Culture*, (Chicago: University of Chicago Press, 1976), 224–25.

25. In 1907, Wister wrote *The Seven Ages of Washington*, a hagiographic biography. The allusion to Washington's spelling comes late in Chapter 6 of *The Virginian*, page 64 of the edition cited herein. From the start, moreover, as Mitchell demonstrates, the Virginian has exercised "rhetorical control" over the schoolteacher, relying on his native wit and essential superiority.

26. Wister may have been following the lead of Cooper, who in *The Spy* (1821) celebrated the Era of Good Feelings by marrying a daughter of a New York Loyalist to a patriot officer from Virginia. In *The Prairie* (1827), Cooper likewise married a Louisiana belle of Hispanic origins to a young American officer of Virginian descent. Wister also had available the example of John William DeForest's *Miss Ravenel's Conversion from Secession to Loyalty* (1867), Reconstructionist fiction of the deepest dye, which ends with a marriage between the titular heroine (who is from New Orleans) and an abolitionist from New England. Wister's attitude toward the "race question," however, reveals his own southern (maternal) heritage, and resulted in *Lady Baltimore* (1906), his only novel after *The Virginian*. As Mitchell demonstrates, Wister uses his fiction to underwrite a highly conservative politics. See also Darwin Payne, *Owen Wister: Chronicler of the West, Gentleman of the East*, (Dallas: Southern Methodist University Press, 1985): "Along with millions of other Americans, four decades after the Emancipation Proclamation, Wister still assumed the black man to be inferior and found evidence of this in the shape of the skulls" (238). Ironically, his bride in 1898, Mary Channing Wister (also called "Molly") was the granddaughter of William Ellery Channing and a tireless civic worker. As Payne demonstrates, the Virginian's honeymoon was inspired by Wister's own.

The Real Davy Crocketts

CREATIVE AUTOBIOGRAPHY

AND THE INVENTION OF HIS LEGEND

Richard Boyd Hauck

The public celebrations, the fresh scholarship, and the media ballyhoo that marked the bicentennial of Crockett's birth in 1986 were not only signs that Davy is well remembered, but also proof that he has escaped the mines of Mexico, the hooks of the hoaxers, the sticky soup of the sentimentalizers, and the dinky darts of his dastardly detractors, and is now emerging in yet another amazing avatar. As Walter Blair says, "'Bout time ol' Davy got borned agin."[1] What will the new Davy Crockett look like? The full-length portrait of him painted by John Gadsby Chapman in 1834 shows that Crockett was not, as legend has it, six feet four in his stocking feet; his hunting clothes were linsey-woolsey with a short fringe, not the extravagantly fringed deerskins he always wears in the movies; and his hat was not made of fur.[2] The revisionist version of Crockett might be a gentle, soft-spoken man, slightly potbellied, middle-aged, fond of whiskey and women, eccentric to the point of being quirky, and every bit of five feet four with his moccasins on. Then again, if such a "realistic" portrayal of Crockett did make him short and plump instead of tall and lean, it would be the first time in history that the growth of his legend was impeded by the facts.

There is, however, one threat to the health of Davy's legend, and I am hopeful that the Crockett renaissance will serve as the cure. It sometimes seems that Davy might be killed off by an overdose of seriousness. Media accounts of the bicentennial and its attendant scholarship have indicated that people are afraid historians will debunk the legend to death. Was Crockett really a hero? If he wasn't, the assumption is, then the legend is merely a fake.

The fact is that the scholarship of the last decade is not at all characterized by debunking. Oddly enough, I have yet to see a newspaper account that properly names James A. Shackford and Stanley J. Folmsbee, whose

John Gadsby Chapman's oil portrait of Congressman Crockett painted in 1834. Harry Ransom Humanities Research Center Art Collection, The University of Texas at Austin.

most important books appeared respectively in 1956 and 1973, as the debunkers of Crockett's legend. Shackford was shocked by expansions wrought upon Crockett's history by Walter Blair and Constance Rourke; Folmsbee fretted about the generous cinematic portrayals of Davy given us by Fess Parker and John Wayne.[3] More recently, scholars from Dan Kilgore in *How Did Davy Die?* to the authors of Michael A. Lofaro's bicentennial collection and the present volume have instead been fascinated by the dynamics of legend building.[4] We have addressed the facts, declared Davy a hero both in spite of and because of the facts, and tried to show that the real excitement of the story lies with the ongoing, ever-expanding collective creation that constitutes the unlimited set of real Davy Crocketts.

The problem, as I see it, starts in a common and understandable misconception about historical factuality, a misconception that afflicts some formal historians as well as laymen. One of the risks in doing history is the easy confusion of the written account with the facts upon which it is based. The word *history* means both things: that which happened, and any record of that which happened. Just as literary critics sometimes forget that their interpretation is not to be confused with the truth that lies in the text interpreted, historians sometimes forget they are, after all, storytellers. The problem also has to do with our natural tendency to forget that we are conscious creatures whose idea of reality is just that — an idea of reality. In short, there once was a real David Crockett, but now his life can be retrieved only as a story. A story always reflects realities outside itself, but it is always a separate reality in itself as well.

The dynamic, ever-expanding legend of Davy Crockett is yet another reality. It is made up of a huge body of facts, one that grew enormously in 1986 as folks everywhere took fresh notice of Davy's story, thus making many new contributions to it. The story of how Davy's legend is constantly re-created tells us more about the people who participate in the process than it does about the original David. Serious-minded historians like Shackford and Folmsbee declared that the artifacts of the legend are lies that get in the way of finding out the truth. Certainly it is necessary to separate legendary artifacts from biography, but to dismiss the legend's artifacts as lies is to miss the rest of the story. The historical David Crockett can be understood very well if he is viewed as a fiction, and the many fictional Davy Crocketts who are the artifacts of the legend can be well understood as facts. In the long run, posterity takes the legendary Crockett to be the primary reality. It is this imaginary construction that expresses, for better or for worse, the hopes and values of Americans, and of a good many people in other countries who are fascinated by the strange and powerful components of the myth of the American West.

The Crockett who is the hero of many different kinds of fiction was of course born of the words and deeds of the living, historical David. This fictional Davy was also shaped by promotional acts performed upon Crockett's image by others, but the appropriate starting point for the study of the whole story is an examination of the historical David's deliberate contributions to his own legend. The dynamic processes that constitute his role include several kinds of artistry: storytelling and joking, theatricality or acting, politicking and oratory, and, above all, the art of creative autobiography.

A creative autobiographer, whether or not he or she ever writes a single word, is one who consciously chooses a life of the imagination after having discovered that the word *history* is synonymous with the word *story*. This person understands that the word *truth* actually refers to an interpretation powerful enough to invite the confidence of enough people willing to agree that it is a truth. The creative autobiographer lives by fiction, and he or she will also be, to a greater or lesser degree, a con artist whose motives are not necessarily selfish.

The tangible autobiography that appears in written form is an act of self-creation at least twice over. It tells the story of how its author created himself, and in the process it re-creates the author as the "voice" of a richly suggestive text. We, the readers, see the person told about—the author as a young man or woman, perhaps; and we also develop an idea of the writer—a picture or image we infer from the voice on the page—that may be quite different from the younger person the writer is telling about. Often, we refer to this voice or presence in the text as a "persona." On top of all this, no autobiographer ever tells the whole truth—it is actually impossible to do so. The writer tells us about the person he *thinks* he is, or more likely, the person he *wants to be*, or most likely, the person he *wants us to think he is*. But no one expects an autobiography to be the mere record of a person's life anyway. We read it to understand the way the author's mind works, to watch him weave a story of his life.

Therefore, even though we usually choose to trust the words of the persona in an autobiography, we interpret the story as if it were a fiction, one that is presumably truth*ful* whether or not it is literally true. Crockett's autobiography, *A Narrative of the Life of David Crockett* (1834), is even more transparently a truthful fiction than many autobiographies. He expresses his own awareness of this when he says his book is designed to portray "the very image of its author."[5] This is not an unsophisticated statement. In it Crockett acknowledges that he is a creating a persona, recognizing that no such picture could ever be purely realistic. He understands that what we readers want is an artful work that evokes in our minds accurate suggestions of the reality to which it refers. Crockett thus has a great deal of control over the picture of him we will develop, and he knows that his first task is to speak in a way that gains our confidence. It is also useful to note that the *Narrative* was written as a campaign autobiography—one of those books carefully designed to show voters why they ought to elect the author to public office.

One of the fortuitous little facts of David Crockett's life is that he owned a copy of Benjamin Franklin's *Autobiography*, and he signed his name in it.[6] He likely got from Franklin the idea of using the common notation "Written by Himself" following the title of his *Narrative*. All this does not tell us, of course, that he read Franklin's book, but I am perfectly confident that he did. I like to think of Benjamin Franklin's *Autobiography* as the first great American comic novel. It is the absolutely definitive example of a self-created story of self-creation, written by America's definitive self-made man.

A comparison of Franklin and Crockett as autobiographers is both enlightening and entertaining. Both men were conscious of their image, developed it, expanded it, and to a considerable extent controlled it. Both loved joking and storytelling. Both led lives that we now view as exemplary of the American tradition of independence and self-reliance: they started out with no money, no name, and no connections and went on to create their own mark on history.

Both men coined aphorisms by paraphrasing and twisting old saws into distinctive American gems of folksy wisdom. Franklin took proverbs dating from antiquity and changed them into "Fish and visitors stink in three days" or "'Tis hard for an empty bag to stand upright." Crockett took Andrew Jackson's complex piece of advice on training troops and transformed it into "Be always sure you're right—then go ahead."[7] Both Franklin and Crockett understood that the person who controls the words—the language we assign to events—is the person who controls events. Fortunately, both were basically honest, good-hearted men who generally put the public welfare ahead of their own interests.

In literary tradition, the figure of the confidence man has two roles: in one he is an image of the satanic deceiver; in the other he is the self-reliant common man who has learned how to beat the devil at his own game. In this latter sense, Franklin is both a man of confidence and a confidence man. He knew how to work, and his *Autobiography* is the Bible of the work ethic, but throughout the book he teaches us also that it isn't enough to work—you have to be sure others see you working. It is regrettable that most people base their judgments upon appearances, but this is a fact of life; therefore, it is wise to pay as much attention to appearances as to realities.

Indeed, it sometimes seems that Franklin recommends that if one is forced to choose, it is best to tend to the appearances. When an army chaplain complained that the troops would not come to meeting, Franklin put him in charge of the daily ration of rum, which the good reverend dispensed every morning and evening—after prayers. "Never," Franklin tells us, "were Prayers more generally and more punctually attended."[8] Franklin says nothing about the reality of any possible connection between attendance at prayer meeting and the spiritual condition of the men. This does not worry him. Elsewhere, he tells how he defended a minister who plagiarized the sermons he gave: "I rather approv'd his giving us good Sermons compos'd by others, than bad ones of his own Manufacture."[9]

In his famous list of thirteen virtues, under "Humility," Franklin recommends, "Imitate Jesus and Socrates." What in the world does this mean? "Imitate" is the first verb of the confidence man's creed. "I cannot," Franklin says, "boast of much Success in acquiring the *Reality* of this Virtue; but I had a good deal with regard to the *Appearance* of it."[10] If he had achieved authentic humility—whatever that is—Franklin says he would have been proud of it.

Franklin tells a story of setting out on a passenger boat from Boston which was becalmed off Block Island. The sailors started fishing and caught a great many codfish, which they cleaned and fried over a stove on deck. "Hitherto," Franklin writes,

> I had stuck to my Resolution of not eating animal Food; and on this Occasion, I consider'd . . . the taking every Fish as a kind of unprovok'd Murder, since none of them had or ever could do us any Injury that might justify the Slaughter. All this seem'd very reasonable. But I had formerly been a great Lover of Fish, and when this came hot out of the Frying Pan, it smelt admirably well. I balanc'd some time between Principle and Inclination: till I recollected, that when the Fish were opened, I saw smaller Fish taken out of their Stomachs: Then, thought I, if you eat one another, I don't see why we mayn't eat you. So I din'd

upon Cod very heartily and continu'd to eat with other People, returning only now and then occasionally to a vegetable Diet. So convenient a thing it is to be a *reasonable Creature*, since it enables one to find or make a Reason for everything one has a mind to do.[11]

It is said that when Franklin went to France to solicit help for the American Revolution, he won the hearts and minds of the court by wearing his fur cap and deerskins. They expected him to look like the very type of the frontiersman, the American backwoods philosopher, so he dressed accordingly (see portrait on p. 156). Was it a disguise? Was it theater? Was it a con game? Was it really the very image of the man? Of course. He made it true. Is this story itself true? If it isn't, it should be.

Indeed, this is the way we seem to feel about the stories of all legendary heroes—if they are not true, they should be. We feel this way because we, the inheritors of the ongoing, ever-expanding story, are ourselves perpetuators of the legend, which is to say we are also coauthors. But the first author of Davy's story really was the David Crockett who was born in 1786 in Tennessee, and it was he who created the first and best ending for it, some fifty years later at the Alamo.

Crockett's autobiography is an imaginative book, and his imagination is one of its subjects. It is a window on the style of the man, a record of how he thought, how he talked, how he joked and told stories. The Crockett legend is a comic legend, and the voice of the historical man himself, as it comes to us in the *Narrative*, is an image against which all other versions of Davy Crockett are measured. With the help of his congressional colleague from Kentucky, Thomas Chilton, Crockett deliberately crafted a style of prose that would evoke backwoods speech.[12] Take any page and note the genuine, downhome American idioms (though quite a few, I suspect, are original inventions): "For I know'd if [the bear] got hold of me, he would hug me altogether too close for comfort. I went to my gun and hastily loaded her again, and shot him the third time, which killed him good." "I thought I could shoot by guess"; "give him a dig with my butcher"; "thinking on what a hobble we had got into"; "the hatchway into the cabin came slap down"; "we were now floating sideways, and the boat I was in was the hindmost as we went"; "I know'd well enough it was neck or nothing, come out or sink"; "I was in a pretty pickle"; and "I reckon I looked like a pretty cracklin' ever to get to Congress."[13]

Like Benjamin Franklin, Crockett is certainly in no hurry to tell us anything about his real faults. He touches instead upon what Franklin called "errata" — typographical errors on the pages of life. Crockett admits to liking whiskey, suggests he prefers hunting and electioneering to hard work, looks honestly and realistically at his role in some very sordid atrocities committed during the Creek wars. But notice how he makes a virtue out of his backwoods naiveté. If he is unlettered, so are most of his constituents; indeed, to be uneducated is to be honest, commonsensible, and forthright. The folks back home do not trust worldly people or rich people, let alone scholars.

Crockett not only tells us that he consciously created his own image, he tells us how he did it. And in telling us, of course, he recapitulates the creation, re-creating himself before our very eyes:

> . . . when I set out electioneering, I would go prepared to put every man on as good footing when I left him as I found him on. I would therefore have me a large buckskin hunting-shirt made, with a couple of pockets holding about a peck each . . . in one I would carry a great big twist of tobacco, and in the other my bottle of liquor; for I knowed when I met a man and offered him a dram, he would throw out his quid of tobacco to take one, and after he had taken his horn, I would out with my twist and give him another chaw. And in this way he would not be worse off than when I found him; and I would be sure to leave him in a first-rate good humour.[14]

Every politician should do so well by us.

This crucial anecdote serves as a model for how Crockett invented his role. Even if he did not really wear such a jacket, his telling of this story creates an image of his attitudes and imagination that spotlights the jacket as its centerpiece. The picture lodges firmly in the mind of the reader. The stereotype of the frontiersman was already established by the time Crockett took it up, but he tailored it to his own purposes, playing the role beautifully, enhancing it, refabricating it, making it very much his own. The act included several parts, all interrelated and coordinated: he was the bear hunter, the common man who spoke directly to the point, a yarnspinner of uncommon talent, an irreverent humorist whose satirical barbs deflated sacred cows like burst balloons, a modest good old boy, the unschooled self-reliant backwoodsman.

Crockett's reputation as a crack shot became the very emblem of his role, and this is true for both the story of his life and the story of his legend. The generative puns spin off easily and in profusion: he displayed a "rifle-shot wit"; he was a "straight-shooter" in all his dealings. The painter John Gadsby Chapman wrote that Crockett's speech "fell upon the ear meaningly and consistent as might the crack of his rifle . . . his ideas flowed most naturally and found most emphatic and unrestrained utterance."[15]

Crockett was a common man who displayed an uncommon style. That he died well at the Alamo is of less importance to his image than the fact that he lived well as a storyteller and comedian. These are not trivial talents. Humor, especially in the face of adversity and danger, is one of the highest forms of courage. Life on the frontier was generally nasty and short, and those last days at the Alamo were certainly brutish. Humor is a weapon, both defensive and offensive, and as a trait it is absolutely central to the strongest American legends and types. Humor in the face of death is of course a mark of unmotivated confidence—faith in spite of all the evidence that faith will not avail. In this sense, humor is pure art, an act of inexplicable creativity.

It is the humor of Crockett's character that persists into his many legendary avatars and binds them together. This humor is distinguished by a handful of powerful components: confidence, wit, and improvisation. Bragging, which appears to be a strong expression of confidence, is best understood as a con game the bragger (not to be confused with "braggart") plays to overcome both his listener's and his own lack of confidence.

Bragging is associated with the tall tale, which is yet another kind of con game, one that is distinguished by the fact that all the players, teller and audience alike, know it is a con game. The teller takes the part of con artist and always begins his yarn by saying, "Now, this is a true story . . . ," and the listeners agree to take the role of the con man's mark, pretending to believe that the story is true. If there is a naive outsider present, this person may become the victim of the game should he either believe the story or challenge the teller's veracity. Otherwise, all the listeners accept the yarn in credulous amazement, though someone may make a *mock* challenge to the teller, in which case the challenger will be up next to tell a story. No one wants the story to be literally true; they ask to have their imaginations stretched. Anyone who gets serious is out of the game.

David Crockett was himself a good teller of tall tales. Moreover, the legendary figure promoted after his death by the perpetrators of the Crockett almanacs—the comic Davy that was resurrected by Constance Rourke and Walter Blair—is often the *hero* of a tall tale. He rode a lightning bolt like a horse, he drank up the Gulf of Mexico, he lit his pipe on the fire of the sun.[16] In the many theatrical versions of Davy's character, this trait persists; it was one of the strongest aspects of both Fess Parker's and John Wayne's portrayals. The first great theatrical expression of the frontiersman type to be linked with David Crockett was Nimrod Wildfire, as played by the great James Hackett, in James Kirke Paulding's *The Lion of the West* (1831), and it is this character who stamped into the American idiom the famous speech, "I'm half horse, half alligator, and I can lick my weight in wildcats."[17] The form of this bragging was already very old, probably having come over from Europe, but in the natural association of Wildfire and Crockett, the hybrid creature was transformed into what *looks* like an indigenous American animal.

That the primary characterizations of Davy from 1831 to the present have been perpetrated upon the stage is another of those fortuitous little facts. Acting is a con game; the con game is a form of theater. The plays and movies depicting Crockett have always retained the spirit of this association. What Frank Mayo's Davy lacked in book learning, he made up in confidence. Fess Parker made Davy's serious ideals convincing and at the same time kept that constant touch of humor. When Parker's Davy first speaks to Congress, he knows they think he's a bumpkin, and he plays to their expectations; but he also knows that they know he knows what they know: that beneath the disguise, or behind the act, is a voice to be reckoned with. Thus they begin by laughing at him, but soon they find themselves laughing with him. I suspect that Parker's portrayal may be very faithful to the kind of success the historical Crockett had when he joked and told stories to win the hearts and minds of his constituents.[18]

One of my favorite moments in John Wayne's movie *The Alamo* occurs when Travis, played by Laurence Harvey, accuses Crockett of making it all up: his clothes are stereotypical, his speech is phony, his mannerisms are a pose, and he has come to the Alamo just to enhance his reputation by getting into the fight. Wayne's Crockett does not deny the charge. Instead, he replies, "Don't tell my Tennesseans that—they think they came to Texas to hunt and get drunk." Then he says he came to the Alamo to fight for what's right.[19] To portray Crockett accurately, John Wayne had only to be himself, drawing on his own image as the self-made American western hero.

But if his image is largely an invention, does this mean Davy Crockett isn't real? Was he *truly* a hero? Asking this is like asking, "Is it true that he climbed the mountain and twisted the tail off the comet?" Only the humorless cynic would deny it. We are entitled to our collective truthful fiction. My own study of Crockett's life and legend reveals him to be less like Superman and more like Huck Finn: naive, good-hearted, and common-sensible, but sometimes confused, often victimized, quick-witted and fleet of foot, but always leaping from one jam into another. He is more like Proteus than Prometheus, elusive and changeable to the point of being malleable: in character, an improviser, but subject also to shapes we, the audience, wish to impose upon him.

As a confidence man, Crockett had only modest success; if he had had the talent for cultivating strong political alliances, he just might have won an election for president. The people of America loved his refreshing, irreverent, straightforward style. He must have gone to the Alamo believing he had chosen the right path to fame and political fortune in Texas. It was not in his nature to settle down in the Red River Valley as land agent, as attractive as that prospect must have been.[20] He belonged on his horse, riding west, meeting the challenge, winning the prize by shooting straighter than anybody else. He saw himself much as the world had come to see him, and he believed in it. If he had been the more powerful, self-interested con man, he would have played it safe and let others pay the cost. But then we would never have found ourselves celebrating his legend.

I believe David Crockett went to the Alamo because he intended to live up to his legend. It had by now expanded far beyond anything he could have imagined, but he had fathered it, and perhaps he saw here the opportunity to reclaim it. His unforeseen sacrifice became the awful but ironically appropriate ending to his act of creative autobiography. I picture him there on March 6, 1836, looking out over the battlement, facing the fate now written clearly in a drama that had, once again, gotten out of his hands. A good day to die, but much too early in the morning. Just time enough for one last joke. "Wal, I'll be shot. I told 'em back home they could go to Hell, and I'd go to Texas. Didn't reckon then that Texas would turn out to be Hell." As a modest contribution to the living truthful fiction of Davy Crockett, this picture is a story that ought to be true, even if it isn't.

NOTES

1. "Heroes," *Chicago Sun Times,* March 2, 1986, Book Week Sec., 27. See also Walter Blair's Introduction to the present volume.

2. The painting, 24½ inches by 16½ inches, oil on canvas, is in the Harry Ransom Humanities Research Center Art Collection, University of Texas at Austin. Recent reprintings include the cover of Richard Boyd Hauck, *Davy Crockett: A Handbook* (Lincoln: University of Nebraska Press, 1986; reprint of *Crockett: A Bio-*

Bibliography, Westport, Conn.: Greenwood Press, 1982), see also p. 107; Michael A. Lofaro, ed., *Davy Crockett: The Man, The Legend, The Legacy, 1786–1986* (Knoxville: University of Tennessee Press, 1985), 6. For commentary on the painting, see Hauck, *Davy Crockett*, 60-67; James A. Shackford, *David Crockett: The Man and the Legend* (Chapel Hill: University of North Carolina Press, 1956; reprint, 1986), 288-89; Curtis Carroll Davis, "A Legend at Full-Length: Mr. Chapman Paints Colonel Crockett—and Tells about It," *Proceedings of the American Antiquarian Society* 69 (1960), 155-74.

3. Shackford's biography of Crockett was published in 1956; after his death, Stanley J. Folmsbee later completed the work that Shackford had begun on an edition of Crockett's autobiography: James A. Shackford and Stanley J. Folmsbee, eds., *A Narrative of the Life of David Crockett of Tennessee* (Knoxville: University of Tennessee Press, 1973), with annotations and introduction, a facsimile of the first edition by Carey & Hart of Philadelphia, 1834; hereafter cited as *Narrative*.

4. *How Did Davy Die?* (College Station: Texas A&M University Press, 1978); Lofaro, *Davy Crockett*.

5. *Narrative*, ii.

6. See Joseph J. Arpad's edition of the *Narrative* (New Haven, Conn.: College & University Press, 1972), 29; and Hauck, *Davy Crockett*, 5-6. For information on Crockett's copy of Franklin's *Autobiography*, see James C. Kelly and Frederick S. Voss, *Davy Crockett, Gentleman from the Cane: An Exhibition Commemorating Crockett's Life and Legend on the 200th Anniversary of His Birth* (Washington: Smithsonian Institution, and Nashville: Tennessee State Museum, 1986), 38-39.

7. Shackford, 26.

8. J.A. Leo Lemay and P.M. Zall, eds., *Benjamin Franklin's Autobiography* (New York: W.W. Norton, 1986), 126-27. The text of this superb edition, which also includes useful notes and critical material, is based on the genetic text prepared by the same editors and published as *The Autobiography of Benjamin Franklin* (Knoxville: The University of Tennessee Press, 1981). A good recent biography that takes account of Franklin's sense of humor and his love of inventive games is Esmond Wright, *Franklin of Philadelphia* (Cambridge, Mass.: Harvard University Press, 1986); see also Richard Boyd Hauck, *A Cheerful Nihilism: Confidence and "The Absurd" in American Humorous Fiction* (Bloomington: Indiana University Press, 1971), 32-39.

9. *Franklin's Autobiography*, 82.

10. Ibid., 67-68, 75.

11. Ibid., 28.

12. *Narrative*, xvi; Hauck, *Davy Crockett*, 4-5; Shackford, 154.

13. *Narrative*, 164, 188, 190, 196, 197, 198.

14. Ibid., 169.

15. Davis, 170; see Hauck, *Davy Crockett*, 60-67.

16. Walter Blair, *Davy Crockett: Legendary Frontier Hero*, rev. ed. (Springfield, Ill.: Lincoln-Herndon Press, 1986); Constance Rourke, *Davy Crockett* (New York: Harcourt, 1934).

17. James Kirke Paulding, *The Lion of the West; Retitled The Kentuckian, or A Trip to New York: A Farce in Two Acts,* ed. James N. Tidwell (Stanford, Calif.: Stanford University Press, 1954). See also Vera Jiji, ed., *Showcasing American Drama: A Handbook of Source Materials on "The Lion of the West"* (Brooklyn: Humanities Institute, Booklyn College, 1983).

18. From 1872 to 1896, Frank Mayo acted in, and continually revised, Frank Murdock's melodrama *Davy Crockett: Or, Be Sure You're Right, Then Go Ahead.* The play can be found in *America's Lost Plays,* ed. Isaac Goldberg and Hubert Heffner (1940; reprint, Bloomington: Indiana University Press, 1963), 4:115-48. Fess Parker starred in *Davy Crockett, King of the Wild Frontier* and *Davy Crockett and the River Pirates,* Walt Disney Productions, 1955, 1956.

19. *The Alamo,* United Artists, 1960. For a discussion of Crockett in the theater and movies, see Hauck, "Making It All Up: Davy Crockett in the Theater," in Lofaro, *Davy Crockett,* 102-23. For a Crockett filmography, see Miles Tanenbaum, "Following Davy's Trail: A Crockett Bibliography," in this volume.

20. See Hauck, *Davy Crockett,* 47-54.

Following Davy's Trail

A CROCKETT BIBLIOGRAPHY

Miles Tanenbaum

"Davy Crockett never a hero, Texas historian [Dan Kilgore] now claims."[1] "Kilgore says Davy Crockett was a flop and a fink and maybe a coward to boot."[2] "'Them's Fightin' Words. Davy's Legend Smudged,' ran the headline of the *Corpus Christi Times*."[3]

These overreactions to Dan Kilgore's controversial study of Crockett's death, *How Did Davy Die?* are just one example of how Crockett scholarship has people "riled up." An incredulous reaction to Michael A. Lofaro's *Davy Crockett: The Man, The Legend, The Legacy, 1786–1986*, was, "He didn't wear a coonskin cap? He didn't amount to much in Congress? He didn't go down fighting at the Alamo? Say it ain't so, Davy Crockett,"[4] and Ann Tillman, a Crockett County (Tennessee) Librarian, said, "We don't care what the scholars say. True or false, he's still our folk hero."[5]

Why are people irate about David Crockett scholarship?[6] The problem is a simple case of mistaken identity. Walter Blair's article "Six Davy Crocketts" (1940) helps to unravel the controversy. Blair identifies six Crocketts — first, the "flesh and blood" David; second, "a Westernized version of a fool character," a creation of the Whig Party when Crockett supported Andrew Jackson; third, "a Westernized version of Poor Richard, uneducated but rich in common sense gained by experience," a creation of Jackson supporters when Crockett was a Jackson supporter; fourth, the backwoodsman portrayed as Crockett number two, but this man was "not only stupid and clownish but also vicious," a creation of Jackson supporters when Crockett became anti-Jackson; fifth, the common-sense Crockett number three magnified, now a "homespun oracle . . . abundantly blessed with unerring horse sense," a creation of the Whigs when Crockett became anti-Jackson; and finally the sixth Crockett, "the mythical demigod whose fantastic life history was unfolded in the almanacs."[7]

In the midst of all this confusion, the real David Crockett was easily obscured and temporarily forgotten, the same problem that exists today when people read modern Crockett scholarship. For example, when Dan Kilgore wrote *How Did Davy Die?* he was writing about the real David Crockett. However, many readers are familiar only with the Davy Crockett films, where he is portrayed by actors like Fess Parker and John Wayne. The film Davy is a cross between the frontier man of principle (Crockett number three) and Davy the superhero (Crockett number six). Readers assumed Kilgore was writing about the Davy they knew, who would never surrender as any other sane man would when his ammunition ran out and he was surrounded by an overwhelming force. And the film Davy did not surrender; he fought bravely (and perhaps foolishly) to the end, battering the enemy with his broken rifle. The real Crockett surrendered, but unfortunately it made no difference. A reader disappointed by the historical Crockett labeled Kilgore "'a mealy-mouth intellectual' who deserved to 'have his mouth washed out with soap,'"[8] but the Crockett identity crisis was not Kilgore's fault.

New scholarship on David and the legendary Davys has created many new trails for the interested reader. This bibliography attempts to clear the pathways by organizing Crockett literature into ten categories, each focusing on different aspects of the man and the legend, to enable readers to choose which of the many Crockett trails they wish to follow.

The bibliography's first section lists primary materials – letters written by David, legal documents (land deeds, marriage licenses, etc.), and pertinent letters written by family members and contemporaries. James Atkins Shackford's doctoral dissertation, "The Autobiography of David Crockett," is the only previous work to list and collect these documents. Shackford located forty-nine Crockett letters (the locations of seventy letters are listed here, plus another twenty listed as sold in *American Book Prices Current*), but unfortunately his work is not easily available to the general public.[9] The letters are listed chronologically followed by information about each letter's whereabouts; most of the letters are scattered across the country in libraries.[10] These documents present the real David in his own words and are not only important historically but provide an intriguing personal view of the man as well.

The second section of the bibliography lists works about the historical David Crockett. Many of these early historical works are tinged with traces of the legendary Davys. Before James Atkins Shackford's definitive biography of Crockett (1956), David Crockett's history was buried in state archives and unpublished letters. Any historical work on Crockett published before

1956, therefore, should be examined warily. Also, several works that examine the historical and legendary Crocketts, like Richard Boyd Hauck's *Crockett: A Bio-Bibliography*, are listed in both the historical and legendary sections.

The Alamo is the subject of the bibliography's third section. Like Crockett, the Alamo has a split personality. According to Paul Andrew Hutton, "There have always been two Alamos—the Alamo of historical fact and the Alamo of our collective imagination."[11] This list contains works about both Alamos but is not a comprehensive bibliography. Only recent works, important older works, and works central to Crockett scholarship are listed here. Hutton's bibliography in *Alamo Images: Changing Perceptions of a Texas Experience*, by Susan Prendergast Schoelwer with Tom W. Glaser, is an excellent follow-up to the works listed here. Also, a new book-length study of the Alamo by Hutton will soon be released.

Crockett-related newspaper articles are listed in the bibliography's next section. These articles are more often a reflection of the authors' and newspapers' opinions of David than they are factual, and many are an accurate gauge of Davy's importance in the public's mind. A comprehensive list of newspaper articles would be impossible to print; this bibliography lists only a selection of articles printed during David's lifetime and major articles from Tennessee and Texas newspapers over the past 150 years.

The next section of the bibliography lists works about the many legendary Davy Crocketts. These Crocketts include the violent, racist superman of the almanacs; the softer, more caring hero of nineteenth-century melodrama; the backwoods humorist; the fabulous hunter; the archetypal hero; and the "wild man." Only their creators' imaginations limit the number and feats of the many legendary Davys. This section is followed by a subsection listing Davy Crockett poems.

Walt Disney Productions' fertile imagination was unintentionally responsible for a Crockett revival and craze in 1955. The bibliography's sixth section is a slightly expanded version of the bibliography that appears with Margaret J. King's article "The Recycled Hero: Walt Disney's Davy Crockett." These works discuss the reasons for, effects of, the reactions to the Crockett craze, along with the broader subject of television's effects on the American public.

Disney was not the only one to produce films about Davy Crockett. The bibliography's seventh section lists works about the many Crockett films plus a Crockett filmography, which originally appeared with Richard Boyd Hauck's article "Making It All Up: Davy Crockett in the Theater."

The Disney films popularized "The Ballad of Davy Crockett," but this is just one in a long line of Crockett songs. The eighth section of the bibliography lists works about Crockett songs and two song chronologies that were originally published with Charles K. Wolfe's article "Davy Crockett Songs: Minstrel to Disney."

The bibliography's ninth section lists children's and juvenile literature dealing with Crockett. (Children's books about the Alamo are not included here; these works are listed in Paul Andrew Hutton's bibliography in *Alamo Images*.) Davy's all-American virtues—his willingness to fight and die for what he believed and his self-made man image—cast him as a role model for America's youth. Apparently Davy is a successful role model, judging from the many versions of his life written especially for children. Comic books and dime novels about Davy are listed in separate subsections at the end of this section.

The final section of the bibliography lists general and thematic works. These are books such as Robert V. Remini's three-volume biography of Andrew Jackson and thematic studies of American literature and culture, like Richard Slotkin's *Regeneration Through Violence: The Mythology of the American Frontier, 1600–1860*, which give a broader perspective on the era.

This bibliography would not be possible without the earlier bibliographic work of James Atkins Shackford, Richard Boyd Hauck, Michael A. Lofaro, Margaret J. King, Charles K. Wolfe, and Paul Andrew Hutton. For allowing me to use and expand upon their work, these scholars have my sincere thanks. In the future, new bibliographers will likely track new trails, for Michael A. Lofaro's statement rings true: "David Crockett is at times a cultural mirror that authors gaze into for various reasons and come away with a reflection of their own interests, hopes, and dreams."[12] A society can measure itself by its heroes, a function David Crockett has served in the past and will serve in the future. When David wrote "My name is making a considerable deal of fuss in the world"[13] in his 1834 autobiography, he did not realize the complete truth of his statement. This bibliography attests to the fact that the name David Crockett has made a "considerable fuss" indeed.

NOTES

1. *The Vancouver Sun,* April 22, 1978.
2. Roger Simon, *Houston Chronicle,* May 7, 1978.

3. Paul Andrew Hutton, Introduction to *Alamo Images: Changing Perspectives of a Texas Experience*, by Susan Prendergast Schoelwer (Dallas: DeGolyer Library and Southern Methodist University Press, 1985), 15–16.

4. John Helyar, "Davy Crockett Was No Great Shakes, The Debunkers Say," *The Wall Street Journal*, July 10, 1986, A-1.

5. Helyar, 14.

6. This article follows the standard practice of referring to the historical Crockett as David and the legendary Crocketts as Davys.

7. Walter Blair, "Six Davy Crocketts," *Southwest Review* 25 (1940): 449–60.

8. Hutton, 16.

9. No complete edition of Crockett's letters exists. This author is currently compiling such an edition.

10. This section of the bibliography would not have been possible without the assistance of many librarians. A special thank you goes out to D. Strong Wyman, University of Tennessee; Marylyn Bell Hughes, Tennessee Historical Society; Charles Crawford, West Tennessee Historical Society; Barbara Kelly, Hofstra University; Karl Kabelac, University of Rochester; Donald R. Lennon, East Carolina University; Lucille Wehner, Newberry Library; Saundra Taylor and Joel Silver, Lilly Library; Jesse Lankford, North Carolina Department of Cultural Resources; Manuscript Department, New York Historical Society; Bernard Crystal, Columbia University; Robert Yampolsky, New York Public Library; Alterman Art Gallery, Dallas, Texas; Edwin Bronner, Haverford Library; Katherine Adams, University of Texas at Austin; John Grabowski, Western Reserve Historical Society; Gerald Krueger, University of Wisconsin–Oshkosh; Bernice Strong, the Library of the Daughters of the Republic of Texas at the Alamo; Herbert Cahoon, Pierpont Morgan Library; Gregory Kendall-Curtis, Maine Historical Society; Pamela Amos, University of Virginia; Robert Clayton, Marietta College; John Rhodehamel, Huntington Library; Leslie A. Morris, Rosenbach Museum and Library; Susan Weinandy, Museum and Library of Maryland History; Laura Monti, Boston Public Library; Richard Shrader, University of North Carolina at Chapel Hill; Miriam Jones, Alabama Department of Archives; Anastacio Teodoro, New York Public Library; George Miles, Yale University; Anne Marie Schaaf, Historical Society of Pennsylvania; Jill Rawnsley, University of the South; Gerald Saxon, University of Texas at Arlington; James Hutson, Library of Congress; Harold Miller, Historical Society of Wisconsin; Ralph Pugh, Chicago Historical Society; Marie Tedesco, East Tennessee State University; Ellen Hanlon, Houston Public Library; Irwin Sexton, San Antonio Public Library; Dora Guerra, University of Texas at San Antonio; Don Wismer, Maine State Library; Barbara Sheffert, Rice University; T. Joan Crouze, North Carolina Department of Cultural Resources; Charles Brown and John Neal Hoover, St. Louis Mercantile Library Association; Yesteryear Book Shop, Atlanta, Georgia; Delanie Ross, Memphis State University; Jennie Rathbun, Harvard University; Mary F. Bell, Buffalo and Erie County Historical Society; Margaret Burri, Johns Hopkins University.

11. Hutton, 3.

12. Michael A. Lofaro, Introduction to the Crockett section of *Houston and Crock-*

ett: Heroes of Tennessee and Texas, ed. Herbert L. Harper (Nashville: Tennessee Historical Commission, 1986), 129.

13. David Crockett, *A Narrative of the Life of David Crockett of the State of Tennessee* (Philadelphia: Carey & Hart, 1834). Facsimile edition with annotations and introduction edited by James A. Shackford and Stanley J. Folmsbee (Knoxville: University of Tennessee Press, 1973), 7.

PRIMARY DOCUMENTS

Letters written by David Crockett are listed chronologically, followed by the names of the libraries in which they are held (when known) and other available information about their locations. The letters have never been collected in an edition; this author is currently working on such an edition.

Abbreviations
   "Photocopied" = Any type of photographic reproduction
   "*ABPC*" = Listed as sold at auction in *American Book Prices Current*
   "Philpott" = Part of the Philpott Texana Collection sold at auction on October
         16–17, 1986, by the Altermann Art Gallery, Dallas, Texas.

October 26, 1820. To John C. McLemore from Lawrence County, Tennessee. The Library of the Daughters of the Republic of Texas at the Alamo.
August 6, 1827. To Mr. C. M. McAllister & Co. from Nashville. Chicago Historical Society.
December 17, 1827. To James L. Totton from Washington, D.C. Transcribed by Emma Inman Williams, *Historic Madison: The Story of Jackson and Madison County, Tennessee* (Jackson, Tenn.: Madison County Historical Society, 1946), 420. Partially quoted by Curtis Bray, "Davy Crockett Autograph," *Hobbies* 43 (1943):17. Transcribed in James Atkins Shackford's doctoral dissertation, "The Autobiography of David Crockett: An Annotated Edition," Vanderbilt University, 1948, 415–16.
February 5, 1828. To James Blackburn from Washington, D.C. Tennessee State Library and Archives. Photocopied in Shackford's dissertation, 417–20. Partially quoted in James Atkins Shackford, *David Crockett: The Man and the Legend*, (Chapel Hill: University of North Carolina Press, 1956), 88.
February 11, 1828. To James L. Totton from Washington, D.C. University of Tennessee Library Special Collections. Transcribed in Williams, *Historic Madison*, 421, and Shackford's dissertation, 421–22. Partially quoted in Shackford's *David Crockett*, 89.
March 11, 1828. To Mr. Seat (in Trenton, Tenn.) from Washington, D.C. Transcribed in A. Garland Adair and M. H. Crockett, Sr., eds., *Heroes of the Alamo: Accounts and Documents of William B. Travis, James Bowie, James B. Bonham and David Crockett, and Their Texas Memorials*, 2nd ed. (New York: Exposition Press, 1957), 86. Photocopied in Shackford's dissertation, 423–25. Partially quoted in Shackford's *David Crockett*, 89.

March 16, 1828. To Dr. Cahern. *ABPC* 80 (1974): 1005.

September 11, 1828. To Dr. Hubbert (in Trenton, Tenn.) from Washington, D.C. Tennessee State Library and Archives. Transcribed in the *American Historical Magazine* 5 (January 1900): 41. Photocopied in Shackford's dissertation, 426–27.

January 3, 1829. To Honorable James Clark of Kentucky. *ABPC* 73 (1967): 1102.

January 26, 1829. To Captain Seat from Washington, D.C. Tennessee State Library and Archives. The University of Tennessee Library Special Collections has a photocopy from a photocopy in the *Nashville Tennessean*, April 13, 1977, 19. Photocopied in the *American Historical Magazine* 2 (April 1897): 178, and in Shackford's dissertation, 428.

January 27, 1829. To George Patton from Washington, D.C. Tennessee State Library and Archives. Transcribed in the *American Historical Magazine* 5 (January 1900): 41–42. Photocopied in Shackford's dissertation, 429–32.

February 23, 1829. To "The Mess at J. Davises" from Washington, D.C. University of Rochester Library, Rochester, New York.

February 23, 1829. To "The Mess at Dowsons" from Washington, D.C. Butler Library, Columbia University.

February 25, 1829. To the "President of the United States," signed by Crockett and others. In volume 3 of the John Davis Batchelder Autograph Collection, Library of Congress.

April 18, 1829. To Gales and Seaton from Huntingdon, Tennessee. Rare Books and Manuscripts Division of the New York Public Library. Photocopied in Shackford's dissertation, 433–35. Quoted entirely in Shackford's *David Crockett*, 124–25.

May 26, 1829. To John Herritage Bryan from Dresden, Weakley County. J. Y. Joyner, East Carolina University.

December 29, 1829. To "His Excellency Andrew Jackson" from Washington, D.C. St. Louis Mercantile Library Association.

1830. To William T. Barry, Postmaster General. *ABPC* 77 (1971): 1045.

January 24, 1830. To Hugh D. Neilson from Washington, D.C. Tennessee State Library and Archives.

May 5, 1830. To Michael C. Sprigg from Steam Boat Courier near Maysville. Philpott. Photocopied in Shackford's dissertation, 436–37.

May 31, 1830. To Major William B. Lewis from Washington, D.C. Philpott.

December 21, 1830. To Henry McClung (in Staunton, Virginia) from Washington, D.C. Historical Society of Pennsylvania. Photocopied in Shackford's dissertation, 438–39. Partially quoted in Shackford's *David Crockett*, 128.

December 22, 1830. To James Kirke Paulding from Washington, D.C. Philpott. According to Shackford this is a spurious letter. See his dissertation, 597–99, for a transcript of the letter and analysis.

January 6, 1831. To Daniel W. Pounds (in Pages Mill, Gibson City, Tennessee) from Washington, D.C. Lilly Library, Indiana University.

February 13, 1831. To A. M. Hughes (in Dresden, Tennessee) from Washington, D.C. Tennessee State Library and Archives. Transcribed in the *American Histori-*

cal Magazine 5 (January 1900): 43–44. Photocopied in Shackford's dissertation, 440–43. Partially quoted in Shackford's *David Crockett*, 118–19.

May 28, 1831. To James Davison from Harrisburgh, Tennessee. Hofstra University Library Special Collections, Long Island, New York.

August 18, 1831. To James Davison from Weakley County, Tennessee. A photocopy and transcript are currently held by the Library of the Daughters of the Republic of Texas at the Alamo.

August 22, 1831. To Dr. Calvin Jones from Weakley County, Tennessee. Southern Historical Collection of University of North Carolina at Chapel Hill Library. A transcript is currently held by the North Carolina Department of Cultural Resources. Transcribed in Williams, *Historic Madison*, 422. Photocopied in Shackford's dissertation, 444–47. Partially quoted in Shackford's *David Crockett*, 133.

January 7, 1832. To Richard Smith from Weakley County, Tennessee. Historical Society of Pennsylvania. Photocopied in Shackford's dissertation, 448. Partially quoted in Shackford's *David Crockett*, 135–36.

November 28, 1833. To Lewis Cass from Washington, D.C. Pierpont Morgan Library, New York City.

December 8, 1833. To A. M. Hughes from Washington, D.C. Tennessee State Library and Archives. Transcribed in the *American Historical Magazine* 5 (January 1900): 44–45. Photocopied in Shackford's dissertation, 449–52. Partially quoted in Shackford's *David Crockett*, 144–45.

December 26, 1833. To John McLean from Washington, D.C. *ABPC*: 47 (1941): 523; and 73 (1967): 1102.

January 8, 1834. To William Rodgers, Esq., (in Caledonia, Henry County, Tennessee) from Washington, D.C. Tennessee State Library and Archives. Transcribed in the *American Historical Magazine* 5 (January 1900): 45–47. Photocopied in Shackford's dissertation, 453–56. Partially quoted in Shackford's *David Crockett*, 147–48.

January 9, 1834. To Henry R. Slorrs (?) from Washington, D.C. Buffalo and Erie County Historical Society.

January 10, 1834. To John W. Crockett (in Trenton, Gibson County, Tennessee) from Washington, D.C. Beinecke Rare Book and Manuscript Collection of Yale University Library. Partly quoted and commented on in a letter by Dr. Alex Dienst, published in Margaret Haynes Gates's master's thesis, "Fact and Fiction in the Early Biographies of David Crockett," University of Illinois, 1929, 152–55. Partly quoted by F. G. Woodard, "Davy Crockett's Autobiography Again," *Peabody Reflector* 11 (August 1938): 308. Photocopied in Shackford's dissertation, 457–60. Partially quoted in Shackford's *David Crockett*, 148.

January 17, 1834. To G. W. McLean from Washington, D.C. A negative photocopy is held in the Miscellaneous Manuscripts Collection of the Library of Congress. Transcribed and photocopied in Gates's master's thesis, 139–42, and in Shackford's dissertation, 461–62. Partially quoted in Shackford's *David Crockett*, 264–65.

January 20, 1834. To John O. Cannon, Esq., (in Madisonville, Tennessee) from

Washington, D.C. Philpott. Transcribed in *Confederate Veteran* 11 (1903): 162, and in Shackford's dissertation with the last page photocopied, 463–66. Partially quoted in Shackford's *David Crockett*, 149–50.

January 28, 1834. To Carey and Hart [publishers of Crockett's autobiography, *A Narrative of the Life of David Crockett of the State of Tennessee*] from Washington, D.C. *ABPC* 13 (1907): 619.

February 3, 1834. To *The Globe* from Washington, D.C. Huntington Library, San Marino, California.

February 3, 1834. To Carey and Hart from Washington, D.C. (According to Shackford, this letter was not written by David Crockett, although it was written for him and with his consent. See Shackford's dissertation, 585.) A photocopy is held by the Tennessee State Library and Archives. Photocopied in Shackford's dissertation, 467–68. Quoted entirely in Shackford's *David Crockett*, 266.

February 23, 1834. To ? concerning a painting of Crockett by S. S. Osgood. The Library of the Daughters of the Republic of Texas at the Alamo.

February 23, 1834. To Carey and Hart from Washington, D.C. Boston Public Library. Photocopied in Shackford's dissertation, 469–72. Quoted entirely in Shackford's *David Crockett*, 267–68.

February 25, 1834. To Carey and Hart from Washington, D.C. Historical Society of Pennsylvania. Photocopied in Shackford's dissertation, 473.

February 26, 1834. To Colonel Thomas Henderson (in Mount Pinson, Madison County, Tennessee) from Washington, D.C. Transcribed in Williams, *Historic Madison*, 423, and in Shackford's dissertation, 474–75. Partially transcribed in "Statement That Frontiersman Couldn't Write Is Protested," by Harry Woodbury, *Memphis Commercial Appeal*, November 23, 1941.

February 28, 1834. To Mrs. Mary Barney from Washington, D.C. Chicago Historical Society.

March 8, 1834. To Carey and Hart from Washington, D.C. New-York Historical Society. Photocopied in Shackford's dissertation, 476.

March 10, 1834. To Colonel Thomas Henderson. Partially quoted in Shackford's *David Crockett*, 151.

March 25, 1834. To Carey and Hart from Washington, D.C. Partially transcribed in Shackford's dissertation, 727. Partially quoted in Shackford's *David Crockett*, 152.

April 4, 1834. To John Drurez. *ABPC* 80 (1974): 1005.

April 9, 1834. To Hiram Favor. *ABPC* 81 (1975): 1065.

April 10, 1834. To Carey and Hart from Washington, D.C. Beinecke Rare Book and Manuscript Collection of Yale University Library. Photocopied in Shackford's dissertation, 477–78. Partially quoted in Shackford's *David Crockett*, 154.

April 11, 1834. To Jacob Dixon from Washington, D.C. *ABPC* 34 (1928): 690; 62 (1956): 397–98; and 67 (1961): 633.

April 12, 1834. To Carey and Hart from Washington, D.C. *ABPC* 38 (1932): 504.

April 23, 1834. Signed note in the album of Octavia Claudia Walton Le Vert. Philpott. Quoted in a Catalogue of the American Autograph Shop, Merion Station,

Pennsylvania, April 1936. Transcribed in Shackford's dissertation, 479–81. Quoted entirely in Shackford's *David Crockett*, 308.

May 4, 1834. Boston. A short autograph note signed. *ABPC* 20 (1914): 665.

May 11, 1834. To Mr. Sanderson (in Philadelphia) from New York. *ABPC* 36 (1930): 623.

May 26, 1834. To Joseph Wallis, Esq. (in Sommerville, Morgan County, North Alabama) from Washington, D.C. Transcribed in A. Garland Adair and M. H. Crockett, Sr., eds., *Heroes of the Alamo*, 87–88. Photocopied in Shackford's dissertation, 482–84. Partially quoted in Shackford's *David Crockett*, 162.

May 27, 1834. To Col. T. J. Dobings (in Brownsville, Tennessee) from Washington, D.C. Lilly Library, Indiana University. Transcribed in S. G. Heiskell, *Andrew Jackson and Early Tennessee History* (Nashville, 1920), 3: 18, and Williams, *Historic Madison*, 424–25. Photocopied in Shackford's dissertation, 485–88. Partially quoted in Shackford's *David Crockett*, 162–63.

May 27, 1834. To Carey and Hart from Washington, D.C. Carl H. Pforzheimer Shelley and his Circle Collection of the New York Public Library.

June 1, 1834. To Carey and Hart from Washington, D.C. Philpott.

June 9, 1834. To William Hack (in Denmark, Madison County, Tennessee) from Washington, D.C. Tennessee State Library and Archives. Transcribed in the *American Historical Magazine* 2 (April 1897): 179–80. Photocopied in Shackford's dissertation, 489–92. Partially quoted in Shackford's *David Crockett*, 163–64.

June 15, 1834. To J. M. Sanderson from Washington, D.C. Historical Society of Pennsylvania. Photocopied in Shackford's dissertation, 495–98. Partially quoted in Shackford's *David Crockett*, 167.

June 15, 1834. To William T. Yeatman (in Fishkill Landing, New York) from Washington, D.C. A transcript is held by the Tennessee State Library and Archives. Quoted in James D. Davis, *History of the City of Memphis* (Memphis: Hite, Crumpton, and Kelley, 1873), 155. Transcribed in Shackford's dissertation, 493–94. Partially quoted in Shackford's *David Crockett*, 167.

August 20, 1834. From Weakley County, Tennessee. *ABPC* 27 (1921): 944.

December 8, 1834. To Nicholas Biddle (in Philadelphia) from Washington, D.C. Historical Society of Pennsylvania. Photocopied in Shackford's dissertation, 499–500. Quoted entirely in Shackford's *David Crockett*, 171.

December 8, 1834. To Carey and Hart from Washington, D.C. Houghton Library, Harvard University.

December 13, 1834. To Carey and Hart from Washington, D.C. Listed for sale at the Historical Ephemera Auction, Wethersfield, Connecticut, February 21, 1987. Partially transcribed in Alex Small, "Davy Crockett Short of Cash, Letter Reveals," *Chicago Sunday Tribune*, May 29, 1955.

December 21, 1834. To Carey and Hart from Washington, D.C. Rosenbach Museum and Library, Philadelphia, Pennsylvania. Photocopied and transcribed in Shackford's dissertation, 731–32, 738. Partially quoted in Shackford's *David Crockett*, 173.

December 24, 1834. To Carey and Hart from Washington, D.C. Dawes Library Slack Collection of Marietta College.

December 25, 1834. To Charles Shultz (in Cincinnati, Ohio) from Washington, D.C. Transcribed (first page) and photocopied (second page) in Shackford's dissertation, 501–2. Partially quoted in Shackford's *David Crockett*, 173–74.

December 27, 1834. To John P. Ash from Washington, D.C. Jessie Ball duPont Library of the University of the South. Transcribed in Williams, *Historic Madison*, 425–27, and in Shackford's dissertation, 503–5. Partially quoted in Shackford's *David Crockett*, 174.

January 1, 1835. To Carey and Hart. *ABPC* 80 (1974): 1005.

January 8, 1835. To Carey and Hart from Washington, D.C. Museum and Library of Maryland History. Photocopied in Shackford's dissertation, 506–8. Quoted entirely in Shackford's *David Crockett*, 176.

Early [10] January 1835. To an editor of a Tennessee newspaper from Washington, D.C. (?) Quoted in the *Niles Register* 47 (February 28, 1835), 452–53. Transcribed in Shackford's dissertation, 509–10. Partially quoted in Shackford's *David Crockett*, 178–79.

January 11, 1835. To Elizabeth Crowder from Washington, D.C. University of Virginia Library.

January 12, 1835. To Carey and Hart from Washington, D.C. New-York Historical Society. Photocopied in Shackford's dissertation, 511–12. Quoted entirely in Shackford's *David Crockett*, 184–85.

January 16, 1835. To Carey and Hart from Washington, D.C. *ABPC* 20 (1913): 755; and 30 (1924): 793. Partially quoted in Shackford's *David Crockett*, 186.

January 22, 1835. To Carey and Hart from Washington, D.C. Rosenbach Museum and Library, Philadelphia, Pennsylvania. Photocopied in Shackford's dissertation, 733–36. Partially quoted in Shackford's *David Crockett*, 187.

February 2, 1835. To R. R. Waldron. *ABPC* 73 (1967): 1102.

February 6, 1835. To Carey and Hart from Washington, D.C. *ABPC* 22 (1916): 857.

February 9, 1835. To Carey and Hart. *ABPC* 59 (1953): 591.

April 16, 1835. To Carey and Hart from Weakley County. Haverford College Library, Haverford, Pennsylvania.

June 26, 1835. To Carey and Hart from Mouth of Sandy, Henry County, Tennessee. *ABPC* 16 (1910): 806.

July 8, 1835. To Carey and Hart from Weakley County. (?) Referred to in Constance M. Rourke, *Davy Crockett* (New York: Harcourt, Brace and Co., 1934), 247–76. Reconstucted from *Texas Exploits* by James A. Shackford and published in his dissertation, 513. Quoted entirely in Shackford's *David Crockett*, 204.

August 10, 1835. To Gales and Seaton from Weakley County. Transcribed in Shackford's dissertation, 728–31.

August 11, 1835. To Carey and Hart from Weakley County, Tennessee. Museum and Library of Maryland History. Photocopied in Shackford's dissertation, 514–17. Partially quoted in Shackford's *David Crockett*, 205–6.

1835. *ABPC* 8 (1902): 593.

August or September 1835. To men of LaGrange, Tennessee, from Weakley County (?). Quoted in Constance M. Rourke, "Davy Crockett: Forgotten Facts and Legends," *Southwest Review* 19 (January 1934): 150. Transcribed in Shackford's dissertation, 518.

October 31, 1835. To George Patton from Weakley County. Photocopied in Shackford's dissertation, 519–522. Quoted entirely in Shackford's *David Crockett*, 210.

January 9, 1836. To Wiley and Margaret Flowers from "St. Agusteen," Texas. The University of Tennessee Library Special Collections and the Tennessee State Library and Archives hold photocopies. Transcribed by Williams, *Historic Madison*, 427–28; Rourke, *Davy Crockett*, 174–76; Rourke, "Forgotten Facts," 149; and Shackford's dissertation, 523–25. Quoted entirely in Shackford's *David Crockett*, 214–15, 216.

January 23, 1836. An order on the Texas government for John Lott from Washington, Texas. Photocopied in Margaret Gates's master's thesis, 149, and Shackford's dissertation, 526. Quoted entirely in Shackford's *David Crockett*, 222.

Other Crockett Documents

October 21, 1805. Marriage license of David Crockett to Margaret Elder. Jefferson County, Tennessee, Courthouse. Photocopied in L. W. Reynolds, "The Pioneer Crockett Family in Tennessee," *DAR Magazine* 55 (April 1921): 190.

August 12, 1806. Marriage bond, Crockett and Thomas Doggett signers, for the marriage between David Crockett and Polly Findley [sic]. Jefferson County, Tennessee, Courthouse. Photocopied in L. W. Reynolds, "The Pioneer Crockett Family in Tennessee," 191. Transcribed in Margaret Gates's master's thesis, "Fact and Fiction in the Early Biographies of David Crockett," 146. Photocopied in Shackford's dissertation, 533.

March 27, 1815. Honorable discharge from "Tennessee Volunteer Mounted Gun-Men," signed by John Coffee, Brigadier General. A transcript is held in the McClung Collection of the East Tennessee Historical Center. Photocopied in the *Knoxville Sunday Journal*, August 17, 1930, B-1.

January 1, 1817. A lease for thirty-eight acres of land to James Penn from David Crockett. State of Alabama Department of Archives and History.

November 25, 1817. David Crockett's commission as justice of the peace, Lawrence County. Photocopied in Shackford's dissertation, 534–35.

April 1, 1818. Five depositions taken before the city commissioners of Lawrenceburg, Lawrence County, Crockett being one of the commissioners. Tennessee State Library and Archives. Photocopied in Shackford's dissertation, 536–53.

May 5, 1818. Legal document. A photocopy is currently held by the University of Texas at Austin Library.

October 10, 1818. Justice of the Peace Execution. Quoted in Edward S. Ellis, *The Life of Colonel David Crockett*. Philadelphia: Porter & Coates, 1884.

November 28, 1818. A legal document signed by David Crockett, J.P. The Library of the Daughters of the Republic of Texas at the Alamo. Transcribed in Margaret Gates's master's thesis, "Fact and Fiction in the Early Biographies of David Crockett," 145.

"February Term" and August 3, 1819. Legal documents signed by David Crockett, J.P. Photocopies are currently held by the University of Texas at Austin Library.

June 2, 1821. A bond issued in Lawrence County, Tennessee, signed by David Crockett. State Historical Society of Wisconsin.

April 14, 1824. The lease of a tract of land on the Obion River, Carroll County, Tennessee. *ABPC* 40 (1939): 291; 66 (1960): 585; and 88 (1982): 34.

February 19, 1825. A promissory note to Armour and Lake, Madison County. Photocopied in Williams, *Historic Madison.* Frontispiece.

August 15, 1826. Bond to Sheriff Needham in a grand jury presentment against Nathan Fiske for unlawful gaming. *ABPC* 90 (1984): 28.

"20 day of 1827." A summons of Crockett by a J.P. Photocopied in Williams, *Historic Madison.* Frontispiece.

September 5, 1827. A bond to Lewis Needham. Signed by four others. *ABPC* 75 (1969): 1320.

February 5, 1828. A Crockett signature appears on a broadside entitled "New Proposals for the *Ohio Monitor,* Published at Columbus, Ohio by David Smith." Crockett was a subscriber. University of Texas at Arlington Library.

May 2, 1828. To Honorable S. L. Southard, Secretary of the Navy, recommending James Madison Lockart of Tennessee as a midshipman. Signed also by James K. Polk and three others. *ABPC* 76 (1970): 1312.

1829. A receipt for attendance as a witness in a lawsuit. Sold by the Yesteryear Book Shop, Atlanta, Georgia, September 1984.

February 17, 1829. Promissory note. A photocopy is currently held by The Library of the Daughters of the Republic of Texas at the Alamo.

February 24, 1829. Promissory note. *ABPC* 67 (1961): 633.

September 2, 1829. Receipt for attendance as a witness in a suit. *ABPC* 90 (1984): 28.

May 3, 1831. A promissory note for $600 to the order of R. E. B. Baylor. *ABPC* 85 (1979): 908.

May 19, 1831. A deed and a bill of sale for a Negro girl, to George Patton from David Crockett in Weakley County. Recorded December 21, 1831, and April 14, 1832. West Tennessee Historical Society.

August 6, 1831. Promissory note to J. H. Ball. *ABPC* 80 (1974): 1005.

November 16, 1832. "Exchange for $1000" to "Crockett & Park." Autograph of Crockett and Park in the handwriting of David Crockett. Haverford College Library, Haverford, Pennsylvania.

October 13, 1833. A bill of sale of a Negro slave woman signed by Crockett. Photocopied in the *Dallas Morning News,* December 25, 1927, Feature Section, 5.

December 3, 1833. A financial bond. *ABPC* 86 (1980): 46.

February 17, 1834. To Levi Woodbury. Recommendation of Issac Brown for appointment as midshipman in the U. S. Navy. Signed by seven others. *ABPC* 74 (1968): 1106.

September 15, 1834. Bond in the administration of an estate. Also signed by two others. *ABPC* 84 (1978): 1162.

October 11, 1834. A promissory note to William Tucker. Photocopied in the *Dallas Morning News*, December 25, 1927, Feature Section, 5. Quoted entirely in Shackford's *David Crockett*, 171.

Other Letters

March 6, 1827. Letter from John W. Crockett (David's son, aged 19) in Paris, Tennessee, to C. G. Dunlap, in Huntingdon, Tennessee. Photocopied in Shackford's dissertation, 554–55. Quoted entirely in Shackford's *David Crockett*, 81.

January 16, 1829. Letter from James K. Polk to Davison M. Millen, Esq. Photocopied in Shackford's dissertation, 556–59.

December 15, 1830. Letter from James K. Paulding to Richard Henry Wilde. New-York Historical Society.

January 13, 1831. To David Crockett from John Ross. Newberry Library, Chicago, Illinois.

February 10 (?) 1833. To James Strange French from William Miner (concerned the copyright on his life of Crockett). Butler Library, Columbia University.

September 9, 1833. Contract signed by James Strange French for his life of Davy Crockett. Butler Library, Columbia University.

January 23, 1835. To the editor of *The Globe* (Washington, D.C.) from H. E. Anderson (Toulon, Hayward County, Tennessee). University of Tennessee Library Special Collections.

1836. Letter from Isaac N. Jones, in Lost Prairie, Arkansas, to Crockett's widow. Transcripts are held in the McClung Collection of the East Tennessee Historical Center and by the Library of the Daughters of the Republic of Texas at the Alamo. Partially quoted in Shackford's *David Crockett*, 214, 235–36.

July 9, 1836. Letter from David's son, John W. Crockett, to his uncle, Captain George Patton. Photocopied in Shackford's dissertation, 560–61. Quoted entirely in Shackford's *David Crockett*, 237–38.

July 11, 1836 [1837]. Letter filed with the court in Bexar County about the heirs of David Crockett. Signed by Robert Crockett. A transcript and photocopy are held by the Library of the Daughters of the Republic of Texas at the Alamo.

August 3, 1837. Letter filed with the court in Bexar County about the heirs of David Crockett. Signed by Robert Crockett, among others. A transcript and photocopy are held by the Library of the Daughters of the Republic of Texas at the Alamo.

December 30, 1879. Letter from Robert Patton Crockett to Smith Rudd. Lilly Library, Indiana University.

June 15, 1880. Letter from Robert Patton Crockett to Smith Rudd. Lilly Library, Indiana University.

March 9, 1881. Letter from Robert Patton Crockett to Smith Rudd. Lilly Library, Indiana University.

November 22, 1884. Letter from John L. Jacobs (Cullasaja, Macon County, North Carolina) to the editor of the *Morristown Gazette*. A transcript is held by the University of Tennessee Library Special Collections.

November 3, 1888. Letter from Marcus J. Wright to James R. Gilmore. Milton S.
Eisenhower Library of John Hopkins University.
January 2, 1907. Letter from John Wesley Crockett to Ben S. Rudd. Lilly Library,
Indiana University.

WORKS DEALING WITH THE HISTORICAL CROCKETT

Works written before 1956, although intended to be historical works, are sometimes
a mixture of historical and legendary materials.

Affleck, J. D. "Colonel David Crockett." *Taylor-Trotwood Magazine* 11 (August 1910):
378–83.
American Historical Magazine 7 (1902): 298–99.
Armstrong, Zella. "Early Marriage Records of East Tennessee." *DAR Magazine* 69
(July 1935): 435–36.
Arpad, Joseph John. "David Crockett, An Original Legendary Eccentricity and
Early American Character." Ph.D. diss., Duke University, 1969.
———, ed. *A Narrative of the Life of David Crockett of the State of Tennessee*. New
Haven, Conn.: College & University Press, 1972.
Baugh, Virgil E. *Rendevous at the Alamo: Highlights in the Lives of Bowie, Crockett,
& Travis*. New York: Pageant Press, 1960. Reprint. Lincoln: University of Ne-
braska Press, 1985.
Beaumont, Hy. Francis. "The Loves of Davy Crockett." *The Alkahest Magazine*
Seventh year, No. 5 (January): 355–59.
Bethune, J. "Davy Crockett's Electioneering Tour." *Harper's New Monthly Maga-
zine* 34 (April 1867): 606–11.
The Birthplace of Davy Crockett. Greeneville, Tenn.: Davy Crockett Birthplace
Association.
Bishop, Curtis. "Davy Crockett, Fabled Texan." *Texas Parade* 15 (May 1955): 34.
Bishop, H. O. "Colonel Crockett Goes Visiting." *National Republic* 17 (October 1929):
24–25, 39.
———. "Colonel Crockett in New York." *National Republic* 17 (November 1929):
28–29, 39.
———. "Davy Crockett – Bear Hunter." *National Republic* 17 (August 1929): 31–37.
Blair, Walter. "Introduction" in Lofaro and Cummings, *Crockett at Two Hundred*,
1–6.
Bracy, Sharen. "Frontiersman." *The Tennessee Conservationist* 52 (July/August 1986):
11–12.
Bray, Curtis. "David Crockett Autographs." *Hobbies* 48 (July 1943): 17.
Burke, James Wakefield. *David Crockett: The Man Behind the Myth*. Austin, Tex.:
Eakin Press, 1984.

Carroll, H. Bailey, ed. "Texas Collection." *Southwestern Historical Quarterly* 47 (1944): 178, 313.

———, ed. "Texas Collection." *Southwestern Historical Quarterly* 54 (January 1951): 229.

Catron, Anna Grace. "The Public Career of David Crockett." Unpublished master's thesis, University of Tennessee, 1955.

Cattermole, E. G. *Famous Frontiersmen, Pioneers, and Scouts: The Vanguards of American Civilization.* Chicago: Donohue, Henneberry & Co., 188?. Reprint. Tarrytown, N.Y.: W. Abbott, 1926.

Cody, William F. *Story of the Wild West and Camp-Fire Chats, by Buffalo Bill, (Hon. W.F. Cody): A Full and Complete History of the Renowned Pioneer Quartette, Boone, Crockett, Carson and Buffalo Bill.* Philadelphia: Historical Publishing Co., 1888. Micropublished in *Western Americana: Frontier History of the Trans-Mississippi West, 1550-1900.* New Haven, Conn.: Research Publication, Inc., 1975.

Confederate Veteran 2 (June 1894): 167.

Connelly, Thomas Lawrence, ed. "Did David Crockett Surrender at the Alamo? A Contemporary Letter." *Journal of Southern History* 26 (1960): 368–76.

Cooper, Texas Jim. "Portrait of a Hero." *Texas Parade* 27 (June 1966): 15–16.

———. "A Study of Some David Crockett Firearms." *East Tennessee Historical Society's Publications* 38 (1966): 62–69. Reprinted in Harper, *Houston and Crockett* 235–41.

Crimmins, M. L. "The Story of David Crockett's Watch." *Frontier Times* 26 (March 1949): 147–48.

Crockett, David. *Address of Mr. Crockett, to the Voters of the Ninth Congressional District of the State of Tennessee.* Washington: Gales and Seaton, 1829.

———. Circular Letters to Constituents, 1824; late 1834; early 1835. This and subsequent entry are from Shackford's *David Crockett.* Thus far I have been able to locate only an October 25, 1834, letter at the Tennessee Historical Society.

———. *David Crockett's Circular. To the Citizens and Voters of the Ninth Congressional District of the State of Tennessee.* Washington: February 24, 1831.

———. *A Narrative of the Life of David Crockett of the State of Tennessee.* Philadelphia: Carey & Hart, 1834. Facsimile edition with annotations and introduction edited by James A. Shackford and Stanley J. Folmsbee. Knoxville: University of Tennessee Press, 1973.

———. "Reply-to-Benton Letters." *National Banner and Nashville Whig,* January 26, 1835, 3.

———. "A Sketch of the REMARKS OF THE HON. DAVID CROCKETT, Representative from Tennessee, On the Bill for Removal of the Indians . . . May 19, 1830." *Speeches on the Passage of the Bill for the Removal of the Indians, Delivered in the Congress of the United States, April and May, 1830.* Boston: Perkins and Marvin, 1830. Reprinted in Walter Blair's, *Davy Crockett—Frontier Hero: The Truth as He Told It—The Legend as His Friends Built It.* New York: Coward-McCann,

1955, 211–15. Reprinted as *Davy Crockett, Legendary Frontier Hero.* Springfield, Ill.: Lincoln-Herndon Press, 1986.

———. *Speech of Mr. Crockett, of Tennessee, on a Bill Proposing to Construct a National Road from Buffalo to New Orleans.* Washington: Duff Green, 1830.

"Crockett Relics in Tennessee." *The Tennessee Conservationist* 21 (June 1955): 10–11.

Culp, Frederick M., and Mrs. Robert E. Ross. *Gibson County: Past and Present.* Trenton, Tenn.: Gibson County Historical Society, 1961.

Cummings, Joe. "Celebrating Crockett in Tennessee." In Lofaro and Cummings, *Crockett at Two Hundred,* 67–82.

———. "Remembering Davy." *The Tennessee Conservationist* 52 (July/August 1986): 16–19.

Davis, Curtis Carroll. "A Legend at Full-Length: Mr. Chapman Paints Colonel Crockett—and Tells about It." *Proceedings of the American Antiquarian Society* 69 (1960): 155–74.

"Davy Crockett vs. Andy Jackson." *Confederate Veteran* 11 (April 1903): 162–63.

"Did Crockett Die at the Alamo? Historian Carmen Perry Says No." *People Weekly,* October 13, 1975, 41.

Downing, Marvin. "Davy Crockett in Gibson County, Tennessee: A Century of Memories." *West Tennessee Historical Society Papers* 37 (1983): 54–61.

———. "Memorial Remembrances of David ("Davy") Crockett in Rutherford." *West Tennessee Historical Society Papers* 35 (1981): 63–82. Reprinted in Harper, *Houston and Crockett,* 260–79.

"Early Times in Weakley County: An Address Delivered by Col. John A. Gardner." *West Tennessee Historical Society Papers* 17 (1963): 68–84.

"East Tennessee Celebrates Crockett." *Southern Living,* August 1986, 29.

Evans, Moina. "David Crockett: An Interpretation." Unpublished master's thesis, Vanderbilt University, 1924.

Felknor, Mrs. A. M. "The Davy Crockett Gun." *The Lookout* [Chattanooga] 72 (October 3, 1947): 7.

Flanagan, Sue. "Davy Crockett: Man & Myth." *Alcalde* [The University of Texas Alumni Magazine] 54 (March 1966): 8–11.

Folmsbee, Stanley J. "David Crockett and his Autobiography." *East Tennessee Historical Society's Publications* 43 (1971): 3–17.

———. "David Crockett and West Tennessee." *West Tennessee Historical Society Papers* 28 (1974): 5–24. Reprinted in Harper, *Houston and Crockett,* 242–59.

Folmsbee, Stanley J., and Anna Grace Catron. "David Crockett: Congressman." *East Tennessee Historical Society's Publications* 29 (1957): 40–78. Reprinted in Harper, *Houston and Crockett,* 158–94.

———. "David Crockett in Texas." *East Tennessee Historical Society's Publications* 30 (1958): 48–74. Reprinted in Harper, *Houston and Crockett,* 195–219.

———. "The Early Career of David Crockett." *East Tennessee Historical Society's Publications* 28 (1956): 58–85. Reprinted in Harper, *Houston and Crockett,* 132–57.

Foreman, Gary L. *Crockett: The Gentleman from the Cane: A Comprehensive View of the Folkhero Americans Thought They Knew*. Dallas, Tex.: Taylor Publishing Company, 1986.

Foster, Austin P. *Counties of Tennessee*. [Nashville]: State of Tennessee, 1923.

————. "David Crockett." *Tennessee Historical Magazine* 9 (October 1925): 166–77.

Franklin, P. L. "Colonel Crockett Visits Boston." *National Republic* 17 (December 1929): 30–31, 45.

————. "Colonel Crockett Gives Advice." *National Republic* 17 (January 1930): 31, 44.

French, Mrs. Stewart, and Zella Armstrong. *The Crockett Family and Connecting Lines*. Bristol, Tenn.: King Printing Co., 1928.

Gates, Bob. "The Start of a Legend." *The Tennessee Conservationist* 52 (July/August 1986): 13–15.

Gates, Margaret Haynes. "Fact and Fiction in the Early Biographies of David Crockett." Unpublished master's thesis, University of Illinois, 1929.

"Gone to Texas." *The Library Development Program Report* [University of Tennessee, Knoxville], 87 (1983–84), 3–4.

Grainger, James M. "David Crockett." In vol. 3 of *Library of Southern Literature*, edited by Edwin Anderson Alderman. Atlanta, Ga. The Martin and Hoyt Company, 1907, 1083–1110.

Hall, Claud V. "Early Days in Red River County." *Bulletin of the East Texas State Teachers College* 14 (June 1931), 49–79.

Harper, Herbert L., ed. *Houston and Crockett: Heroes of Tennessee and Texas*. Nashville: Tennessee Historical Commission, 1986.

————. "Tennessee is Crockett Country." *The Tennessee Conservationist* 52 (July/August 1986): 20–21.

Hauck, Richard Boyd. *Crockett: A Bio-Bibliography*. Westport, Conn.: Greenwood Press, 1982. Reprinted as *Davy Crockett: A Handbook*. Lincoln: University of Nebraska Press, 1986.

————. "The Man in the Buckskin Hunting Shirt: Fact and Fiction in the Crockett Story." In *Davy Crockett*, edited by Michael A. Lofaro. Knoxville: University of Tennessee Press, 1985, 3–20.

————. "The Real Davy Crocketts: Creative Autobiography and the Invention of His Legend." In Lofaro and Cummings, *Crockett at Two Hundred*, 179–91.

Heale, M. J. "The Role of the Frontier in Jacksonian Politics: David Crockett and the Myth of the Self-Made Man." *Western Historical Quarterly* 4 (1973): 405–23.

Henderson, Mrs. Jessie Arn. "Unmarked Historic Spots of Franklin County." *Tennessee Historical Magazine*, series 2, vol.3 (January 1935): 111–20.

Hicklin, J. R. "The Carson-Vance Duel." *The State* [North Carolina] 6 (December 10, 1938), 9.

Historical Program of Dedication of the Davy Crockett Birthplace Park. Limestone, Tenn., August 17, 1958.

Hogue, Albert Ross. *Davy Crockett and Others in Fentress County Who Have Given the County a Prominent Place in History*. Jamestown, Tenn., 1955.

Hunter, Marvin J. "Crockett's Colorful Career Ended in Texas." *Frontier Times* 15 (1938): 139–40.

Hunter, Mary Kate. "David Crockett—of Tennessee and Texas." *East Texas*, June 1928, 23, 39.

Hutton, Paul Andrew. "Davy Crockett: An Exposition in Hero Worship." In Lofaro and Cummings, *Crockett at Two Hundred*, 20–41.

———. "Davy Crockett, Still King of the Wild Frontier." *Texas Monthly*, November 1986, 122–28, 130, 244–48.

———, ed. *A Narrative of the Life of David Crockett of the State of Tennessee Written by Himself.* Lincoln: University of Nebraska Press, 1987.

Jenkins, John H. "Did Davy Crockett Survive the Alamo?" *Texana* 1 (Summer 1963): 284–87.

The John Crockett Tavern and Pioneer Museum. 1958. [A copy is held at the University of Tennessee Library Special Collections, Knoxville.]

Kelly, James C. "The Gentleman from the Cane." *The Tennessee Conservationist* 52 (July/August 1986): 6–8.

Kelly, James C., and Frederick S. Voss. *Davy Crockett: Gentleman from the Cane.* Washington, D.C.: National Portrait Gallery, and Nashville: Tennessee State Museum, 1986.

Kilgore, Dan. *How Did Davy Die?* College Station: Texas A&M University Press, 1978.

———. "Why Davy Didn't Die." In Lofaro and Cummings, *Crockett at Two Hundred*, 7–19.

Kirk, Donald W. "Tennessee's Davy Crockett: A Close Look." *Blackpowder Annual*, 1987, 12–15, 81–84.

Lake, Mary Daggett. "David Crockett's Widow. The Pioneer Wife and Mother Who Was Widowed by the Fall of the Alamo." *Texas Monthly* 2 (December 1928): 703–8.

———. "The Family of David Crockett in Texas." *Tennessee Historical Magazine* Series 2, vol. 3 (1935), 174–78.

Little, Lucius Powhattan. *Ben Hardin: His Times and Contemporaries, With Selections from his Speeches.* Louisville: Courier-Journal Job Printing Co., 1887.

Lofaro, Michael A., and Joe Cummings, eds. *Crockett at Two Hundred: New Perspectives on the Man and the Myth.* Knoxville: University of Tennessee Press, 1989.

Loomis, C. Grant. "Davy Crockett Visits Boston." *The New England Quarterly* 20 (1947): 396–400.

McBride, Robert M. "David Crockett and His Memorials in Tennessee." *Tennessee Historical Quarterly* 26 (1967): 219–39. Reprinted in *More Landmarks of Tennessee History*. Nashville: Tennessee Historical Society and Tennessee Historical Commission, 1969. Also reprinted in Harper, *Houston and Crockett*, 220–34.

McSpadden, J. Walter. *Pioneer Heroes.* New York: Thomas Y. Crowell, 1929.

Miles, Guy S. "David Crockett Evolves, 1821–1824." *American Quarterly* 8 (1956): 53–60.

Mills, Larry, comp. *The Sayings of Davy Crockett in his Own Language.* [n.p.], 1938. [A copy is held at the University of Texas at Austin Library.]

Montgomery, Michael. "David Crockett and the Rhetoric of Tennessee Politics." In Lofaro and Cummings, *Crockett at Two Hundred*, 42–66.

Mooney, Chase C. "The Political Career of Adam Huntsman." *Tennessee Historical Quarterly* 10 (1951): 99–126.

Morrison, John F., Jr. *Life of David Crockett in Lawrence County.* Nashville: Department of Conservation, Division of State Parks, 1967.

Morrison, John (Judge), and Colonel Bob Hamsley. *The Real David Crockett.* Lawrenceburg, Tenn., n.p., 1955.

Morrow, Temple Houston. "Address of Temple Houston Morrow Delivered at the Unveiling of Monument to David Crockett at His Old Home near Trenton, Tennessee, October 13, 1950." *West Tennessee Historical Society Papers* 5 (1951): 5–13. Reprinted in Harper, *Houston and Crockett*, 280–87.

Null, Marion Michael. *The Forgotten Pioneer, The Life of Davy Crockett.* New York: Vantage Press, 1954.

Palmquist, Robert F. "High Private: David Crockett at the Alamo." *Real West: True Tales of the American Frontier*, December 1981, 12–15, 41–43.

Pearson, Josephine A. "The Tennessee Woman Trecker – Elizabeth – Widow of David Crockett." *Tennessee Historical Magazine*, Series 2, vol. 3 (1935), 169–73.

Polatnick, Florence. "Davy Crockett, the Man." In *Showcasing American Drama: A Handbook of Source Materials on "The Lion of the West" by J.K. Paulding*, edited by Vera Jiji. Brooklyn: Humanities Institute, 1983, [15]–[18].

Pollard, Claude. *David Crockett, the Representative Man; Address Before the David Crockett Memorial Association at Crockett, Houston County, Texas, on March First, 1929.* Austin, Tex.: Tobin's, 1929?

Potter, R. M. "Colonel David Crockett." *Magazine of American History* 11 (February 1884): 177–78.

Randolph, J. Ralph. "David Crockett." In *Heroes of Tennessee*, edited by Billy M. Jones. Memphis: Memphis State University Press, 1979, 69–82.

Register of Debates in Congress. Vols. 3–11. Washington: Gales and Seaton, 1827–35.

"Reminiscences of Davy Crockett." *Every Saturday* 11 (November 25, 1871): 515.

Reynolds, Louise Wilson. "The Pioneer Crockett Family in Tennessee." *DAR Magazine* 55 (April 1921): 186–91.

Richardson, T. C. "The Girl Davy Left Behind." *Farm and Ranch* 25 (June 1927): 3, 11.

Roberts, Harry B. *Davy Crockett: Explained and Defended.* 2 vols. Greeneville, Tenn.: Privately printed for Harry B. Roberts, 1986.

Rothrock, Mary V. "David Crockett, the Legend and the Man." *The Tennessee Teacher* 22 (March 1955): 8–11.

Shackford, James Atkins. "The Author of David Crockett's Autobiography." *Boston Public Library Quarterly* 3 (October 1951): 294–304.

———. "The Autobiography of David Crockett: An Annotated Edition." Ph.D. diss., Vanderbilt University, 1948.

———. "David Crockett and North Carolina." *North Carolina Historical Review* 28 (July 1951): 298–315.

———. "David Crockett, the Legend and the Symbol." In *The Frontier Humorists: Critical Views*, edited by M. Thomas Inge. Hamden, Conn.: Archon Books, 1975, 208–18.

————. *David Crockett: The Man and the Legend*, edited by John B. Shackford. Chapel Hill: University of North Carolina Press, 1956. Reprinted with a new introduction by Michael A. Lofaro. Chapel Hill: University of North Carolina Press, 1986.

Silver, Marty. "Early Days." *The Tennessee Conservationist* 52 (July/August 1986): 9–10.

Smith, Samuel D. *Historical Background and Archaeological Testing of the Davy Crockett Birthplace State Historic Area, Greene County, Tennessee.* Nashville: Division of Archaeology, Tennessee Department of Conservation, 1980.

Stout, Dr. S. H. "David Crockett." *American Historical Magazine* 7 (January 1902): 3–21.

Tanenbaum, Miles. "Following Davy's Trail: A Crockett Bibliography." In Lofaro and Cummings, *Crockett at Two Hundred*, 192–241.

————. *Hunting Davy Crockett: A Guide to Crockett Studies.* Nashville: Tennessee Department of Conservation and Tennessee State Museum, 1986.

Taylor, Alfred A. "Davy Crockett: An Address." In Paul Deresco Augsburg, *Bob and Alf Taylor: Their Lives and Lectures.* Morristown, Tenn.: Morristown Book Company, Inc., 1925, 276–78.

Torrence, Helen H. Leeds, and Robert M. Torrence. "Davy Crockett at 'Old Springdale.'" *Maryland Historical Magazine* 50 (September 1955): 263–66.

Torrence, Robert M., and Robert L. Whittenburg. *Colonel "Davy" Crockett.* [A genealogy.] Washington, D.C.: Homer Fagan, 1956.

Turner, H. S. "Andrew Jackson and David Crockett: Reminiscences of Colonel Chester." *Magazine of American History* 27 (May 1892): 385–87.

Wade, John Donald. "The Authorship of David Crockett's 'Autobiography.'" *Georgia Historical Quarterly* 6 (September 1922): 265–68.

Williams, Emma Inman. *Historic Madison, the Story of Jackson, and Madison County, Tennessee, from Prehistoric Moundbuilders to 1917.* Jackson, Tenn.: Madison County Historical Society, 1946.

————, ed. "Letters of Adam Huntsman to James K. Polk." *Tennessee Historical Quarterly* 6 (December 1947): 337–69.

Woodward, F. G. "Davy Crockett's Autobiography Again." *Peabody Reflector* 11 (August 1938): 300–302.

Worner, William Frederick. "David Crockett in Columbia." *Lancaster County [Pennsylvania] History Society Papers* 27 (December 1923): 176–77.

Wright, Marcus J. "Colonel David Crockett of Tennessee." *Magazine of American History* 10 (December 1883): 484–89. Reprinted in *Publications of the Southern History Association* 1 (January 1897): 53–60.

WORKS DEALING WITH THE ALAMO
AND TEXAS INDEPENDENCE

Works on the Alamo which focus primarily on Crockett, like Dan Kilgore's *How Did Davy Die?* are listed with the historical Crockett materials.

Adair, A. Garland, and M. H. Crockett, Sr., eds. *Heroes of the Alamo: Accounts and Documents of William B. Travis, James Bowie, James B. Bonham and David Crockett, and Their Texas Memorials.* 2d ed. New York: Exposition Press, 1957.

Allison, Zoe. "Notes on the Journal of the Proceedings of the General Council of the Republic of Texas Held at San Felipe De Austin, November 14, 1835 – March 11, 1836." *Bulletin of East Texas State Teachers College* 14 (June 1931): 84–88.

American History Illustrated: Special Texas Sesquicentennial Issue 20 (March 1986).

Becerra, Francisco. *A Mexican Sergeant's Recollections of the Alamo and San Jacinto.* Austin: Jenkins Publishing Co., 1980.

Binkley, William C. *The Texas Revolution.* Baton Rouge: Louisiana State University Press, 1952.

Boyd, Bob. *The Texas Revolution: A Day-by-Day Account.* San Angelo: San Angelo Standard, Inc., 1986.

Bryant, Christopher. *The Bee Hunter.* New York: Pageant Press, 1966.

Burke, James Wakefield. *The Blazing Dawn.* New York: Pyramid Books, 1975.

Crawford, Ann Fears, ed. *The Eagle: The Autobiography of Santa Anna.* Austin: Pemberton Press, 1967.

Eaton, Jack D. *Excavations at the Alamo Shrine (Mission San Antonio de Valero).* San Antonio: University of Texas at San Antonio, Center for Archaeological Research, 1980.

Elfer, Maurice. *Madam Candelaria, Unsung Heroine of the Alamo: Including a Personal Account of the Faithful Woman who, Staying in the Mission When the Battle Raged and the Doomed Men Sold Their Lives as Dearly as Possible, Obeyed Sam Houston's Trust and was Wounded by Mexican Bayonets While Trying to Protect Dying Bowie.* Houston, Tex.: The Rein Co., 1933.

Fehrenbach, T. R. *Lone Star: A History of Texas and Texans.* New York: The Macmillan Company, 1968.

Frantz, Joe B. "The Alamo." In *Battles of Texas.* Waco, Tex.: Texian Press, 1967.

Gaddy, Jerry J., comp. *Texas in Revolt: Contemporary Newspaper Accounts of the Texas Revolution.* Fort Collins, Colo.: Old Army Press, 1973.

Galloway, G. Norton. "Sketch of San Antonio, The Fall of the Alamo." *Magazine of American History* 15 (June 1886): 521–40.

Groneman, Bill, and Phil Rosenthal. *Roll Call at the Alamo.* Fort Collins, Colo.: Old Army Press, 1985.

Guerra, Mary Ann Noonan. *The Alamo.* San Antonio: Alamo Press, 1983.

Haley, J. Evetts. *The Alamo Mission Bell.* Austin: Encino Press, 1974.

Heroes of Texas. Waco, Tex.: Texian Press, 1964.

Hutton, Paul Andrew. "The Alamo: An American Epic." *American History Illustrated* 20 (March 1986): 12–26, 35–37.

———. "Continuing Battles for the Alamo." *American History Illustrated* 20 (March 1986): 52–57.

———. Introduction to Susan Prendergast Schoelwer's *Alamo Images.* Dallas: De-Golyer Library and Southern Methodist University Press, 1985.

———. "A Tale of Two Alamos." *SMU Mustang* 36 (Spring 1986): 16–27.

James, Marquis. *The Raven: A Biography of Sam Houston.* New York: Blue Ribbon Books, Inc., 1929; Paperback Library, 1962.

Jenkins, John H., ed. *The Papers of the Texas Revolution, 1835–1836.* 10 vols. Austin: Presidial Press, 1973.

Jones, Oakah L., Jr. *Santa Anna.* New York: Twayne Books, 1968.

LaFay, Howard. "Texas!" *National Geographic* 157 (1980): 440–83.

"Letters to the Editor." *Smithsonian* 17 (May 1986): 14.

Lord, Walter. "Myths and Realities of the Alamo." *American West* 5 (May 1968): 18–25. Reprinted in *The Republic of Texas*, edited by Stephen B. Oates. Palo Alto, Calif.: American West Publishing Co. and Texas State Historical Association, 1968, 18–25.

———. *A Time to Stand.* New York: Harper & Row, 1961.

Marks, Paula Mitchell. "The Men of Gonzales." *American History Illustrated* 20 (March 1986): 46–47.

McDonald, Archie P. "Lone Star Rising." *American History Illustrated* 20 (March 1986): 48–51.

McWilliams, Perry. "The Alamo Story: From Fact to Fable." *Journal of the Folklore Institute* 15 (September – December 1978): 221–33.

The Mexican Side of the Texan Revolution [1836] by the Chief Mexican Participants. Translated by Carlos Castaneda. Dallas: P. L. Turner, 1928. Reprint. Washington, D.C.: Documentary Publications, 1971.

Michener, James A. *Texas.* New York: Random House, 1985.

Myers, John M. *The Alamo.* New York: E. P. Dutton and Co., 1947.

Nance, Joseph Milton. *After San Jacinto, The Texas-Mexican Frontier, 1836–1841.* Austin: University of Texas Press, 1963.

———. *Attack and Counterattack, The Texas-Mexican Frontier, 1842.* Austin: University of Texas Press, 1964.

Nevin, David. *The Texans.* New York: Time-Life Books, 1975.

Peña, José Enrique de la. *With Santa Anna in Texas: A Personal Narrative of the Revolution.* Translated and edited by Carmen Perry. College Station: Texas A&M University Press, 1975.

Pohl, James W., and Stephen L. Hardin. "The Military History of the Texas Revolution." *Southwestern Historical Quarterly* 89 (January 1986): 269–308.

Potter, Reuben M. "The Fall of the Alamo." *Magazine of American History* 2 (January 1878): 1–21.

———. "The Legendary Alamo." *Magazine of American History* 16 (August 1886): 200–202.

Santos, Richard G. *Santa Anna's Campaign Against Texas, 1835–1836, Featuring the Field Commands Issued to Major General Vicente Filisola.* 2d ed., rev. Salisbury, N.C.: Documentary Publication, 1981.

Schoelwer, Susan Prendergast. "Alamo Images." *American History Illustrated* 20 (March 1986): 38–45.

———, with Tom W. Glaser. *Alamo Images: Changing Perceptions of a Texas Experience.* Introduction by Paul Andrew Hutton. Dallas: DeGolyer Library and Southern Methodist University Press, 1985.

Tinkle, Lon. *Thirteen Days to Glory.* New York: McGraw-Hill Book Company, Inc., 1958.

Vigness, David M. *The Revolutionary Decades: The Saga of Texas, 1810–1836.* Austin: Steck Vaughn Co., 1965.

Von Schmidt, Eric. "How is the Alamo Remembered?" *Smithsonian* 16 (March 1986): 54–67.

Weber, David J. *The Mexican Frontier, 1821–1846: The American Southwest Under Mexico.* Albuquerque: University of New Mexico Press, 1982.

Williams, Amelia W. "A Critical Study of the Siege of the Alamo and of the Personnel of Its Defenders." Ph.D. diss., University of Texas, 1931. Published in abridged form in the *Southwest Historical Quarterly* 36 (April 1933): 251–87; 37 (July 1933): 1–44; 37 (October 1933): 79–115; 37 (January 1934): 157–84; 37 (April 1934), 237–312.

———, and Eugene C. Barker, eds. *The Writings of Sam Houston, 1813–1863.* 8 vols. Austin: University of Texas Press, 1938.

Wisehart, M. K. *Sam Houston, American Giant.* Washington: Robert B. Luce, Inc., 1962.

Zuber, W. P. "An Excape from the Alamo." In *Texas Almanac for 1873,* 80–85.

———. "The Escape of Rose from the Alamo." *The Quarterly of the Texas State Historical Association* 5 (1901): 1–11.

———. "Rose's Escape from the Alamo." *The Quarterly of the Texas State Historical Association* 6 (1902): 67–69.

SELECTED NEWSPAPER ARTICLES
DEALING WITH CROCKETT

For more information about nineteenth-century newspaper articles on Crockett, see James Atkins Shackford's "The Autobiography of David Crockett," Ph.D. diss., Vanderbilt University, 1948, 693–96, and *David Crockett: The Man and the Legend* (Chapel Hill: University of North Carolina Press, 1956), 320.

Armstrong, Zella. "Davy Crockett, Boy and Man." *Chattanooga Sunday Times,* August 30, 1936, Magazine Section, 4.

Barclay, Dolores. "Davy Crockett a Hero with a Song." *San Antonio Express-News,* March 7, 1986.

Blair, Walter. "'Bout Time ol' Davy Crockett Got Borned Agin." *Chicago Sun-Times,* March 2, 1986, 27.

Branston, John. "The Life & Made-Up-Times of David Crockett." *Mid-South* [The *Memphis Commercial Appeal* Magazine], April 20, 1986, 4–7.

Brooks, Ray. "Governor McAlister and Other Dignitaries Join Thousands of East Tennesseans in Reviving Days of Davy Crockett, Alamo's Famed Defender." *Knoxville Journal,* August 18, 1936, 1, 12.

Burchard, Hank. "'Davy Crockett': He Put Up a Good Frontier." *The Washington Post,* June 27, 1986.

Burke, James Wakefield. "David Crockett: The Man Behind the Myth." *San Antonio Light* [magazine section], February 24, 1985, 19–23.

Cincinnati Gazette, July 14, 1834.

Columbia Spy [Pennsylvania], July 12, 1834.

"Coonskin cap a myth, experts say." *USA Today*, August 15–17, 1986, A–1.

Cooper, Texas Jim. "Peña's Diary: How Did David Crockett Die?" *Carrollton Star* [Texas], November 6, 1975, Sec. 2, p. 8.

Crumbaker, Marge. "That Crockett Named Davy." *Texas Tempo*, January 28, 1968.

Cummings, Joe. "'Great Deal of Fuss' Still Being Made About Crockett." *The Greeneville* [Tennessee] *Sun*, August 9, 1986, 13.

———, ed. *The Crockett Bicentennial Times*. Supplement to *The Greeneville* [Tennessee] *Sun*, August 8, 1986.

Daffan, Miss Katie. "With Davy Crockett." *The Fort Worth Record*, March 31, 1907.

Daily Evening Transcript [Boston], June 21, 1833; November 21, 1833; November 30, 1833; January 8, 1834; May 6, 1834; July 8, 1834; July 31, 1834; August 1, 1834; July 27, 1835.

Dallas Morning News, December 25, 1927, 5.

"David Crockett Not the Idol You Think, Debunkers Say." *Tennessee Town & City*, September 29, 1986.

"David Crockett's Motto Lives a Hundred Years After." *San Antonio Express*, March 1, 1936, D–1.

Davis, Louise. "Davy Crockett: Fact or Fiction?" *The Nashville Tennessean*, October 12, 1986, E–1.

"Davy Crockett Bicentennial Edition." *The Greeneville* [Tennessee] *Sun*, August 8, 1986.

"Davy Crockett, Dead-Shot Pioneer, Who Went to Congress." *The Kansas City Star*, February 10, 1925.

"Davy Crockett Landmarks." *Knoxville Journal Cavalcade*, June 5, 1955, D–1.

"Davy Crockett 200th Birthday Celebrates Legend, History." *Columbia* [Tennessee] *Daily Herald*, July 27, 1986.

"Davy Fans Flock to Festival." *The Greeneville* [Tennessee] *Sun*, August 16, 1986.

"Davy's Last Stand at the Alamo as Visualized by Bob Dale, Express Cartoonist." *San Antonio Express*, June 19, 1955, G–1.

"Did Crockett Surrender?" *San Antonio Express*, March 6, 1985, B–1.

Dobie, J. Frank. "Alamo Hero Loved a Gun and a Girl." *San Antonio Light*, March 2, 1941.

———. "Texas' Crockett Relics." *San Antonio Light*, June 12, 1955.

Donovan, Dick. "Ol' Davy Crockett Was No Big Deal." *Weekly World News*, September 9, 1986.

Downing Gazette [Portland, Maine], February 28, 1835; March 14, 1835; May 23, 1835; May 30, 1835; June 13, 1835; August 1, 1835.

Dykeman, Wilma. "Books to Brighten Homecoming '86." *Knoxville News-Sentinel*, December 1, 1985, F–1.

Eblen, Tom. "It Was a Big Birthday for Crockett Country." *The Atlanta Constitution*, August 18, 1986, B–1.

"1836 Paper Tells Story of Davy's Death." *Knoxville News-Sentinel,* May 5, 1955.

Elledge, Tim. "'King of the Wild Frontier' Dies Hard by the Pen of Lofaro the Giant Legend Killer." *Context* [University of Tennessee], April 16, 1986.

Essig, Trisha. "Crockett: A Man for All Centuries." *Knoxville Journal,* August 15, 1986, A–3.

Fields, Franklin. "Last Man Alive at the Alamo?" *The Houston Chronicle Rotogravure Magazine,* February 28, 1954.

Furneaux, John. "Giant of the Alamo." *The Houston Chronicle Rotogravure Magazine,* June 5, 1955, 6–7.

Gibson, Dorothy. "Davy Crockett *Did* Wear a Coonskin Cap." *The Washington Post,* July 5, 1986, A–21.

"Grandson Writes View of Elizabeth Crockett, Wife of Alamo Hero." *Hood County News* [Granbury, Texas], June 27, 1976.

Haguewood, J. L. "Was Crockett Sacrificed By His Friends at Bloody Alamo?" *Memphis Commercial Appeal,* December 18, 1932.

Harris, Roger. "Communities Plan Davy Crockett Celebrations." *Knoxville News-Sentinel,* April 27, 1986, K–4.

Helyar, John. "Davy Crockett Was No Great Shakes, The Debunkers Say." *The Wall Street Journal,* July 10, 1986, A–1.

Hope, Sherlock. "Crockett's Descendant Would Solve Mystery—Davy's 'Extra Child.'" *Knoxville Journal,* July 10, 1958, 1.

Hurley, Bob. "Celebration Could Match Size of Crockett Legend." *The Greeneville* [Tennessee] *Sun,* March 26, 1986, 1.

———. "Our Own Davy Crockett: 200 Years and 1,000 Famous Caps." *The Greeneville* [Tennessee] *Sun,* March 12, 1986.

Hurst, Jack. "Legendary Davy Crockett a Good Ole Boy at Heart." *Chicago Tribune,* August 17, 1986, Sec. 2, p. 3.

Jackson [Tennessee] *Gazette,* July, 2, 1824; August 6, 1824; October 30, 1824; November 13, 1824; July 30, 1825; April 4, 1829; August 15, 1829; May 1, 1830.

Jackson [Tennessee] *Tribune and Sun,* July 9, 1882.

Johnson, Mrs. H. Clay. "Davy Crockett's Kinsmen in Texas." *The Dallas Morning News,* July 26, 1925.

Jones, Cecil. "Crockett in Lawrence." *Nashville Tennessean Magazine,* November 3, 1946, 7–8.

Judd, Cameron. "Davy Crockett Birthday Bash Under Way." *The Greeneville* [Tennessee] *Sun,* August 15, 1986, p. 1.

Kirkland, Tom. "Davy Crockett: King of the Wild Frontier." *Johnson City* [Tennessee] *Press,* August 16, 1986, 1.

———. "Period Re-enactors Enliven Crockett Days Celebration." *Johnson City* [Tennessee] *Press,* August 17, 1986, 1.

———. "Who, What was the Real David Crockett?" *Johnson City* [Tennessee] *Press,* August 15, 1986, 1.

Lake, Mary Daggett. "History and Genealogy of the Family of David Crockett." *San Antonio Express,* January 12, 1930.

Laurence, Charles. "Davy Crockett: Another Great American Myth." [London] *Daily Telegraph,* August-September 1986.

Lofaro, Michael A. "Davy Crockett's Legend Grew Just Like America." *Perspective, The Atlanta Journal-The Atlanta Constitution,* June 1, 1986, D–1.

Lollar, Michael. "In Limestone, Lore and Legend Lose Their Luster." *Memphis Commercial Appeal,* January 25, 1986.

Lumpkin, John. "Did Santa Anna 'Execute' Crockett?" *San Antonio Light,* September 9, 1975, A–1.

McCoy, George W. "Research Shows Crockett's Connection With WNC." *Asheville* [North Carolina] *Citizen Times,* August 12, 1951.

Missouri Republican, July-August 1829.

Morning Courier and New York Enquirer, December 15, 1830; April 27, 1831; June 3, 1831; November 21, 1831.

Morris, Doug. "Don't Go to Trashing Davy Crockett." *Knoxville Journal,* April 19, 1986, A–4.

"*MW* Recommends *Davy Crockett: Gentleman from the Cane.*" *Museum Washington,* June-July 1986, 22.

Nashville Tennessean, March 6, 1938; February 1, 1948, A–14.

Natchez Courier, [account of Crockett's death, printed in Walter Lord's *A Time to Stand* (New York: Harper & Row, 1961), 170].

National Banner and Nashville Whig, August 14, 1822; September 4, 1822; September 29, 1823; October 6, 1823; October 13, 1823; September 27, 1824; November 25, 1828; January 9, 1829; January 23, 1829; January 21, 1835; January 26, 1835; February 23, 1835.

National Intelligencer, September 2, 1835.

Neal, Suzanne Force. "Crockett Exhibit an Honor to UT [University of Tennessee]." *Knoxville News-Sentinel,* August 20, 1986, W–1.

New York Evening Post, August 27, 1831.

New York Mirror, December 18, 1830.

Niles Weekly Register. Edited by H. Niles. Baltimore: At the Franklin Press, Sept. 1811–August 27, 1842. Important Crockett-related volumes–41, pp. 150, 332; 45, p. 21; 46, pp. 148, 149, 173, 252, 280, 321; 47, pp. 390, 452–453; 49, pp. 229, 281; 50, pp. 121–23, 432–33; 54, pp. 242–43, 258; 55, p. 15; 57, pp. 319, 399; 58, pp. 128, 224, 255; 59, pp. 270, 318, 394, 407.

"On Davy Crockett's Trail." *Chattanooga News-Free Press,* August 17, 1986, L–7.

Pasztor, David. "Hero or Hoax?" *Dallas Times Herald,* August 16, 1986, A–1.

Patton, E. E. "B'ar Hunter a Poet Too." *Knoxville Journal,* August 17, 1930, 1.

Phelan, Charlotte. "The Davy Crockett Affray." *The Houston Post,* April 4, 1976, 7.

Poulson's American Daily Advertiser [Philadelphia], July 7, 1834.

"Professor Shoots Holes in Crockett Myth." *The Knoxville Journal,* April 17, 1986, D–1.

"Remembering the Alamo." *Homecoming Times* [Tenn.], April 1986, 16.

Rhea, David. "Improvements Coming to Crockett Birthplace." *The Greeneville* [Tennessee] *Sun,* July 24, 1985, 12.

Ridgway, William Alexander. "The Only Man Alive Who Knew Davy Crockett." *San Antonio Express,* June 16, 1912.

Ross, Margaret Smith. "Davy Crockett in Arkansas." *Arkansas Gazette Sunday Magazine,* May 15, 1955.

"Saluting a Folk Hero." *Knoxville News-Sentinel,* August 16, 1986, A–1.

San Antonio Daily Express, February 11, 1899.

San Antonio Light, February 19, 1899.

Schidlovsky, John. "Davy Crockett: The Right Man for the 1950's." *San Antonio Light,* August 17, 1986.

———. "Davy, Davy Crockett." *Baltimore Sun,* August 5, 1986, C–1.

Shemanski, Frances. "Tennessee Celebrating Davy Crockett." *The Dallas Morning News,* August 10, 1986, G–1.

"Tenn. Paper of 1836 Tells of Crockett Death at Alamo." *Morristown* [Tennessee] *Gazette and Mail,* April 14, 1960, 1.

Tully, Andrew. "Crockett Used Rough-and-Ready Frontier Humor in His Speeches." *Knoxville News-Sentinel,* May 1, 1955.

Umbreit, Kristi. "Loyal Davy Crockett Fans Mark His 200th Birthday, Alamo Death." *Knoxville Journal,* August 11, 1986, A–5.

———. "Remembering: Tennesseans Mark 200th Birthday of Frontiersman Davy Crockett." *Chattanooga Times,* August 16, 1986.

Vaughn, Renee. "Davy Crockett's Battle Not Over." *Nashville Tennessean,* April 17, 1986, 1.

West, Felton, "How Crockett Died Still Stirs Furor." *The Houston Post,* November 22, 1985, B–2.

"The Wilderness Man Takes His Pen in Hand." *Fort Worth Star-Telegram,* March 10, 1929.

Woodbury, Harry. "Statement That Frontiersman Couldn't Write is Protested." *Memphis Commercial Appeal,* November 23, 1941.

Yarbrough, Willard. "Renovation of Neglected Davy Crockett Park Sought." *Knoxville News-Sentinel,* December 20, 1981, B–1. 1, cols. 1–6.

Young, Kevin R. "Facts & Footnotes." *The Texian Express,* February 4, 1987.

WORKS DEALING WITH THE LEGENDARY CROCKETT

Abbott, John S. C. *David Crockett.* New York: Dodd, Mead, 1874.

Aderman, Ralph M., ed. *The Letters of James Kirke Paulding.* Madison: University of Wisconsin Press, 1962.

Adkins, N. F. "James K. Paulding's *Lion of the West.*" *American Literature* 3 (November 1931): 249–58.

Albanese, Catherine. "Citizen Crockett: Myth, History, and Nature Religion." *Soundings: An Interdisciplinary Journal* 61 (1978): 87–104.

———. "Davy Crockett and the Wild Man; Or, The Metaphysics of the *Longue Durée.*" In Lofaro, *Davy Crockett,* 80–101.

———. "King Crockett: Nature and Civility on the American Frontier." *Proceedings of the American Antiquarian Society* 88 (1978): 225–49.

———. "Savage, Sinner, and Saved: Davy Crockett, Camp Meetings, and the Wild Frontier." *American Quarterly* 33 (Winter 1981): 482–501.

Allen, Charles Fletcher. *David Crockett, Scout, Small Boy, Pilgrim, Mountaineer, Soldier, Bear-Hunter, and Congressman, Defender of the Alamo.* Philadelphia: J. B. Lippincott, 1911.

———. "The Men Who Died in the Alamo." *Sports Afield* 45 (October 1910): 297–306.

Ardman, Harvey. "The Life of Davy Crockett: Frontier Hero & Humorist." *The American Legion Magazine* December 1972: 16–20, 40–47.

Armstrong, A. B. *Backwoods to Border.* Publications of the Texas Folklore Society, vol. 18, 1943.

Arpad, Joseph John. "The Fight Story: Quotation and Originality in Native American Humor." *Journal of the Folklore Institute* 10 (1973): 141–72.

———. "John Wesley Jarvis, James Kirke Paulding, and Colonel Nimrod Wildfire." *New York Folklore Quarterly* 21 (1965): 92–106.

Bezanson, W. E. "Go Ahead Davy Crockett." *Journal of Rutgers University Library* 12 (June 1949): 32–37.

Bird, Robert Montgomery. *Nick of the Woods; or, the Jibbenainosay.* Edited by Curtis Dahl. New Haven: College & University Press, 1967.

Blair, Walter. "Americanized Comic Braggarts." *Critical Inquiry* 4 (Winter 1977): 331–49.

———. "Davy Crockett, Tennessee Settler" and "Davy Crockett, Soldier, Congressman and Comet Licker." In Blair's *Tall Tale America: A Legendary History of Our Humorous Heroes.* New York: Coward-McCann, 1944, 66–94, 259. Reprint. Chicago: University of Chicago Press, 1987.

———. *Horse Sense in American Humor: From Benjamin Franklin to Ogden Nash.* Chicago: University of Chicago Press, 1942. Reprint. New York: Russell & Russell, 1962.

———. "Introduction" in Lofaro and Cummings, *Crockett at Two Hundred,* 1–6.

———. "Six Davy Crocketts." *Southwest Review* 25 (1940): 443–62.

Blair, Walters, and Hamlin Hill. *America's Humor: From Poor Richard to Doonesbury.* New York: Oxford University Press, 1978.

Blair, Walter, and Franklin J. Meine, eds. *Half Horse Half Alligator: The Growth of the Mike Fink Legend.* Chicago: University of Chicago Press, 1956. Reprint. New York: Arno Press, 1977.

Boone and Crockett Club, Brief History of, With Officers, Constitution, and List of Members for the Year 1910. Edited by George Bird Grinnell. New York: Forest and Stream Publishing Company.

Boorstin, Daniel. "Heroes or Clowns? Comic Supermen from a Subliterature." In Boorstin's *The Americans: The National Experience.* New York: Random House, 1965, 327–37. Selections reprinted in *Showcasing American Drama,* edited by Vera Jiji. Brooklyn: Humanities Institute, 1983, [21].

Brady, Cyrus T. "David Crockett and the Most Desperate Defense in American History." *The Idler* 21 (July 1902): 522–33.

Bright, Verne. "Davy Crockett Legend and Tales in the Oregon Country." *Oregon Historical Quarterly* 51 (1950): 207–15.

Brown, Dee. *Wave High the Banner: A Novel Based on the Life of Davy Crockett.* Philadelphia: Macrae-Smith, 1942.

Campbell, Mrs. A. A. "David Crockett, the 'Go-ahead' Man." *Confederate Veteran* 28 (March 1920): 104–5.

Carmer, Carl. "Confab with Crockett: A Radio Play." In *Plays of Democracy*, edited by Margaret Mayorga. New York: Dodd, Mead & Company, 1944, 107–15.

Caruthers, William Alexander. *The Kentuckian in New York; Or, The Adventures of Three Southerns.* New York: Harper & Bros., 1834. Reprint. Ridgewood, N.J.: Gregg Press, 1968.

Chadwicke, Alice (William Braun). *Davy Crockett: A Robust Comedy Drama in Three Acts Based on the Life of America's Heroic Young Backwoodsman.* New York: Samuel French, Inc., 1956.

Chittick, V. L. O. "Review of *Davy Crockett* and the *Adventures of Davy Crockett*." *American Literature* 6 (November 1934): 368–70.

———, ed. *Ring-Tailed Roarers: Tall Tales of the American Frontier, 1830–60.* Caldwell, Idaho: Caxton Printers, 1941.

Clark, William Bedford. "*Col. Crockett's Exploits and Adventures in Texas*: Death and Transfiguration." *Studies in American Humor* I (June 1982): 66–76.

Crockett, David (probable author, William Clark). *An Account of Colonel Crockett's Tour to the North and Down East.* Philadelphia: Carey & Hart, 1835.

———. *The Adventures of Davy Crockett, Told Mostly by Himself.* New York: Charles Scribner's Sons, 1934.

——— [Richard Penn Smith]. *Colonel Crockett's Exploits and Adventures in Texas, Written by Himself.* Philadelphia: Carey & Hart, 1836.

———. *The Life of David Crockett, the Original Humorist and Irrespressible Backwoodsman: An Autobiography.* Philadelphia: Porter & Coates, 1869.

———(probable author, Augustin Smith Clayton). *The Life of Martin Van Buren, Hair-Apparent to the "Government," and the Appointed Successor of General Jackson.* Philadelphia: Robert White, 1835.

———[Mathew St. Clair Clarke]. *The Life and Adventures of Colonel David Crockett of West Tennessee.* Cincinnati: Published for the Proprietor, 1833. Reprinted the same year as *Sketches and Eccentricities of Colonel David Crockett of West Tennessee.* New York: J. & J. Harper, 1833.

Crockett almanacs. 1835–56.

Crowell, C. T. "Davy Crockett." *American Mercury* 4 (January 1925): 109–15.

Daugherty, James, ed. *Their Weight in Wildcats: Tales of the Frontier.* Boston: Houghton Mifflin Company, 1936.

"Davy Crockett's Almanack." *The Library Development Program Report* [University of Tennessee, Knoxville] 79 (1975–1976): 6–7.

Davy Crockett's Almanac of Wild Sports in the West, Life in the Backwoods, & Sketches of Texas. 1837. Nashville, Tenn: Published by the heirs of Col. Crockett. Reprinted in facsimile with an introduction by James Thorpe, San Marino, Calif. The Huntington Library and Art Gallery, 1971.

Dorson, Richard M. *America in Legend: Folklore from the Colonial Period to the Present.* New York: Random House, 1973.

———, ed. *Davy Crockett: American Comic Legend.* New York: Spiral Press for Rockland Editions, 1939. Reprint. Salem, N.H.: Ayer Publishing Co., 1977.

———. "Davy Crockett and the Heroic Age." *Southern Folklore Quarterly* 6 (June 1942): 95–102.

———. "The Sources of *Davy Crockett, American Comic Legend.*" *Midwest Folklore* 8 (1958): 143–49.

Durrett, John. "David Crockett and the Fall of the Alamo: Being Some Leaves from His Notebook." *Methodist Quarterly Review* 76 (October 1927): 615–24.

Eggleston, George Cary. *David Crockett.* New York: Dodd, Mead Company, 1875.

Ellis, Edward S. *The Life of Colonel David Crockett.* Philadelphia: Porter & Coates, 1884.

———. *Sockdolager! A Tale of Davy Crockett, in which the Old Tennessee Bear Hunter Meets up with the Constitution of the United States.* 1876. Reprint. Richmond: Virginia Commission on Constitutional Government, 1961.

Ellms, Charles. *The Pirates Own Book.* Boston: Samuel N. Dickinson, 1837.

French, James Strange. *Elkswatawa; Or, The Prophet of the West: A Tale of the Frontier.* New York: Harper & Bros., 1836.

Garland, Hamlin, ed. *The Autobiography of David Crockett.* New York: Charles Scribner's Sons, 1923.

"'Go Ahead,' or Crockett Again." *The Library Development Review* [University of Tennessee, Knoxville] (1985/1986): 10–11.

Hamilton, Elizabeth B., ed. *How Big They Started: Nine Famous Men Begin Their Careers.* New York: Harcourt, Brace and Company, 1937.

Harrison, Lowell H. "Davy Crockett: The Making of a Folk Hero." *Kentucky Folklore Record* 15 (1969): 87–90.

Hauck, Richard Boyd. *Crockett: A Bio-Biliography.* Westport, Conn.: Greenwood Press, 1982. Reprinted as *Davy Crockett: A Handbook. Lincoln: University of Nebraska Press,* 1986.

———. "The Man in the Buckskin Hunting Shirt: Fact and Fiction in the Crockett Story." In Lofaro, *Davy Crockett,* 3–20.

———. "The Real Davy Crocketts: Creative Autobiography and the Invention of His Legend." In Lofaro and Cummings, *Crockett at Two Hundred,* 179–91.

Hoffman, Daniel G. "The Deaths and Three Resurrections of Davy Crockett." *Antioch Review* 21 (Spring 1961): 5–13.

Hoover, John Neal. "Treasures of the Mercantile." *News of Note: A Quarterly Publication of the St. Louis Mercantile Library Association* 1 (September 1986): 3.

Hough, Emerson. "Davy Crockett." *Outing Magazine* 42 (July 1903): 440–48.

———. *The Way to the West, and the Lives of Three Early Americans: Boone– Crockett– Carson.* Indianapolis: Bobbs-Merrill, 1903.

Hyde, Stuart W. "The Ring-Tailed Roarer in American Drama." *Southern Folklore Quarterly* 19 (September 1955): 171–78.

Jiji, Vera, ed. *Showcasing American Drama: A Handbook of Source Materials on "The Lion of the West" by J. K. Paulding.* Brooklyn: Humanities Institute, 1983.

Jones, Howard Mumford. Foreword to *Davy Crockett: American Comic Legend,* by Richard M. Dorson. Reprint. Salem, N.H.: Ayer Publishing Co., 1977.

Kelly, C. C. (Sen.) *Tennessee's Hero of the Alamo, Col. David Crockett, and Business Men's Directory.* Lawrenceburg, Tenn., 1922.

Leach, Joseph. "Crockett Almanacs and the Typical Texan." *Southwest Review* 35 (Spring 1950): 88–95.

———. *The Typical Texan: Biography of an American Myth.* Dallas: Southern Methodist University Press, 1952.

Leithead, Edward J. "Legendary Heroes and the Dime Novel." *American Book Collector* 18, no. 7 (1968), 22–27.

Lemay, J. A. Leo. "The Frontiersman from Lout to Hero: Notes on the Significance of the Comparative Method and the Stage Theory in Early American Literature and Culture." *Proceedings of the American Antiquarian Society* 88, Pt. 2 (1978): 187–223.

Lipper, Mark. "Comic Caricatures in Early American Newspapers as Indicators of the National Character." Ph.D. diss., Southern Illinois University, 1972.

Lofaro, Michael A., ed. *Davy Crockett: The Man, The Legend, The Legacy, 1786–1986.* Knoxville: University of Tennessee Press, 1985.

———. "From Boone to Crockett: The Beginnings of Frontier Humor." *Mississippi Folklore Register* 14 (1980): 57–74.

———. "The Hidden 'Hero' of the Nashville Crockett Almanacs." In Lofaro, *Davy Crockett,* 46–79.

———. Introduction to the Crockett section in *Houston and Crockett,* edited by Herbert L. Harper. Nashville: Tennessee Historical Commission, 1986, 127–31.

———. Introduction to the new edition of James Atkins Shackford's *David Crockett: The Man and the Legend,* edited by John B. Shackford. 1956. Reprint. Chapel Hill: University of North Carolina Press, 1986, ix–xx.

———. "The Legendary Davy Crockett." *The Tennessee Conservationist* 52 (July/August 1986): 2–5.

———. "Riproarious Shemales: Legendary Women in the Tall Tale World of Davy Crockett." In Lofaro and Cummings, *Crockett at Two Hundred,* 114–52.

———, ed. *The Tall Tales of Davy Crockett: The Second Nashville Series of Crockett Almanacs, 1839–1841.* Knoxville: University of Tennessee Press, 1987.

Lofaro, Michael, and Joe Cummings, eds. *Crockett at Two Hundred: New Perspectives on the Man and the Myth.* Knoxville: University of Tennessee Press, 1989.

Loney, Glenn. "Acting in Period Plays." In *Showcasing American Drama,* edited by Vera Jiji. Brooklyn: Humanities Institute, 1983, [11]–[13].

Mason, Melvin R. "*The Lion of the West:* Davy Crockett and Frances Trollope." *Studies by Members of SCMLA* 19 (Winter 1969): 143–45.

Mayer, Edwin Justus. *Sunrise in My Pocket, Or The Last Days of Davy Crockett: An American Saga.* New York: Julian Messner, 1941.

McKernan, Frank. *David Crockett—Scout.* New York: J. B. Lippincott Company, 1911.

Meine, Franklin J., ed. *The Crockett Almanacks: Nashville Series, 1835–1838.* Chicago: The Caxton Club, 1955.

Milhous, John Philip. "Davy Crockett: Half Horse, Half Alligator." *The Carolina Playbook* [University of North Carolina] 6 (March 1933): 5–24. Reprinted in *American Folk Plays,* edited by F. H. Koch. New York, 1939, 29–58.

Miller, Marilyn. "Yankee Theater." In *Showcasing American Drama,* edited by Vera Jiji, [2]–[3]. Brooklyn: Humanities Institute, 1983.

Murdock, Frank. *Davy Crockett; Or, Be Sure You're Right, Then Go Ahead.* In *Davy Crockett and Other Plays,* vol. 4 of *America's Lost Plays,* edited by Isaac Goldberg and Hubert Heffner. Princeton, N.J.: Princeton University Press, 1940. Reprint. Bloomington: Indiana University Press, 1963, 115–48.

Newmill, P. M. "Davy Crockett Explains a Vote. Backwoods Statesman and Alamo Hero Tells of When He Wept Like a Child." *Bunker's [Texas] Monthly* 1 (June 1928): 926–40.

Owens, Harry J. ". . . And Laugh Out Loud." In *The Crockett Almanacks,* edited by Franklin J. Meine. Chicago: The Caxton Club, 1955, xxvii–xxxvi.

Parrington, Vernon Louis. "The Crockett Myth." In *Main Currents in American Thought.* New York: Harcourt, 1927, 2, 172–79.

Paulding, James Kirke. "The American People." In *Showcasing American Drama,* edited by Vera Jiji. Brooklyn: Humanities Institute, 1983, [18].

———. *The Lion of the West; Retitled the Kentuckian, or A Trip to New York: A Farce in Two Acts.* Revised by John Augustus Stone and William Bayle Bernard. Edited by James N. Tidwell. Stanford, Calif.: Stanford University Press, 1954.

Paulsen, Barbara. "Say It Ain't So, Davy." *Texas Monthly,* November 1986, 129.

Porter, Kenneth W. "Davy Crockett and John Horse: A Possible Origin of the Coonskin Story." *American Literature* 15 (1943): 10–15.

Price, Shirley. "Davy Crockett." *The Tennessee Conservationist* 35 (June 1969): 1–3.

"Real Davy Crockett, Politician, Bear-hunter, Hero." *Literary Digest* 84 (February 7, 1925), 46–53.

Roche, James Jeffery. *The Story of the Filibusters. To Which is Added the Life of Colonel David Crockett.* London: T. Fisher Unwin, 1891.

Rourke, Constance. *Davy Crockett.* New York: Harcourt, 1934.

———. "Davy Crockett, Forgotten Facts and Legends." *Southwest Review* 19 (1934): 149–61.

Seelye, John. "Cats, Coons, Cocketts, and Other Furry Critters: Or, Why Davy Wears an Animal for a Hat." In Lofaro and Cummings, *Crockett at Two Hundred,* 153–78.

———. "A Well-Wrought Crockett: Or, How the Fakelorists Passed through the Credibility Gap and Discovered Kentucky." In Lofaro, *Davy Crockett,* 21–45.

Seitz, Don Carlos. *Uncommon Americans, Pencil Portraits of Men and Women Who Have Broken the Rules.* Indianapolis: The Bobbs-Merrill Company, 1925.

Shapiro, Irwin. "All American Hero." *Saturday Review of Literature* 27 (April 1, 1944): 10–11.

Shaw, Russell. *Davy Crockett: Fabulous Frontier Fighter.* Gatlinburg, Tenn.: Russell Shaw Guides, 1955.

Simms, William Gilmore. *Michael Bonham: Or, The Fall of Bexar.* Richmond: John R. Thompson, 1852.

"*Sketches and Eccentricities* Reviewed." *Monthly Review* [London] 134 (June 1834): 254–59.

"Slick, Crockett, Downing, etc." [Review]. *The London and Westminster Review* 32 (December 1838–April 1839): 136–45.

Smith-Rosenberg, Carroll. "Davy [*sic*] Crockett as Trickster: Pornography, Liminality and Symbolic Inversion in Victorian America." *Journal of Contemporary History* 17 (1982): 325–50. Reprinted in *Disorderly Conduct: Visions of Gender in Victorian America*, edited by Carroll Smith-Rosenberg. New York: A. A. Knopf, 1985, 90–108.

Smith, Seba. *The Life and Writings of Major Jack Downing, of Downingville, Away Down East in the State of Maine, Written by Himself.* Boston: Lilly, Wait, Colman, & Holden, 1833. Reprint. New York: AMS Press, 1973.

———. *My Thirty Years Out of the Senate.* New York: Oaksmith and Co., 1859.

Sprague, William C. *Davy Crockett.* New York: The Macmillan Company, 1915.

Stiffler, Stuart A. "Davy Crockett: The Genesis of Heroic Myth." *Tennessee Historical Quarterly* 16 (1957): 134–40.

Stone, Irving. "Four Loves Had Davy Crockett." *The American Weekly,* June 5, 1955, 3–5; 7, 13–14; June 12, 1955, 14–15.

Taylor, Joshua C. *America as Art.* Washington, D.C.: Smithsonian Institution Press, 1976, 88–94.

"*Texas Exploits* Reviewed." *Fraser's Magazine* [London] 16 (November 1837): 610–27.

"*Texas Exploits*, Review of London Edition." *Monthly Review* [London] 143 (May 1837): 215–33.

Thompson, Ernest T. *The Fabulous David Crockett.* Rutherford, Tenn.: Davy Crockett Memorial Association, 1956.

Thompson, Samuel H. "Hunter Hero." In *Southern Hero Tales.* Morrison, Tenn.: Globe Book Company, 1914, 51–63.

Thorne, Creath S. "The Crockett Almanacs: What Makes A Tall Tale Tall?" *Southern Folklore Quarterly* 44 (1980): 93–104.

Trollope, Frances. "Selections from *Domestic Manners of the Americans.*" In *Showcasing American Drama*, edited by Vera Jiji. Brooklyn: Humanities Institute, 1983, [21]–[22].

Van Doren, Carl. Foreword to *Sunrise in My Pocket, Or The Last Days of Davy Crockett: An American Saga*, by Edwin Justus Mayer. New York: Julian Messner, 1941.

Warren, Robert Penn. "A Dearth of Heroes." *American Heritage* 23 (October 1972): 4–7.

Warshaver, Gerald E. "*The Lion of the West*: A Text for National Identity." In *Show-*

casing American Drama, edited by Vera Jiji. Brooklyn: Humanities Institute, 1983, [18]–[21].

Watkins, Floyd C. "James K. Paulding's Early Ring-Tailed Roarer." *Southern Folklore Quarterly* 15 (September 1951): 183–87.

Wecter, Dixon. *The Hero in America: A Chronicle of Hero-Worship.* 1941. Reprinted with an introduction by Robert Penn Warren. New York: Charles Scribner's Sons, 1972.

West, James L. W. III. "Early Backwoods Humor in The Greenville *Mountaineer,* 1826–1840." *Mississippi Quarterly* 25 (Winter 1971): 69–82.

Zanger, Jules. "The Frontiersman in Popular Fiction, 1820–1860." In *The Frontier Re-examined,* edited by John Francis McDermott. Urbana: University of Illinois Press, 1967, 141–53.

Poems

Caruthers, William Alexander. *David Crockett; or, The Nimrod of the West. The Only Cure for Hard Times.* 1837. Manuscript poem, never completed. Held by the Library of Congress.

"Colonel David Crockett's Only Poem." In *Tennessee's Hero of the Alamo, Col. David Crockett, and Business Men's Directory,* by C. C. Kelly. Lawrenceburg, Tenn., 1922, inside back cover.

Crockett, M. H., Sr. "Davy Crockett." In *Heroes of the Alamo: Accounts and Documents of William B. Travis, James Bowie, James B. Bonham and David Crockett, and Their Texas Memorials,* edited by A. Garland Adair and M. H. Crockett, Sr. 2d ed. New York: Exposition Press, 1957, 66.

Glassford, Cora Carleton. "The Alamo." In Adair and Crockett, *Heroes of the Alamo,* 25.

"His Parting Blessing: The Only Poem Composed by Davy Crockett." In *Gibson County: Past and Present,* by Frederick M. Culp and Mrs. Robert E. Ross. Trenton, Tenn. Gibson County Historical Society, 1961, 25.

Hughes, Fannie May. "The Legend of Crockett." [n.p., n.d.; A copy is held at the University of Texas at Austin Library.]

"Hymn of the Alamo." In *Tennessee's Hero of the Alamo, Col. David Crockett, and Business Men's Directory,* by C. C. Kelly. Lawrenceburg, Tenn., 1922, back cover. Reprinted in Adair and Crockett, *Heroes of the Alamo,* 77.

"Lines on the Death of the Late David Crockett Who Fell At Bejai." In "Seven Patriotic Poems from New Orleans Newspapers on the War for Texas Independence," edited by Hennig Cohen. *Southwestern Historical Quarterly* 54 (January 1951): 337–43.

Smith, T. F. "On the Death of Colonel Crockett." In *Field's Scrapbook.* Philadelphia: Claxton, Remsen, & Haffelfinger, 1878, 42. Reprinted in Adair and Crockett, *Heroes of the Alamo,* 47.

WORKS DEALING WITH THE WALT DISNEY–INSPIRED CROCKETT
CRAZE AND WITH TELEVISION'S EFFECTS ON AMERICAN CULTURE

Blair, Walter. "R.I.P. King of the Wild Frontier." *Saturday Review,* July 21, 1956, 26.
"Braggarts of the Backwoods." *Life,* April 11, 1960, 99–100.
"Coonskin Superman." *New York Times Magazine,* April 24, 1955, 20.
"Crockett and Circulation." *Newsweek,* July 18, 1955, 60,
"Davy: Row and a Riddle." *Newsweek,* July 4, 1955, 56.
"Davy Crockett Craze on the Wane." *New York Times Magazine,* December 11, 1955, 27.
"Davy Crockett 'Elected.'" *New York Times,* May 19, 1955, 32.
"Davy Crockett: 'King of the Wild Frontier. . . .'" *The Tennessee Conservationist* 21 (June 1955): 6–7.
"Davy in Bean Town." *Time,* August 8, 1955, 59.
"Decline of a Hero." *Collier's,* November 25, 1955, 102.
Dichter, Ernest. "Fads: What Starts Them, What Keeps Them Going, Why They Die." *Tide,* November 1958, 20ff.
Dorson, Richard. Letter to the Editor. *Saturday Review,* August 6, 1955, 23.
"Fess Parker as 'Davy Crockett' Vividly Portrays Frontier Days in Tennessee." *The Tennessee Conservationist* 21 (June 1955): 8–9.
Finch, Christopher. *The Art of Walt Disney, from Mickey Mouse to the Magic Kingdoms.* New York: Harry N. Abrams, 1973.
Fischer, John. "The Embarrassing Truth About Davy Crockett." *Harper's* 211 (July 1955): 16–18.
Graham, Keith. "Frontier King Image Still Tails Fess Parker." *The Atlanta Constitution,* August 18, 1986, B–1.
Greene, Bob. "King of the Wild Frontier." *Esquire,* March 1982, 13–16.
Harrigan, Stephen. "The Ballad of Fess Parker." *Texas Monthly,* November 1986, 131.
Haverstick, John. "The Two Davy Crocketts." *Saturday Review,* July 9, 1955, 19.
Johnson, Nicholas. *How to Talk Back to Your Television Set.* New York: Bantam Books, 1970.
Jones, Landon. *Great Expectations: America and the Baby Boom Generation.* New York: Ballantine, 1980.
Kahn, E. J., Jr. "Be Sure You're Right, Then Go Ahead." *New Yorker,* September 3, 1955, 64–70.
Kalb, Bernard. "Dan'l, Dan'l Boone." *New York Times Magazine,* October 9, 1955, 42.
King, Margaret Jane. "The Davy Crockett Craze: A Case Study in Popular Culture." Ph.D. diss., University of Hawaii, 1976.
———. "The Disney Sensibility." Unpublished master's thesis, Bowling Green State University, 1972.
———. "The Recycled Hero: Walt Disney's Davy Crockett." In *Davy Crockett,* edited by Michael A. Lofaro. Knoxville: University of Tennessee Press, 1985, 137–58.
"King Davy and Friends." *Time,* August 1, 1955, 30.

Leebron, Elizabeth and Lynn Gartley. *Walt Disney: A Guide to References and Resources*. Boston: G. K. Hall & Inc., 1979.

Letters. *Harper's Magazine* 211 (September 1955): 4, 6.

Letters. *New York Times*, May 8, 1955, Sec. 4, p. 4, col. 4.

Maltin, Leonard. *The Disney Films*. New York: Crown, 1973.

"The Mark of Zorro." *Life*, August 18, 1958, 69–75.

McLuhan, Marshall. *Understanding Media: The Extensions of Man*. New York: Signet Books, 1964.

"Meet Davy Crockett." *Look*, July 26, 1955, 36.

"Mr. Crockett is Dead Shot as Salesman." *New York Times*, June 1, 1955, 38.

Packard, Vance. *The Hidden Persuaders*. New York: David McKay, 1957.

"Random Notes from Washington: Hero Stands in for Davy Crockett." *New York Times*, June 20, 1955, 12.

Reston, James. "Even Davy Crockett Can't Do Everything." *New York Times*, May 22, 1955, Sec. 4, p. 8.

Rourke, Constance. Letter to the Editor. *Saturday Review*, July 30, 1955, 23.

"The Saga of Davy Crockett." *The Disney Channel Magazine*, June 22–August 2, 1986, 8.

Sann, Paul. "The King of Nothing: Davy Crockett." In *Fads, Follies and Delusions of the American People*. New York: Crown Publishers, 1967, 27–30.

Schickel, Richard. *The Disney Version*. New York: Avon, 1968.

"Taxridden Hoppy to Unsaddle Enterprises." *Business Week*, January 19, 1952, 151.

"U.S. Again is Subdued by Davy." *Life*, April 25, 1955, 27–33.

Walt Disney Productions, Publicity Department. "Davy Crockett, King of the Wild Frontier." Production story, [1954].

————. Publicity office memos nos. 22871, 22874, 22875, 22876; (no dates) concerning the re-release (about 1972–73) of the Davy Crockett film series for television.

"Where Are You, Davy, When We Need You?" [interview with Fess Parker by Cobey Black], *Honolulu Advertiser*, October 28, 1975, B–1.

White, Peter. "Ex-King of the Wild Frontier." *New York Times Magazine*, December 11, 1955, 27.

"The Wild Frontier." *Time*, May 23, 1955, 90–92.

"A Wonderful World: Growing Impact of the Disney Art." *Newsweek*, April 18, 1955, 60.

Woolsey, Bill. "Davy Crockett, Disney Style." *Nashville Tennessean Magazine*, October 3, 1954, 8–9.

Wright, John P. "In Defense of Davy." In Letters to the Editor, *Harper's* 211 (September 1955): 4.

Wyllie, Irvin. "The Embarrassing Truth about Davy Crockett, the Yoknapatawpha County and Other Dear Myths." *Harper's* 211 (July 1955): 16–18.

The Disney Television Shows

"Davy Crockett, Indian Fighter." Walt Disney, 1954.

"Davy Crockett Goes to Congress." Walt Disney, 1955.

"Davy Crockett at the Alamo." Walt Disney, 1955.
"Davy Crockett's Keelboat Race." Walt Disney, 1955.
"Davy Crockett and the River Pirates." Walt Disney, 1955.
"Davy Crockett: Rainbow in the Thunder." Walt Disney, 1988.

Disney Movies
Davy Crockett, King of the Wild Frontier. Walt Disney, 1955.
Davy Crockett and the River Pirates. Walt Disney, 1956.

The above bibliography is a slightly enlarged version of the one in Margaret Jane King's "The Recycled Hero: Walt Disney's Davy Crockett," in *Davy Crockett*, edited by Michael A. Lofaro. Knoxville: University of Tennessee Press, 1985, 157–58.

WORKS DEALING WITH CROCKETT FILMS AND A CROCKETT FILMOGRAPHY

"*The Alamo.*" A review. *Filmfacts* 3 (1960): 255–57.
"*The Alamo.*" A review. *Time* November 7, 1960, 76.
Beaufort, John. "*Davy Crockett* on Screen." *Christian Science Monitor*, May 1, 1955.
Birdwell, Russell. *A News Release: John Wayne's "The Alamo."* New York: Russell Birdwell, 1960.
Bruce, Norman. "A Newly Discovered Silent Film: An Article on *Davy Crockett* (Oliver Morosco Photoplay Co.)." In *Davy Crockett*, edited by Michael A. Lofaro. Knoxville: University of Tennessee Press, 1985, 125–36.
"Film Review: *Davy Crockett, King of the Wild Frontier.*" *Variety*, May 18, 1955, 8.
Graham, Don. *Cowboys and Cadillacs: How Hollywood Looks at Texas.* Austin: Texas Monthly Press, 1983.
———. "Remembering the Alamo: The Story of the Texas Revolution in Popular Culture." *Southwestern Historical Quarterly* 89 (July 1985): 35–66.
Hauck, Richard Boyd. "Making It All Up: Davy Crockett in the Theater." In *Davy Crockett*, edited by Michael A. Lofaro. Knoxville: University of Tennessee Press, 1985, 102–23.
Hutton, Paul Andrew. "The Celluloid Alamo." *Arizona & the West* 28 (Spring 1986): 5–22.
Jamborsky, William Eric. "Davy Crockett and the Tradition of the Westerner in American Cinema." In *Crockett at Two Hundred: New Perspectives on the Man and the Myth.* Eds. Michael A. Lofaro and Joe Cummings. Knoxville: University of Tennessee Press, 1989, 97–113.
———. "Moviemakers and the Myth." *The Crockett Bicentennial Times*, supplement to *The Greeneville* [Tennessee] Sun, August 8, 1986, 14–15.
Lamkin, Ken. "Thirteen Days to Glory: *The Alamo.*" *American Cinematographer* 68 (February 1987): 54–58.
Levine, Paul G. "Remember the Alamo?" *American Film* 7 (January-February 1982): 47–49.
Rouch, Matt. "NBC's 'Alamo' surrenders to the usual hokum." *USA Today*, January 26, 1987, D-3.

Films dealing with Crockett are listed chronologically in the categories silent films, talkies, and television films.

Silent Films
Davy Crockett — in Hearts United. New York Motion Pictures, 1909.
Davy Crockett. Selig Polyscope, 1910.
The Immortal Alamo. Melies, 1911.
Davy Crockett Up-to-Date. United Film Service, 1915.
The Martyrs of the Alamo. Fine Arts-Triangle, 1915.
Davy Crockett. Pallas (Paramount), 1916.
Davy Crockett at the Fall of the Alamo. Sunset, 1926.

Talkies
Heroes of the Alamo. Columbia, 1937.
Man of Conquest. Republic, 1939.
Davy Crockett, Indian Scout. Reliance Pictures, 1950.
Man from the Alamo. Universal, 1953.
Davy Crockett, King of the Wild Frontier. Walt Disney, 1955.
Last Command. Republic, 1955.
Davy Crockett and the River Pirates. Walt Disney, 1956.
The First Texan. Allied Artists, 1956.
Alias Jesse James. United Artists, 1959.
The Alamo. United Artists, 1960.

Television Films
Sequin. PBS, 1982.
The Alamo: Thirteen Days to Glory. NBC, 1987.
[See also Disney films in the Crockett Craze section.]

The above filmography is a slightly enlarged version of the one in Richard Boyd Hauck's "Making It All Up: Davy Crockett in the Theater," in *Davy Crockett*, edited by Michael A. Lofaro. Knoxville: University of Tennessee Press, 1985, 122–23.

Additional, but minor television appearances by Crockett include "Alamo episodes" in the 1960s science-fiction series "Time Tunnel," and "You Are There" (1971, with Fred Gwynne as Davy) and small parts in the "Alamo Jobe" episode of "Amazing Stories" (1986) and in "Houston: The Legend of Texas" (1986).

WORKS DEALING WITH CROCKETT SONGS

Brewton, John E. "Folk Rimes of Southern Children." *Tennessee Folklore Society Bulletin* 26 (1960): 92–99.
Combs, Josiah. *Folk-Songs of the Southern United States.* Edited by D. K. Wiggins. Austin: University of Texas Press/American Folklore Society, 1967.

Crockett's Free-and-Easy Song Book: A New Collection of the Most Popular Stage Songs, as Given By the Best Vocalists of the Present Day: and also of Favorite Dinner and Parlour Songs. Philadelphia: J. Kay, Jr. & Bro., 1837.

Crockett's Free-and-Easy Songbook: Comic, Sentimental, Amatory, Sporting, African, Scotch, Irish, Western and Texian National, Military, Naval and Anacreontic: A New Collection of the Most Popular Stage Songs, Together with Glees, Duets, Recitations, and Medleys. 2d ed. Philadelphia: Kay and Troutman, and Pittsburgh: C. H. Kay, 1846.

Randolph, Vance. *Ozark Mountain Folks.* New York: Vanguard, 1932.

Sandburg, Carl. *The American Song Bag.* New York: Harcourt Brace and Co., 1927.

Toll, Robert C. *Blacking Up: The Minstrel Show in Nineteenth Century America.* New York: Oxford University Press, 1974.

Wolfe, Charles K. "Crockett and 19th-Century Music." In *Crockett at Two Hundred: New Perspectives on the Man and the Myth.* Eds. Michael A. Lofaro and Joe Cummings. Knoxville: University of Tennessee Press, 1989, 83–96.

———. "Davy Crockett Songs: Minstrels to Disney." In *Davy Crockett,* edited by Michael A. Lofaro. Knoxville: University of Tennessee Press, 1985, 159–90.

———. "Davy Crockett's Dance and Old Hickory's Fandango." *The Devil's Box* 16 (September 1982): 34–41.

———. *Kentucky Country: Folk and Country Music of Kentucky.* Lexington: University Press of Kentucky, 1982.

Printed Twentieth-Century Versions
of Traditional "Davy Crockett" Songs

1910	H. M. Belden, ed. *Song-Ballads and Other Popular Poetry.* No. 59. n.p., n.d.
1925	Josiah H. Combs, ed. *Folk-songs du midi des Etats-Unis.* Paris: 1925; translation reprinted as *Folk-Songs of the Southern United States,* edited by D. K. Wilgus. Austin: University of Texas Press/American Folklore Society, 1967, 182–83.
1925	John H. Cox, ed. *Folk-Songs of the South.* Cambridge: Harvard University Press, 494–500. No. 177.
1925	Dorothy Scarborough. *On the Trail of Negro Folk-Songs.* Cambridge: Harvard University Press, 177–78. (Possibly not a "Pompey Smash" variant.)
1927	Julia Beazley. "The Ballad of Davy Crockett." *Texas Folk-Lore Society Publications* 6 (1927): 205–6. Reprinted in *American Ballads and Folk Songs,* edited by Alan and John Lomax. New York: Macmillan, 1934, 251–53; in *A Treasury of American Folklore,* edited by B. A. Botkin. New York: Crown, 1944, 15–16. Reprint. New York: Bantam, 1980; in *The American People,* edited by B. A. Botkin. London: Pilot Press, 1946, 33; and in *Texas Folk Songs,* by William Owens. Austin: Texas Folklore Society, 1950.
1932	Vance Randolph. *Ozark Mountain Folks.* New York: Vanguard, 138–39.

1949   Vance Randolph. *Ozark Folk Songs*. Vol. 3, 165–67. Columbia: University of Missouri Press, 1949. Reprint edition, 1980; abridged edition, edited by Norm Cohen. Urbana: University of Illinois Press, 1982, 338–40.

1965   Archie Green. "Notes" for Sarah Ogan Gunning, *Girl of Constant Sorrow*. (Folk Legacy LP record FSA–26). Sharon, Conn.: Folk Legacy, 1965, 23–24.

Commercial (*) and Noncommercial Recordings
of "Davy Crockett/Pompey Smash" Songs

1931   *   "Davey Crockett." Sung by Chubby Parker, with harmonica and banjo accompaniment. New York, Conqueror Records No. 7895.

1936   "Pompey Smash." Sung by David Rice, Springfield, Missouri (recorded by Sidney Robertson). Library of Congress No. 3208 B1 and B2.

1937   "Davy Crockett." Sung by Mrs. Minnie Floyd, Murrells Inlet, South Carolina (recorded by John A. Lomax). Library of Congress No. 1046 B1.

1938   "Davy Crockett." Sung by Lester Wells, Traverse City, Michigan (recorded by Alan Lomax). Library of Congress No. 2305 B1.

1938   "Davy Crockett." Sung by Mrs. Pormola Eddy, Daybrook, Monongalia County, West Virginia (recorded by Louis Watson Cappell). WVU Archives disc 362.

1939   "Davy Crockett." Sung by Worthy Perkins, Wirt County, West Virginia (recorded by Louis Watson Chappell). WVU Archives disc 160.

1939   "Davy Crockett." Spoken by Finley Adams, Dunham, Kentucky (recorded by Herbert Halpert). Library of Congress No. 2772 B2.

1939   "Davy Crockett." Sung by Elmer Barton, Quebec, Vermont (recorded by Alan Lomax and Helen Hartness Flanders). Library of Congress No. 3694 B1.

1939   "Old Zippy Coon." Sung by Lafe Cogar, Calhoun County, West Virginia (recorded by Louis Watson Chappell). WVU Archives disc 222.

1940   "Zip Coon." Sung by Tom Whit, Mingo County, West Virginia (recorded by Louis Watson Chappell). WVU Archives disc 422.

1941   "Davy Crockett." Sung by Pearl Brewer, Ozarks (exact location unknown) (recorded by Vance Randolph). Library of Congress No. 12036 B23.

1941   "Davy Crockett." Sung by Mrs. Will Redden, Ozarks (exact location unknown) (recorded by Vance Randolph). Library of Congress No. 13131 B3.

1954   *   "Davy Crockett." Sung by Hermes Nye with guitar accompaniment, Dallas, Texas. Folkways Records No. FH 5004 (*Ballads of the Civil War*).

ca.1964*   "Ballad of Davy Crockett." Sung by Mrs. Melton, Central Texas. Candid Records no. 8026 (*A Treasury of Field Recordings*).

1965   *   "Davy Crockett." Sung by Sarah Ogan Gunning, southeastern Kentucky. Folkways Records No. FSA-26 (*Girl of Constant Sorrow*).

1978   *   "Davy Crockett." Sung by Dee Hicks, Fentress County, Tennessee. TFS Records No. TFS 103 (*Tennessee Folk Heritage: The Mountains*).

Other Davy Crockett Songs

1835   "'Go Ahead' A March Dedicated to Colonel Crockett." Sheet music. New York: Firth and Hall. See Wolfe, "Davy Crockett Songs," in Lofaro, *Davy Crockett*, 161.

1839   "Colonel Crockett: A Virginia Reel." George P. Knauff. Baltimore: Published by George Willig, Jr. See Wolfe, "Davy Crockett Songs," in Lofaro, *Davy Crockett*, 162.

1954   "The Ballad of Davy Crockett." Sheet music. Lyrics by Tom Blackburn; music by George Bruns. New York: Wonderland Music Company. See Wolfe, "Davy Crockett Songs," in Lofaro, *Davy Crockett*, 178–81.

1955   Tennessee Ernie Ford. "The Ballad of Davy Crockett." Capitol Records.

1955   Bill Hayes. "The Ballad of Davy Crockett." Cadence Records.

1955   Bill Hayes. "The Real Story of Davy Crockett." Folkways, FP 205.

1955   Red River Dave McEnery. "When Davy Crockett Met San Antonio Rose." Decca.

n.d.   (probably 1955 or shortly thereafter; see Wolfe, "Davy Crockett Songs," in Lofaro, *Davy Crockett*, 184–85).

    Irving Field. "Davy Crockett Mambo."

    Stephin Fetchit. "Davy Crockett Boogie."

    Fess Parker and Buddy Ebsen. "Davy Crockett's Motto — Be Sure You're Right (Then Go Ahead)," and "Old Betsy," (written by George Bruns and Gill George), Columbia, issue 40510.

    Burl Ives. "Davy Crockett's Motto — Be Sure You're Right (Then Go Ahead)," and "Old Betsy." Decca.

    Red Kirk. "Davy Crockett Blues." Republic.

    Lala Guerrero. "Pancho Lopez." Real Records.

    Mickey Katz. "David Crockett." Capitol.

    Homer Haynes and Jethro Burns. "The Ballad of Davy Crewcut." RCA Victor.

n.d.   Jane Bowers. "Remember the Alamo." Sung by the Kingston Trio on *The Kingston Trio at Large*, Capital, T1199.

The first two song chronologies are from Charles Wolfe's "Davy Crockett Songs: Minstrels to Disney," in *Davy Crockett*, edited by Michael A. Lofaro. Knoxville: University of Tennessee Press, 1985, 188–90.

CHILDREN'S AND JUVENILE LITERATURE
DEALING WITH DAVID CROCKETT

Beals, Frank L. *Davy Crockett*. Evanston, Ill.: Row, Peterson and Co., 1941.

Beecher, Elizabeth. *Walt Disney's Davy Crockett King of the Wild Frontier*. Illustrated. New York: Simon and Schuster, 1955.

Bishop, Lee. *Davy Crockett: Frontier Fighter*. American Explorer Series, No. 11. New York: Dell, 1983.

Blair, Walter. *Davy Crockett — Frontier Hero: The Truth as He Told It — The Legend as His Friends Built It.* New York: Coward-McCann, 1955. Reprinted as *Davy Crockett, Legendary Frontier Hero.* Springfield, Ill.: Lincoln-Herndon Press, 1986.

Blassingame, Wyatt. *How Davy Crockett Got a Bearskin Coat.* Illustrated by Mimi Korach. Champaign, Ill.: Garrard Publishing Co., 1972.

Brady, Cyrus Townsend. *Border Fights and Fighters.* Garden City, N.Y.: Doubleday, Page and Co., 1916.

Burton, Ardis E. *Walt Disney Legends of Davy Crockett.* Illustrated. Racine, Wis.: Whitman Publishing Co., 1955.

Carmer, Carl. *The Hurricane's Children.* Illustrated by Elizabeth Black Carmer. David McKay, 1937, 1965.

Coatsworth, Elizabeth Jane. *Old Whirlwind: A Story of Davy Crockett.* Illustrated. New York: Macmillan, 1953.

Cohen, Caron Lee. *Sally Ann Thunder Ann Whirlwind Crockett.* Illustrated by Ariane Dewey. New York: Greenwillow Books, 1985.

Corby, Jane. *The Story of David Crockett.* New York: Barse and Hopkins, 1922.

Davis, Hazel H. *Davy Crockett: Frontiersman and Indian Scout.* Illustrated. New York: Random House, 1955.

Disney (Walt) Productions. *Walt Disney's Crockett and Mike Fink: The Adventures of the King of the Wild Frontier and the King of the River, on the Ohio and the Mighty Mississippi.* Illustrated. New York: Simon and Schuster, 1955.

Driskill, Frank A. *Davy Crockett: The Untold Story.* Illustrated. Austin, Texas: Eakin Press, 1981.

Evatt, Harriet. *Davy Crockett, Big Indian, and Little Bear.* Illustrated. Indianapolis: Bobbs-Merrill, 1955.

Evernden, Margery. *Davy Crockett & His Coonskin Cap.* Coach House, 1956.

Farr, Naunerle C. *Davy Crockett—Daniel Boone.* Illustrated by Fred Carrillo and Nestor Redondo. West Haven, Conn.: Pendulum Press, 1979.

Fitzhugh, Percy Keese. *The Boys' Book of Scouts.* New York: Thomas Y. Crowell Company, 1917.

Ford, Anne. *Davy Crockett: A See and Read Biography.* Illustrated by Leonard Vosburgh. New York: G. P. Putnam's Sons, 1961.

Frank, Janet. *Davy Crockett and the Indians.* Variant title, *Straight-shootin' Davy.* Illustrated. Philadelphia: J. C. Winston Co., 1955.

Grant, Bruce. *Davy Crockett, American Hero.* Illustrated. Chicago: Rand McNally, 1955.

Grant, Matthew G. *Davy Crockett, Frontier Adventurer.* Illustrated by Jack Norman. Mankato, Minn.: Creative Education, Inc., 1973.

Hazan, Barbara. *Davy Crockett: Indian Fighter.* Illustrated by Joseph Guarino. New York: Pyramid Publishers, Co., 1975.

Holbrook, Stewart H. *Davy Crockett: From the Backwoods of Tennessee to the Alamo.* New York: Random House, 1955.

Johnston, Charles Haven Ladd. *Famous Scouts, Including Trappers, Pioneers, and Soldiers of Fortune.* Boston: The Page Company, 1910.

Kittredge, Belden. *The Truth about Casey Jones and other Fabulous American He-*

roes, including Johnny Appleseed, Davy Crockett, Roy Bean, and Mike Fink. Girard, Kans.: Haldeman-Julius Publications, 1945.

Lawrence, James Duncan. *Davy Crockett and the Indian Secret.* Illustrated. New York: Books, Inc., 1955.

Lenvers, Leo. *Davy Crockett; Le Coureur des Bois.* [France]: Fernand Nathan, 1984.

Le Sueur, Meridel. *Chanticleer of the Wilderness Road: A Story of Davy Crockett.* Illustrated. New York: Alfred A. Knopf, 1951.

Littlejohn, Elbridge Gerry. *Texas History Stories. Houston, Austin, Crockett, La-Salle.* Galveston, Tex.: E. G. Littlejohn, 1897.

McIntyre, John T. *In Texas With Davy Crockett.* Philadelphia: Penn Publishing Co., 1926.

McNeil, Everett. *In Texas with Davy Crockett: A Story of the Texas War of Independence.* New York: E. P. Dutton and Co., 1908.

Meadowcroft, Enid L. *The Story of Davy Crockett.* Illustrated by Charles B. Falls. New York: Grosset and Dunlap, 1952.

Moseley, Elizabeth R. *Davy Crockett: Hero of the Wild Frontier.* Illustrated by Thomas Beecham. Champaign, Ill.: Garrard, 1967.

Munroe, Kirk. *With Crockett and Bowie, or Fighting for the Lone-Star Flag.* New York: Charles Scribner's Sons, 1905.

Murphy, Keith. *Battle of the Alamo.* Illustrated by Trevor Parkin. Milwaukee: Raintree Publishers, 1979.

Parks, Aileen Wells. *Davy Crockett: Young Rifleman.* Illustrated by Justin Pearson. Indianapolis: Bobbs-Merrill Co., 1949. Reprint. New York: Macmillan, 1983, 1986.

Perry, Frances M., and Katherine Beebe. *Our American Pioneers: Daniel Boone, George Rogers Clark, David Crockett, Kit Carson.* New York: The American Book Co., 1900.

Quackenbush, Robert M. *Quit Pulling My Leg!: A Story of Davy Crockett.* New York: Prentice-Hall Books for Young Readers, 1987.

Rourke, Constance. *Davy Crockett.* New York: Harcourt, 1934.

Sabin, Edwin L. *Boys Book of Border Battles.* Philadelphia: George W. Jacobs & Co., 1920.

Santrey, Laurence. *Davy Crockett: Young Pioneer.* Illustrated by Francis Livingston. Mahwah, N.J.: Troll, 1983.

Schaare, C.R. *The Life of Davy Crockett in Picture and Story.* New York: Cupples and Leon Company, 1935.

Shapiro, Irwin. *Davy Crockett's Keelboat Race.* Illustrated. New York: Simon and Schuster, 1955.

———. *Walt Disney's Davy Crockett, King of the Wild Frontier.* Illustrated. New York: Simon and Schuster, 1955.

———. *Walt Disney's Davy Crockett Stamp Book.* New York: Simon and Schuster, 1955.

———. *Yankee Thunder: The Legendary Life of Davy Crockett.* Illustrated by James Henry Daugherty. New York: J. Messner, Inc., 1944.

Steele, William O. *Davy Crockett's Earthquake*. Illustrated. New York: Harcourt Brace, 1956.

Sutton, Felix. *The Picture Story of Davy Crockett*. Illustrated by H. B. Vestal. New York: Wonder Books, 1955.

Tappan, Eva March. *American Hero Stories*. Boston and New York: Houghton Mifflin Co., 1906.

Taylor, Vincent Frank. *David Crockett: The Bravest of Them All Who Died in the Alamo*. Illustrated. San Antonio: Naylor Co., 1955. Reprint 1967.

Tolliver, Arthur. *The Wild Adventures of Davy Crockett: Based Mainly on the Writings of the Hero of the Alamo*. Girard, Kansas: Haldeman-Julius Publishers, 1944.

Trotman, Felicity, and Shirley Greenway, eds. *Davy Crockett*. Milwaukee, Wis.: Raintree Children's Books, 1985. Reprint. New York: Torstar Books, 1986.

Warren, Robert Penn. *Remember the Alamo!* New York: Random House, 1958.

Wayne, Bennett. *Men of the Wild Frontier*. Illustrated. Champaign, Ill.: Garrard Publishing Co., 1974.

Wilson, Nat. *The Adventures of Davy Crockett*. New York: Triple Nickel Books, 1955.

Comic Books

Christmas Book, (no date). Sears giveaway.

Davy Crockett, [Classics Illustrated] series 1 (November 1955); series 2, no. 129 (September 1966). New York: Gilberton Co.

Davy Crockett, no. 34 (March 1970). Milan, Italy: Editoriale Cepim/Daim Press.

Davy Crockett, no. 12, (1977). New York: King Features Syndicate.

Davy Crockett and the River Pirates, [Walt Disney] no. 671 (1955). Dell; Four Color Comics.

Davy Crockett at the Alamo, [Walt Disney] no. 639 (1955). Dell; Four Color Comics.

Davy Crockett Frontier Fighter, no. 1 (August 1955); no. 8 (1957). Derby, Conn.: Charlton Comics Group.

Davy Crockett, King of the Wild Frontier, no. 1, 2. (1955 – no. 2, 1963; no. 1, 1963; no. 2, 1969). Dell Publishing Company.

Davy Crockett, Indian Fighter, [Walt Disney] no. 631 (1955). Dell; Four Color Comics.

Davy Crockett in the Great Keelboat Race, [Walt Disney] no. 664 (1955). Dell; Four Color Comics.

Fighting Davy Crockett, no. 9 (October-November 1955). New York: Avon Periodicals.

Frontier Fighter Davy Crockett, no. 1 (1951). New York: Avon Periodicals.

Hunting with Davy Crockett, (1955). Ben Franklin Store giveaway.

In the Raid at Piney Creek, (1955). American Motors giveaway.

It's Gametime, no. 1 (September-October 1955). National Periodical Publications.

Safety Trails, (1955). Cities Service giveaway.

Tex Granger, no. 20 (January 1949). Chicago: Commended Comics, Parents Magazine.

"True Comics: Davy Crockett – At the Height of the Battle." *Chicago Sun*, ca. 1949.

Western Tales, no. 31 (October 1955); no. 32 (1956). Harvey Publications.

Dime Novels

Aiken, Albert W. *The Prairie Mazeppa, or, The Madman of the Plains: a Strange Story of the Texas Frontier. Saturday Journal*, Vol. 2, No. 102, February 1872, to Vol. 3, No. 116, June 1872. Reprinted as Twenty Cent Novel No. 6. New York: Beadle & Adams, 1875.

"An Old Scout." *Davy Crockett, Jr., or, "Be Sure You're Right, Then Go Ahead."* Pluck and Luck No. 372, 1905.

————. *Dead Game, or, Davy Crockett's Double*. Pluck and Luck No. 412, 1906. Reprinted No. 1213, 1921.

————. *Young Davy Crockett, or, The Hero of Silver Gulch*. Pluck and Luck No. 1014, 1917.

Clyde, Kit. *Davy Crockett's Vow, or, His Last Shot for Vengeance*. The Five Cent Wide Awake Library (Tousey) No. 729, 1886.

Comstock, Captain. *Kill-Bar, the Guide; Or The Long Trail*. Starr's American Novel Series No. 18. New York: Beadle & Adams, 1869.

Ellis, Edward S. ("Harry Hazard"). *The Bear-Hunter; or Davy Crockett as a Spy*. Starr's American Novel Series No. 11. New York: Beadle & Adams, 1873. Reprinted as New Dime Novel No. 357, 1876; New Dime Novel No. 590, 1885.

————("Charles E. Lasalle"). *Col. Crockett, the Bear King*. Beadle's Boy's Library No. 139. New York: Beadle & Adams, 1886.

————. *The Life of Colonel David Crockett*. Lives of Great Americans No. 7. New York: Beadle & Adams, 1876.

————("Charles E. Lasalle"). *The Texas Trailer; or, Davy Crockett's Last Bear Hunt*. Dime Novel No. 231. New York: Beadle & Adams, 1871. Reprinted as *Col. Crockett, the Texan Trailer*. Pocket Novel No. 9, 1878.

St. George, Harry. *Daring Davy, the Young Bear Killer; or The Trail of the Border Wolf*. Half-Dime Library No. 108. New York: Beadle & Adams, 1879.

Warren, Ensign Charles Dudley. *Killb'ar, the Guide, or, Davy Crockett's Crooked Trail*. Beadle's Half-Dime Library No. 266. New York: Beadle & Adams, 1882. Reprinted as *Rocky Rover Kit; or Davy Crockett's Crooked Trail*. Pocket Library No. 233. New York: Beadle & Adams, 1888.

"Wild Bill." *Young Davy Crockett, or, The Hero of Silver Gulch*. Wide Awake Library (Tousey) No. 652. Reprinted Pluck and Luck No. 213.

Willett, Edward. *Davy Crockett's Boy Hunter*. Beadle's Frontier Series No. 11. Cleveland: Arthur Westbrook Co., 1908. Also New York: Ivers, 1908.

GENERAL, THEMATIC, AND REFERENCE WORKS

Abernethy, Thomas P. *From Frontier to Plantation in Tennessee: A Study in Frontier Democracy*. Chapel Hill: University of North Carolina Press, 1932. Reprint. Westport, Conn.: Greenwood Press, 1979.

Bergeron, Paul. *Antebellum Politics in Tennessee*. Lexington: The University Press of Kentucky, 1982.

Berkhofer, Robert F., Jr. *The White Man's Indian: Images of the American Indian from Columbus to the Present.* New York: Knopf, 1978.

Bernheimer, Richard. *Wild Men in the Middle Ages: A Study in Art, Sentiment, and Demonology.* Cambridge, Mass.: Harvard University Press, 1952.

Blankenship, Russell. *American Literature as an Expression of the National Mind.* New York: Henry Holt, 1931. Rev. ed. 1949.

Botkin, Benjamin A., ed. *A Treasury of American Folklore.* New York: Crown Publishers, 1944.

Bowers, Claude G. *The Party Battles of the Jackson Period.* Boston and New York: Houghton Mifflin Company, 1922.

Braden, Waldo. *The Oral Tradition in the South.* Baton Rouge: Louisiana State University Press, 1983.

Cawelti, John G. *Adventure, Mystery, and Romance: Formula Stories as Art and Popular Culture.* Chicago: University of Chicago Press, 1976.

————. *Apostles of the Self-made Man.* Chicago: University of Chicago Press, 1965, 39–76.

————. *The Six-Gun Mystique.* 2d ed. Bowling Green, Ohio: Bowling Green University Popular Press, 1984.

Cohen, Hennig, and William Dillingham, eds. *Humor of the Old Southwest.* Boston: Houghton Mifflin, 1964. 2d ed. Athens: University of Georgia Press, 1975.

Corlew, Robert E. *Tennessee: A Short History.* 2d ed. Knoxville: The University of Tennessee Press, 1981.

Cox, James M. "Humor of Old Southwest." In *The Comic Imagination in American Literature,* edited by Louis B. Rubin, Jr. New Brunswick, N.J.: Rutgers University Press, 1973, 101–12.

Davis, James D. *History of the City of Memphis.* Memphis: Hite, Crumpton, and Kelley, 1873.

Derby, J. S. *Fifty Years Among Authors, Books, and Publishers.* New York: G. W. Carleton, 1884.

DeVoto, Bernard. *Mark Twain's America.* Boston: Houghton Mifflin, 1932.

Dimmit, Richard B. *A Title Guide to the Talkies.* New York: Scarecrow Press, 1965.

Dorson, Richard M. *Folklore and Fakelore.* Cambridge, Mass.: Harvard University Press, 1976.

Dudley, Edward, and Maximillian E. Novak. *The Wild Man Within: An Image in Western Thought from the Renaissance to Romanticism.* Pittsburgh: University of Pittsburgh Press, 1972.

The Film Index: A Bibliography. New York: Museum of Modern Art Film Library and H. K. Wilson, 1941. Reprint. New York: Arno Press, 1966. Vol.1.

Fishwick, Marshall W. *American Heroes: Myth and Reality.* Washington, D.C.: Public Affairs Press, 1954.

————. *The Hero, American Style.* New York: David McKay, 1969.

Folsom, James K. *The American Western Novel.* New Haven: College and University Press, 1966.

Gunn, Giles, ed. *New World Metaphysics: Readings on the Religious Meaning of the American Experience.* New York: Oxford University Press, 1981.

Halbert, H. S., and T. H. Ball. *The Creek War of 1813–1814*. Chicago: Donohue and Hennebury, 1895. Reprint. Montgomery: University of Alabama Press, 1969.

Halliwell, Leslie. *The Filmgoer's Companion*. 6th ed. New York: Hill & Wang, 1977.

Hammond, Bray. "Jackson, Biddle, and the Bank of the United States." *Journal of Economic History* 7 (May 1947): 1–23.

Heiskell, S. G. *Andrew Jackson and Early Tennessee History*. 3 vols. Nashville, 1920.

Herold, Amos L. *James Kirke Paulding, Versatile American*. New York: Columbia University Press, 1926.

Hofstadter, Richard. *Anti-intellectualism in American Life*. New York: Alfred A. Knopf, 1966.

Hubbell, Jay B. *The South in American Literature, 1607–1900*. Durham, N.C.: Duke University Press, 1954.

Inge, M. Thomas. *The Frontier Humorists: Critical Views*. Hamden, Conn.: Archon Books, 1975.

Jackson, Andrew. *The Correspondence of Andrew Jackson*. Edited by John Spencer Bassett and J. Franklin Jameson. 7 vols. Washington, D.C.: Carnegie Institute, 1926–1935.

Jacobs, Robert D. "*Tobacco Road*: Lowlife and the Comic Tradition." In *The American South: Portrait of a Culture*, edited Louis D. Rubin, Jr. Baton Rouge: Louisiana State University Press, 1980, 206–26.

Johannsen, Albert. *The House of Beadle and Adams and Its Dime and Nickel Novels: The Story of a Vanished Literature*. Norman: University of Oklahoma Press, 1950, Vol. 1.

Levi-Strauss, Claude. *Totemism*. Boston: Beacon Press, 1963.

Lewis, R. W. B. *The American Adam: Innocence, Tragedy, and Tradition in the Nineteenth Century*. Chicago: University of Chicago Press, 1955.

Link, Samuel Albert. *Pioneers of Southern Literature*. Nashville, Tenn.: M. E. Church, 1899. Vol. 2.

Lovejoy, Arthur O., and George Boas. *Primitivism and Related Ideas in Antiquity*. 1935. Reprint. New York: Octagon Books, 1965.

Meine, Franklin J. *Talltales of the Southwest: An Anthology of Southern and Southwestern Humor, 1830–1860*. New York: Alfred A. Knopf, 1933.

Meyers, Marvin. *The Jacksonian Persuasion: Politics & Belief*. New York: Random House, 1957.

Moore, Arthur Keister. *The Frontier Mind*. Lexington: University of Kentucky Press, 1957.

Murrels, Joseph. *The Book of Golden Discs*. Rev. ed. London: Barrie and Jenkins, 1978.

Paine, Gregory. *Southern Prose Writers*. Edited by Harry Hayden Clark. New York: American Book Co., 1947.

Paulding, William I. *Literary Life of James K. Paulding*. New York: Charles Scribner's Sons, 1867.

Pearce, Roy Harvey. *The Savages of America: A Study of the Indian and the Idea of Civilization*. Baltimore: Johns Hopkins Press, 1953. Reprinted as *Savagism and Civilization: A Study of the Indian and the American Mind*. Baltimore: John Hopkins Press, 1965.

Percy, Walker. "Decline of the Western." *Commonweal* 68 (May 16, 1958): 181–83.

Pickard, Roy. *Who Played Who in the Movies.* London: Frederick Muller, 1979.

Radin, Paul. *Trickster: A Study in American Indian Mythology.* New York: Schocken, 1956.

Remini, Robert V. *Andrew Jackson and the Course of American Democracy, 1833–1845.* Vol. 3. New York: Harper & Row, 1984.

———. *Andrew Jackson and the Course of American Freedom, 1767–1821.* Vol. 1. New York: Harper & Row, 1977.

———. *Andrew Jackson and the Course of American Freedom, 1822–1832.* Vol. 2. New York: Harper & Row, 1981.

Rickels, Milton. "The Grotesque Body of Southwestern Humor." In *Critical Essays in American Humor,* edited by William Bedford Clark and W. Craig Turner. Boston: G. K. Hall, 1984, 155–66.

Robbins, J. Albert, et. al. *American Literary Manuscripts: A Checklist of Holdings in Academic, Historical, and Public Libraries, Museums, and Authors' Homes in the United States.* 2d ed. Athens: University of Georgia Press, 1977.

Rourke, Constance. *American Humor: A Study of the National Character.* New York: Harcourt, 1931.

Schlesinger, Arthur M., Jr. *The Age of Jackson.* Boston: Little, Brown and Co., 1945.

Schmitt, Peter J. *Back to Nature.* New York: Oxford University Press, 1969.

Seelye, John. "Root and Branch: Washington Irving and American Humor." *Nineteenth-Century Fiction* 38 (1984): 415–26.

Sellers, Charles G., Jr. "Banking and Politics in Jackson's Tennessee, 1817–1827." *Mississippi Valley Historical Review* 41 (June 1954): 61–74.

———. *James K. Polk, Jacksonian, 1795–1843.* Princeton: Princeton University Press, 1957.

Shapiro, Nat, ed. *Popular Music: An Annotated Index of American Popular Songs.* New York: Adrian Press, 1964. Vol 1.

Slotkin, Richard. *The Fatal Environment: The Myth of the Frontier in the Age of Industrialization, 1800–1890.* New York: Atheneum, 1985.

———. *Regeneration Through Violence: The Mythology of the American Frontier, 1600–1860.* Middletown, Conn.: Wesleyan University Press, 1973.

Smith, Henry Nash. *Virgin Land: The American West as Symbol and Myth.* Cambridge: Harvard University Press, 1950. Reprint. 1972.

Taubman, Howard. *The Making of the American Theatre.* New York: Coward McCann, Inc., 1965.

Turner, Frederick Jackson. *The Frontier in American History.* New York: Henry Holt and Company, 1920. Reprint. New York: Holt, Rinehart and Winston, 1962.

Van Deusen, Glyndon G. *The Jacksonian Era.* New York: Harper & Row, 1959.

Ward, John William. *Andrew Jackson: Symbol for an Age.* New York: Oxford University Press, 1955.

Williamson, Edward C. *American Political Writers, 1801–1973.* Boston: Twayne, 1981.

Wright, Joseph, ed. *The English Dialect Dictionary.* London: Henry Frowde, 1898. Reprint. New York: Hacker Art Books, 1962. Vol. 2.

Wyllie, Irvin G. *The Self-Made Man in America: The Myth of Rags to Riches.* New York, 1966.

Yates, Norris W. *The American Humorist: Conscience of the Twentieth Century.* Ames, Iowa: Iowa State University Press, 1964.

————. *William T. Porter and the* Spirit of the Times: *A Study of the BIG BEAR School of Humor.* Baton Rouge: Louisiana State University Press, 1957.

Contributors

WALTER BLAIR is considered by many to be the dean of Crockett studies. From the famous *Native American Humor* (New York: American Book Company, 1937) to *America's Humor: From Poor Richard to Doonesbury* with Hamlin Hill (New York: Oxford Press, 1978), his books and articles discussing the role of the famous frontiersman in the American comic tradition span over fifty years of scholarship. His famous 1940 article on "The Six Davy Crocketts" serves as the starting point for modern studies of Crockett. Recently his 1955 classic work on the Tennessee backwoodsman was reissued as *Davy Crockett: Legendary Frontier Hero* (Springfield, Ill: Lincoln-Herndon Press, 1986). Dr. Blair is Professor Emeritus of the University of Chicago's Department of English Language and Literature.

JOE CUMMINGS was the Coordinator for the Crockett Bicentennial Celebration for the State of Tennessee in 1986; he was also the editor of the special Crockett edition of *The Tennessee Conservationist* (Jul/Aug 1986) and *The Crockett Bicentennial Times* (Greeneville, Tenn.: Greeneville Sun Publishing Co., 1986). He is also the author of "Remembering Davy" and other articles on Crockett.

RICHARD BOYD HAUCK, a specialist in tall tales and American humor, is the author of *A Cheerful Nihilism: Confidence and the Absurd in American Humorous Fiction* (Bloomington: Indiana University Press, 1971) and *Crockett: A Bio-Bibliography* (Westport, Conn.: Greenwood Press, 1982) which was recently reissued as *Davy Crockett: A Handbook* (Lincoln: University of Nebraska Press, 1986). He is also Abe Levin Professor of English at the University of West Florida.

PAUL ANDREW HUTTON is the author of "Davy Crockett, Still King of the Wild Frontier" (*Texas Monthly* 36 [November 1986]), "A Tale of Two Alamos" (*SMU Mustang* 36 [Spring 1986]), and the introduction to *Alamo Images: Changing Perceptions of a Texas Experience* (by Susan Prendergast Schoelwer with Tom W. Glaser, [Dallas: Southern Methodist University Press, 1986]). He has also written *Phil Sheridan and His*

Army (Lincoln: University of Nebraska Press, 1985), a forthcoming book on the Alamo, and numerous articles on Western folk heroes. He is the editor of *Soldiers West: Biographies from the Military Frontier* (Lincoln: University of Nebraska Press, 1987). Dr. Hutton is an Associate Professor of History at the University of New Mexico and editor of the *New Mexico Historical Review.*

WILLIAM ERIC JAMBORSKY is the author of "The Alamo: Moviemakers and the Myth" in *The Crockett Bicentennial Times* (Greeneville, Tenn.: Greeneville Sun Publishing Co., 1986). Presently, he is a graduate student in the Department of History at the University of Tennessee.

DAN KILGORE is the author of *How Did Davy Die?* (College Station, Tex.: Texas A&M University Press, 1978) as well as many other articles on Texas history. He is the past president of the Texas State Historical Association.

MICHAEL A. LOFARO is the editor of *Davy Crockett: The Man, the Legend, the Legacy, 1786–1986* (Knoxville: University of Tennessee Press, 1985) and of *The Tall Tales of Davy Crockett: The Second Nashville Series of Crockett Almanacs, 1839–1841* (Knoxville: University of Tennessee Press, 1987). He is also the author of *The Life and Adventures of Daniel Boone* (Lexington: University Press of Kentucky, 1978, 2d ed., rev., 1986). Dr. Lofaro is Professor of English at the University of Tennessee.

MICHAEL MONTGOMERY is the editor of *Language Variety in the South: Perspectives in Black and White* (Tuscaloosa: University of Alabama Press, 1986) and co-editor of the *Annotated Bibliography of Southern American English* (2d edition). He also serves as consulting editor of languages and dialects for *The Encyclopedia of Southern Culture* (Chapel Hill: University of North Carolina Press, 1987). Dr. Montgomery is an Associate Professor of English at the University of South Carolina.

JOHN SEELYE is the author of *Prophetic Waters: The River in Early American Life and Literature* (New York: Oxford University Press, 1977). His other major works include *Mark Twain in the Movies: A Meditation with Pictures* (New York: Viking Press, 1977), *The True Adventures of Huckleberry Finn, As Told by John Seelye* (Evanston, Ill: Northwestern University Press, 1970; second edition, Urbana: University of Illinois Press, 1987), and *Melville: The Ironic Diagram* (Evanston, Ill: Northwestern University Press, 1970). Dr. Seelye is Graduate Research Professor of American Literature at the University of Florida.

MILES TANENBAUM is the author of *Hunting Davy Crockett: A Guide to*

Crockett Studies (Nashville: Tennessee Department of Conservation and the Tennessee State Museum, 1986). Presently, he is a post-doctoral instructor in the Department of English at the University of Tennessee.

CHARLES K. WOLFE is the author of many works on traditional and popular music. Among his books are *Everybody's Grandpa: Fifty Years Behind the Mike* (by Louis M. "Grandpa" Jones with Charles K. Wolfe, Knoxville: University of Tennessee Press, 1984), *Kentucky Country: Folk and Country Music of Kentucky* (Lexington: University Press of Kentucky, 1982), *Tom Ashley, Sam McGee, Bukka White: Tennessee Traditional Singers* (coauthor, Knoxville: University of Tennessee Press, 1980), *Tennessee Strings: The Story of Country Music in Tennessee* (Knoxville: University of Tennessee Press, 1977), and *Grand Ole Opry: The Early Years* (London: Old Time Music Press, 1975). Dr. Wolfe is Professor of English at Middle Tennessee State University.

Index

Crockett at Two Hundred was designed by Dariel Mayer, composed by Lithocraft, Inc., and printed and bound by Braun-Brumfield, Inc. The book is set in Plantin. Text stock is 60-lb. Glatfelter Natural Smooth.